Quick Guide

This guide is organized
looking birds are shown
color-coded as follows:

WATERFOWL (Whistling-Ducks, Geese, Swans, Ducks)

GAMEBIRDS (Quail, Grouse, Chukar, Pheasant, Turkey) – GREBES – PIGEONS AND DOVES

CUCKOO, ANI, AND ROADRUNNER – NIGHTHAWKS – NIGHTJARS – SWIFTS – HUMMINGBIRDS

RAILS – COOT – CRANE – SHOREBIRDS (STILT, AVOCET, Plovers, Jacana, Sandpipers, Dowitchers, Snipe, Phalaropes)

JAEGERS – GULLS – SKIMMER – TERNS – LOONS – STORK – FRIGATEDBIRD

BOOBIES – CORMORANTS – PELICANS – WADING BIRDS (Bitterns, Herons, Egrets, Ibises, Spoonbill)

VULTURES – DIURNAL RAPTORS (OSPREY, Eagles, Kites, Hawks) – OWLS

TROGONS – KINGFISHERS – WOODPECKERS – FALCONS – LOVEBIRD AND PARAKEET

BECARDS – FLYCATCHERS (Tyrannulet, Pewees, Flycatchers, Phoebes, Kingbirds)

SHRIKES – VIREOS – CORVIDS (Jays, Nutcracker, Magpie, Crow, Ravens) – LARK – SWALLOWS

CHICKADEES – TITMICE – VERDIN – BUSHTIT – KINGLETS – NUTHATCHES – CREEPER – GNATCATCHERS – WRENS – DIPPER – CATBIRD – MOCKINGBIRDS – THRASHERS

BLUEBIRDS – SOLITAIRES – THRUSHES – ROBINS – WAXWING – PHAINOPEPLA – PIPITS – STARLING – HOUSE SPARROW

FINCHES – ("HOUSE" FINCHES, PINE GROSBEAK, CROSSBILL, ROSY-FINCHES, SISKIN, GOLDFINCHES)

LONGSPURS – NATIVE SPARROWS (SPARROWS, JUNCOS, TOWHEES)

BLACKBIRDS (DICKCISSEL, BOBOLINK, MEADOWLARKS, BLACKBIRDS, COWBIRDS, GRACKLES, ORIOLES)

WARBLERS (OLIVE WARBLER, WOOD WARBLERS, CHAT)

TANAGERS – CARDINAL – PYRRHULOXIA – GROSBEAKS – BUNTINGS

BIRDS
OF
ARIZONA

By

Richard Cachor Taylor

R.W. Morse Company
Olympia, Washington

For Barbara Bickel and Kathy Olmstead
Friends and birding companions

Published by R.W. Morse Company, Olympia, Washington

Library of Congress Control Number: 2019948484

EAN 9780999073612   **$26.95 Softcover**
First Edition 2022   **© 2022 R.W. Morse Company**
First Printing 2022

Printed: China, Imago Group

Author: Richard Cachor Taylor

Publisher, Editor: Christina Duchesne Morse

Cover, Interior Design: Christina Merwin

Bird Range Maps: Richard Cachor Taylor

State of Arizona Map: Eric G. Taylor

Bird Drawings: Eric Kraig

Front Cover Photographer: Gilded Flicker, Charlie Trapani

Back Cover Photographers: Clark's Grebe, Bruce D. Talbert
Eared Quetzal, A. R. Donaldson
Rivoli's Hummingbird, Bruce D. Talbert

Contents

Common Arizona Birds

These are some of the most common birds in Arizona.
For more information about each bird, go to its Species Account.

Widespread Birds

Rock Pigeon
p. 71

Eurasian
Collared-Dove
p. 73

White-winged
Dove
p. 73

Mourning
Dove
p. 73

Black-chinned
Hummingbird
p. 95

Turkey
Vulture
p. 191

Red-tailed
Hawk
p. 211

Great Horned
Owl
p. 221

Common Raven
p. 307

Barn Swallow
p. 315

House
Sparrow
p. 367

European
Starling
p. 367

House
Finch
p. 369

Lesser
Goldfinch
p. 377

Great-tailed Grackle
p. 423

Yellow-rumped
Warbler
p. 437

Water Birds

American Wigeon
p. 33

Mallard
p. 35

Northern Shoveler
p. 39

Pied-billed Grebe
p. 65

Killdeer
p. 117

Ring-billed Gull
p. 149

Double-crested Cormorant
p. 171

Great Blue Heron
p. 177

Osprey
p. 193

Belted Kingfisher
p. 233

Marsh Wren
p. 339

Song Sparrow
p. 399

Red-winged Blackbird
p. 417

Yellow Warbler
p. 435

Common Yellowthroat
p. 463

Desert Birds

Gambel's Quail
p. 57

Anna's Hummingbird
p. 97

Costa's Hummingbird
p. 97

Elf Owl
p. 225

Harris's Hawk
p. 205

Gila Woodpecker
p. 239

Vermilion Flycatcher
p. 273

Verdin
p. 321

Cactus Wren
p. 331

Curve-billed Thrasher
p. 345

Northern Mockingbird
p. 341

Phainopepla
p. 363

Lucy's Warbler
p. 431

Black-throated Sparrow
p. 385

Northern Cardinal
p. 471

Mountain Birds

Wild Turkey
p. 63

Band-tailed Pigeon
p. 71

Broad-tailed Hummingbird
p. 99

Northern Pygmy-Owl
p. 223

Acorn Woodpecker
p. 235

Hairy Woodpecker
p. 241

Mexican Jay
p. 299

Steller's Jay
p. 301

Mountain Chickadee
p. 317

White-breasted Nuthatch
p. 325

"Gray-headed" Dark-eyed Junco
p. 405

Spotted Towhee
p. 409

Black-throated Gray Warbler
p. 441

Painted Redstart
p. 459

Grace's Warbler
p. 447

Elevation Ranges of Arizona Hummingbirds

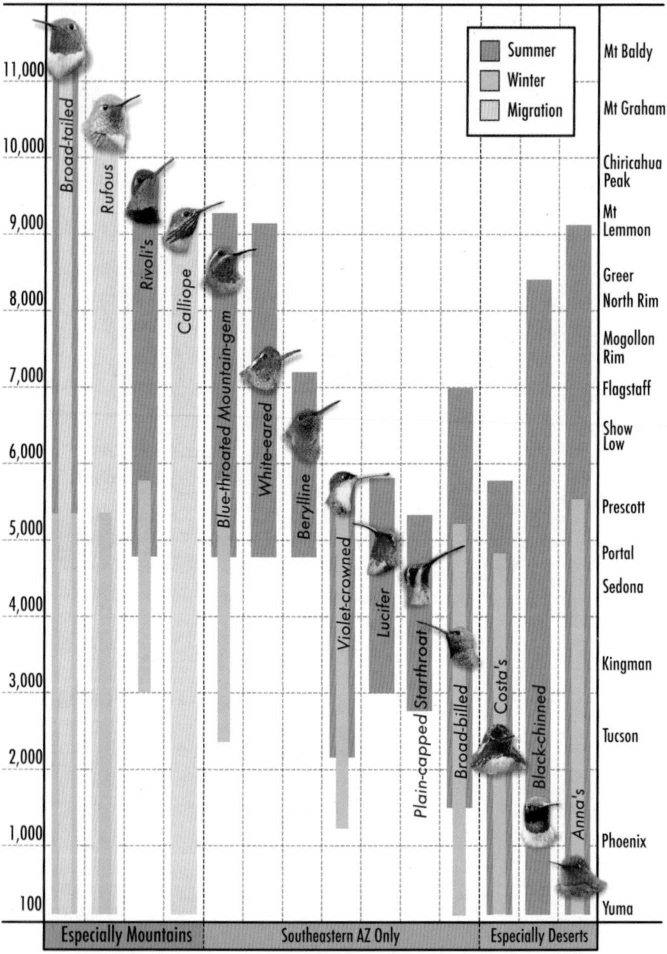

Summer
Winter
Migration
11,000
10,000
9,000
8,000
7,000
6,000
5,000
4,000
3,000
2,000
1,000
100
Broad-tailed
Rufous
Rivoli's
Calliope
Blue-throated Mountain-gem
White-eared
Berylline
Violet-crowned
Lucifer
Plain-capped Starthroat
Broad-billed
Costa's
Black-chinned
Anna's
Mt Baldy
Mt Graham
Chiricahua Peak
Mt Lemmon
Greer
North Rim
Mogollon Rim
Flagstaff
Show Low
Prescott
Portal
Sedona
Kingman
Tucson
Phoenix
Yuma
Especially Mountains
Southeastern AZ Only
Especially Deserts

Introduction

The hummingbirds on the facing page illustrate the importance of geographic location in shaping Arizona's avifauna. The Rocky Mountains contribute 3 high elevation species, the Sierra Madres account for 7 high and mid-elevation hummingbirds, and deserts—2 species from the Mohave-Sonoran, 1 from the Great Basin and arid Interior West, and 1 from the Chihuahuan Desert—yield the remainder. Wandering Allen's from the West Coast, Ruby-throated Hummingbirds from the Eastern U.S., plus a wayward Cinnamon Hummingbird from Mexico and Central America give Arizona a total of 17 members of this charismatic tribe. No other state can match the hummingbird diversity of Arizona. Linked to the Pacific Ocean by 35 miles of the Colorado River valley in Mexico, water dependent species also have a corridor directly into the state. Given the variety of Arizona's habitats, it is not surprising that more than half of all the birds of the United States and Canada have been recorded in an area that occupies less than 1.5 percent of the land area of North America. *Birds of Arizona* is a handbook for all birdwatchers who wish to identify and enjoy the birds in this uniquely positioned corner of the world.

From Yuma at the four corners of California, Baja California, and Sonora, to the Four Corners where Utah, Colorado, and New Mexico converge, *Birds of Arizona* encompasses all of the regularly occurring birds within the Grand Canyon State. Many of these same species range from the Pacific Ocean to West Texas, and *Birds of Arizona* should help provide a solid foundation for understanding the avian dynamics of the American Southwest. Because they attract birders from throughout the U.S., all of the recent Mexican specialties, regardless of their abundance, are also included. Naturally the abundance, seasonality, and even the behavior of birds will vary with changes in the environment. Those differences can help illuminate the environmental factors that shape the life of a bird, as well as the irreducible requirements for its future conservation.

HABITAT CHANGE

Rainfall patterns and drought affecting food availability and overall habitat quality—locally and in surrounding states—impacts both resident and migratory birds. Although the distribution and seasonal numbers of birds fluctuate every year, three of the past five years have been the warmest Arizona has experienced since climate records for our area were inaugurated in 1895. Beginning in 1994, long-term drought has squeezed our region and reduced water storage in the Colorado River reservoirs by about 50 percent. In 2020 wildfires consumed 978,500 acres, including vast tracts of the forests that formerly spread across the Kaibab Plateau, the White Mountains, and the archipelago of sky islands in Southeastern Arizona. Regardless of whether mankind is responsible for climate change, reversing the amount of greenhouse gases in the atmosphere is something only humans can achieve.

CONSERVATION

A diverse and thriving avifauna is perhaps the best indication of a healthy environment. Arizona has seen rapid development surround its larger cities. With pavement and concrete come heat islands that have seen the average temperature of Phoenix rise by 1.4 degrees since 1980. Another consequence of clearing native vegetation is the loss of habitat vital to the survival of not only birds, but also to the entire community of wildlife. Because the majority of birds are active during the day when most mammals are hidden, they are the most observable form of wildlife. Their presence or absence and their relative abundance will tell us just how well we are succeeding in the preservation of our natural heritage, as well as the patrimony we are leaving our children. A knowledge of birds may help turn progress down pathways that benefit not only our human communities, but also the native birds and wildlife with whom we share these desert valleys.

Identifying Birds

Initially, learning to identify birds may seem difficult. Many birds are very small, move quickly, remain hidden in dense cover, and many resemble other birds. First, look at the general shape, size, and color of the bird. Check the habitat categories in the Common Arizona Birds (pages vi - ix) and see if it is there. If not, scan through the Species Account pages. Read the description—especially the boldfaced text—to see how it matches your bird. Compare similar species, voice, and habitat. Check the elevation and the seasons of its occurrence. Keep comparing until you have a match.

The colors and patterns of a bird's feathering ("plumage") and bare parts (bill, legs, feet, eyes) provide some of the best clues for identification. With bill shape to place it in a family, birds often can be identified by head pattern alone. Be aware, however, that plumages may vary within the same species between the sexes, between adults and younger birds, by season, and by geographical location. Learn the parts of a bird; consult the diagrams on pages 4 and 5.

Some examples of birds where the male and the female have distinctly different plumages are Cinnamon Teal, Anna's Hummingbird, Elegant Trogon, Olive Warbler, and Scott's Oriole. Usually males display more brilliant colors meant to attract a mate, while females have muted colors that serve as camouflage when they sit immobile on a nest. Other species such as Black-bellied Whistling-Duck, Elf Owl, Violet-crowned Hummingbird, Bridled Titmouse, and Western Meadowlark show no obvious plumage differences between the sexes. In a few species, such as the phalaropes, where the males are responsible for incubation, females are more brightly colored than males.

Most birds seen in our area in spring and summer display what is known as their breeding—or "alternate"—plumage. Birds present in winter are usually in their nonbreeding—or "basic"—plumage. To attract mates at the onset of spring, both sexes—but especially males—transition out of their worn and drab basic plumage into

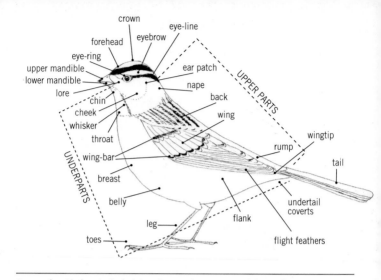

Parts of a Bird. It is helpful to know the names of the different parts of a bird. These sketches of a White-crowned Sparrow and a Mallard in flight show the terms used to describe bird topography in this guide.

fresher and more colorful alternate plumage. Note, however, that some birds, many flycatchers, for example, molt their worn feathers after breeding, just before migration. These birds are at their brightest in the fall. When molt timing helps identify a species it is noted in the text.

Most birds also display different plumages as they mature. Some birds, such as California Gulls, require up to four years to attain adult plumage. Other birds, such as Cactus Wrens, however, essentially look like adults from the moment they leave the nest. With the exception of precocial species like Killdeer and Wild Turkey, most species appear full-sized when they fledge.

The term "juvenile plumage" refers to the first true plumage worn by a young bird—a juvenile—after it molts its downy feathers. Some species only retain this plumage for a few weeks after fledging,

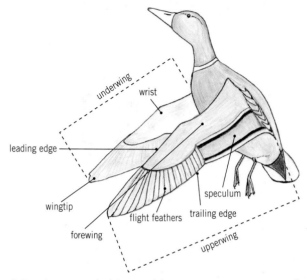

underwing

wrist

leading edge

wingtip

flight feathers

forewing

speculum

trailing edge

upperwing

while others may hold it until late winter. "Immature" refers to all plumages before the bird gains its adult plumage. For many species, juvenile males resemble females. Young male hummingbirds are an example of this precept.

Plumage colors and patterning may also vary considerably within birds of the same species across geographical populations. For instance, the nearly black race of Red-tailed Hawk that occasionally winters in Arizona, the "Harlan's Hawk," is quite different from the extremely pale "Fuertes" subspecies that breeds in our region. This book will highlight the structural elements and plumage patterns necessary to identify either color "morph" adult as a Red-tailed Hawk.

Finally, do not expect every bird you see to look exactly like the photographs in this guide. Like people, birds express individual variation. Male Lucifer Hummingbirds, for example, show a range of gorget patterns. Some have straight edges at the bottom, others have major V's, and still others have jagged lower margins, as if trimmed with pinking shears. To survive birds must be able to distinguish their mates and—among social species—members of their particular flock.

In this book the birds are presented in family groupings, as shown in the Quick Guide to Arizona Birds (opposite the map inside the front cover). Learning the characteristics of the different bird families will make bird identification easier. Birds in the same family tend to show similarities in appearance and behavior. A bird's structure, including bill shape, general body shape, and the relative length of its wings, tail, and legs, provide important clues to both the family to which it belongs and to its species.

Taxonomy: It should be noted that birds in this book do not always appear in the most recent American Ornithological Society taxonomic sequence. Current taxonomy, based on genomic sequencing, inserts Willet between Greater and Lesser Yellowlegs, a species which resembles neither. Similarly, Streaked-backed Oriole separates Baltimore and Bullock's Orioles, apparent siblings so closely aligned by structure, plumage pattern, and songs that some interbreed where their ranges overlap—a fact that led taxonomists to lump them as "Northern Oriole" from 1973-1995. Egrets, for example, are members of the heron family that appear similar by virtue of their entirely white plumage, but which are not necessarily closely related. To facilitate identification, both Yellowlegs, the two former "Northern Orioles," and all three white egrets are yoked together on single pages where they can easily be compared.

Although *Birds of Arizona* focuses on visual field marks, the identification of a bird is often clinched by its voice. Experienced birders can recognize most of this region's species by ear. In this book I've tried to transcribe bird calls and songs into English language sounds or words, hoping to help make it possible to positively identify heard birds at night, in poor light, or in dense cover. With practice, the unique quality or pattern of a vocalization may enable you to identify birds without even catching a glimpse of the songster itself. Some transient and wintering species are largely silent. This information is noted for those birds.

Bird Habitats of Arizona

With the exception of such generalists as Common Raven, birds typically require specialized habitats. These are areas where topography combines with temperature and rainfall to create a distinctive plant community. In Arizona temperatures decrease about four degrees Fahrenheit per thousand feet of elevation gain as the air grows thinner, and annual rainfall increases approximately four inches per thousand feet of elevation gain. The giant saguaro cactus that grace the Sonoran Desert below 4,000' are symbolic of a habitat that bears no resemblance to the Canadian fir and aspen forests that green our mountaintops above elevations of 8,000'. Cactus Wrens found in southern Arizona from the Colorado River to the New Mexico state line occur in conjunction with the thorny plants of the desert. Mountain Chickadees are found almost a vertical mile higher in the boreal forests of Arizona's highland areas. Cactus Wrens and Mountain Chickadees require completely different habitats. Under normal circumstances, these two species would never encounter one another in the wild. For the birder, knowledge of a species' habitat preferences is the key to finding that bird. Throughout *Birds of Arizona* reference is made to the following 11 habitats.

STREAMS AND RIVERS; PONDS AND LAKES: 100-10,000'

Surface water constitutes less than 1 percent of Arizona, yet many families of birds that occur here are utterly dependent on water for food and shelter, regardless of whether they are simply migrating through or actually nesting in our region. Among the list of water-dependent bird families are ducks and geese, rails and coots, avocets and stilts, plovers and sandpipers, gulls and terns, cormorants and pelicans, and herons and egrets. The importance of artificial impoundments—regardless of size—cannot be overstated. From murky stock tanks with less than a surface acre of water, to large metropolitan sewage treatment ponds, to recreation lakes whose length is measured in miles, any body of water in Arizona is a magnet for birds. In our area the Colorado River and its string of blue reservoirs provides habitat for many species that also occur in the Sea of Cortez, 35 miles farther south. Almost all birds can easily fly 100 miles in a single night, and waterbirds seem to regard the Colorado as an extension of the upper gulf. The Colorado River and its major tributary the Gila River drain virtually the entirety of the state. These two watersheds are major conduits into the most remote corners of Arizona. Mountain streams, marshes and wet meadows at their headwaters permit birds as diverse as Spotted Sandpiper, Bald Eagle, Belted Kingfisher, and American Dipper to find appropriate habitat to nest and raise their young.

DESERTSCRUB: 100-6,500'

Approximately 42 percent of Arizona is desert. All four corners of Arizona are in or near four major deserts. Lowest and largest is the Sonoran Desert, a ragged triangle spreading north from Yuma up the Colorado River Valley to Bullhead City and southeast to Phoenix and Tucson. Where it has not been altered by man, this low-lying area is characterized by saguaro cactus, cholla, and other drouth adapted succulents. Farther up the Colorado River Valley north of Bullhead City, weird, alphabet-shaped Joshua Trees are emblematic of the Mohave Desert. The lower valleys of Northern Arizona's high, wind-swept Colorado Plateau are dotted with blue-gray sagebrush from the Great Basin Desert. Elevations are generally above 3,000' in the valleys east of Tucson, but thorny, cold-tolerant fingers of the Chihuahuan Desert from west Texas and the Interior Valley of Mexico reach high up into the foothills of the border ranges. Bendire's Thrasher breeds in all four deserts. Other birds—Gilded Flicker in the Sonoran Desert, Sage Thrasher in the Great Basin Desert, and Scaled Quail in the Chihuahuan Desert—are largely confined as breeding species to a single North American desert.

VALLEY GRASSLAND; AGRICULTURAL FIELDS: 100-6,500'

Historically, Arizona supported some of North America's richest grasslands. One quarter of Arizona was originally blanketed with savanna. Overgrazing, agriculture, water withdrawal, fire suppression, and the elimination of millions of Black-tailed Prairie Dogs have all contributed to reducing the size of these grasslands. Nonetheless, many species are still dependent on grasslands or—in lieu of native savanna—large agricultural fields for their existence. Among these are Ferruginous Hawk, Sandhill Crane, Mountain Plover, Horned Lark, Thick-billed and Chestnut-collared Longspurs, and Eastern Meadowlark. Sadly, the last certain record of a wild Aplomado Falcon in 1942 coincides with the extirpation of prairie dogs from Southeastern Arizona. Black-tailed Prairie Dogs were reintroduced to Las Cienegas National Wildlife Area in 2008; Gunnison's Prairie Dogs still survive north of the Mogollon Rim.

VALLEY GROVES, PECAN FARMS, AND DESERT OASES: 100-6,500'

Where water lies near or on the surface in the Colorado, Virgin, Little Colorado, Gila, Salt, Verde, Santa Cruz, and San Pedro River Valleys, green ribbons of Fremont cottonwood and willow trees mark the flow. Introduced tamarisk trees have supplanted native trees in parts of most of these watersheds. The "cienega" or swampy area near the town of Arivaca is an example of smaller, but important groves of big trees otherwise surrounded by an arid landscape. These corridors of food, water, and shelter not only harbor a community of riparian obligate-nesting birds, such as Gray Hawks, Yellow-billed Cuckoos, Tropical Kingbirds, and Summer Tanagers, they also provide a safe flyway for hundreds of species of migrants. Nearly 250 species of birds have been recorded using the Hassayampa River Preserve near Wickenberg, and over 300 different species of birds are regular migrants in the San Pedro River National Conservation Area east of Sierra Vista.

Mankind has replaced the native trees with enormous tracts of pecans in several areas of Arizona. While lacking any understory, pecan farms seem to afford some birds many of the same benefits as cottonwood groves. Lowland urban areas with parks and artificial plantings provide birds with a third important woodland habitat. Tucson is reputed to have one of the highest concentrations of Cooper's Hawks in the entire United States. The Arizona-Sonora Desert Museum, a desert oasis boasting only a dozen cottonwoods on the grounds, still supports a breeding enclave of Hooded Orioles and a bird list of nearly 200 species.

FOOTHILL GROVES: 2,500-6,500'

Often at higher elevations than valley groves, often with sycamores mixed with the gallery forest, foothill groves attract a unique subset of the riparian birds. Included among these are some of Arizona's most sought-after species. Common Black Hawks breed in all the major streams that drain south from the Mogollon Rim. After arriving in Arizona in 1958, Thick-billed Kingbirds have spread from the border with New Mexico to the California state line.

FOOTHILL THORNSCRUB: 3,500-5,000'

Above 3,500' and below 5,000' the walls of foothill canyons near the border are often armored with an impenetrable layer of spiny shrubbery. A suite of Mexican tropical species follows these tendrils of thornscrub across the Arizona border into legendary birding areas such as Sycamore Canyon and California Gulch in the Atascosa Mountains; Sonoita Creek—especially downstream from the town of Patagonia to Patagonia Lake; lower Madera Canyon, lower Florida Canyon, and lower Montosa Canyon in the Santa Rita Mountains; and the San Bernadino Ranch and Guadalupe Canyon east of Douglas in the extreme southeast corner of the state. Inhabitants of thornscrub slopes include Buff-collared Nightjar, Black-capped Gnatcatcher, Varied Bunting, and Five-striped Sparrow.

MOUNTAIN INTERIOR CHAPARRAL AND PINYON-JUNIPER WOODLAND: 4,000-7,500'

In almost all of Arizona, cold winter nights in the mountains eliminate many of the spiny plants that characterize the subtropical thornscrub of the lower border foothills. Dense stands of mountain mahogany on thin limestone substrates and thickets of manzanita on volcanic soils form an interior chaparral at elevations between 4,000 and 7,500'. Usually pinyon pine and junipers punctuate the chaparral, and in much of Northern Arizona, pinyon-juniper may mantle plateaus and the broad skirts of mountain highlands. These habitats are especially attractive to species derived from the Great Basin. Some of the breeding birds include Gray Vireo, Woodhouse's Scrub-Jay, Juniper Titmouse, Virginia's Warbler, and Black-chinned Sparrow. Roving flocks of Pinyon Jays are nomadic "residents" in central and northern Arizona.

MADREAN PINE-OAK WOODLAND: 5,000-7,000'

Mexico's single largest habitat is Sierra Madrean pine-oak woodland. The border ranges of Southeastern Arizona, usually between elevations of 5,000-7,000', mark the northernmost limits of this admixture of spring deciduous oaks and fire-tolerant pines. In Sycamore Canyon in the Atascosa Mountains, however, a relict pine-oak woodland occurs more than 1,000' lower in elevation. Upper Sycamore Canyon—situated between elevations of 3,600-4,000'—shares the Montezuma Quail, Whiskered Screech-Owls, Arizona Woodpeckers, Mexican Jays, Bridled Titmouse, Painted Redstarts, and Hepatic Tanagers that typify some of Arizona most famous mid-elevation birding locales.

MOUNTAIN CANYON GROVES: 5,000-9,500'

Elegant, white-barked Arizona sycamore belies the presence of permanent water, either a live stream or significant flow just below the surface. Between elevations of 5,000 and 6,500' the floor of larger mountain canyons in Arizona support an ivory latticework of these water dependent trees, and they in turn provide homes for such "Mexican" birds as Elegant Trogon and Sulphur-bellied Flycatcher in the south, and Bald Eagles in the north. Trees, shrubs, and vines flourish in the deeper, better-watered soils along the canyon floor, and food, shelter, and water are all more available to birds here than on the adjacent slopes. Madera Canyon, Ramsey Canyon, and Cave Creek Canyon near Portal exemplify this bird rich habitat in southern Arizona. Probably the most famous canyon hotspot in northern Arizona is Oak Creek upstream from Sedona, but dozens of other streams pour off the Mogollon Rim and shelter breeding enclaves of Common Mergansers and Belted Kingfishers. At higher elevations in east-central Arizona, snow melt in the White Mountains gives rise to a broad wheel of streams. Here species as diverse as Dusky Flycatcher, Winter Wren, and MacGillivray's Warbler thread the willow and alder thickets.

MOUNTAIN CONIFEROUS FOREST: 6,500-11,300'

More than 15 percent of Arizona is covered in conifers. A 200-mile-long escarpment called the Mogollon Rim bisects central Arizona and arcs southeast from the San Francisco Peaks to the White Mountains on the border of New Mexico. The Mogollon Rim supports the largest stand of Ponderosa pine in North America. North of the Grand Canyon the Kaibab Plateau is an elevated limestone block with lush, grassy parks, tall timber, and expansive aspen glades. Forests also mantle isolated higher peaks in Northern Arizona such as the Chuskas on Navajo Nation lands, and the Hualapai Mountains outside of Kingman. The term "Sky Islands" is often used to describe the larger mountains of Southeastern Arizona. With elevations approaching or exceeding 10,000' in the Pinaleños and Chiricahuas, and well above 9,000' in the Santa Catalina, Santa Rita and Huachuca Mountains, these ranges sustain stands of pine, fir, and quaking aspen. Naturally, the bird communities that occupy these highlands are reminiscent of Colorado's Rocky Mountains. Some of the birds to watch for are Northern Saw-whet Owl, Hairy Woodpecker, Steller's Jay, and Pygmy Nuthatch. Dusky Grouse, Olive-sided Flycatcher, and Gray Jay which reach the southern limits of their breeding distribution in central Arizona. Other birds such as Greater Pewee, Olive Warbler, and Yellow-eyed Junco—essentially confined in the U.S. to Arizona—underscore the Sierra Madrean influence on our region's avifauna.

MOUNTAIN TUNDRA: 11,000-12,633'

Only the two highest mountains in Arizona rise above timberline. Highest of six volcanic summits in the San Francisco Peaks is Mt. Humphreys, elevation 12,633 feet. A ring of windswept low scrub and bristlecone pines constitute a habitat called krummholz—German for "crooked wood"—providing a transition from the arctic-alpine zone to tall spruce forest below 11,000 feet. In eastern Arizona the highest point of the White Mountains is Mt. Baldy, the culmination of a long alpine meadow that gradually climbs to 11,409 feet. After spring snowmelt, the summits of both mountains are festooned in wildflowers. Others visit but short summers with the possibility of snow and freezing temperatures in any month limit the breeding bird community to American Pipit, the only species hardy enough to endure this extreme environment.

Helpful Resources

ARIZONA BIRD BOOKS AND AUDIO:

Babbitt, Charles J. 2019. *Birding Arizona*. R. W. Morse Company.

Brown, David E. 1985. *Arizona Wetlands and Waterfowl*. University of Arizona Press.

_____. 1989. *Arizona Game Birds*. University of Arizona Press and the Arizona Game and Fish Department.

Burns, Jim. 2008. *Arizona Birds from Backyard to the Backwoods*. University of Arizona Press.

Corman, Troy E., and Cathryn Wise-Gervais, editors. 2005. *Arizona Breeding Bird Atlas*. University of New Mexico Press.

Detwiler, Henry. 2013. *Finding Birds in Yuma County, Arizona*.

Doyle, Diane. 2019. *SE Arizona Birds: The Missing Tracks* (5 disc set). Diana@birding aboard.org.

Glinski, Richard L., editor. 1998. *The Raptors of Arizona.* University of Arizona Press.

Jacobs, Brad. 1986. *Birding on the Navajo and Hopi Reservations.* Jacobs Publishing Company.

Keller, Geoffrey A. 2001. *Bird Songs of Southeastern Arizona and Sonora, Mexico* (2 CD set). Cornell Laboratory of Ornithology.

Monson, Gale, and Allan R. Phillips. 1981. *Annotated Checklist of the Birds of Arizona.* University of Arizona Press.

Phillips, Alan, Joe Marshall, and Gale Monson. 1964. *The Birds of Arizona.* University of Arizona Press.

Rosenberg, Gary H., and Dave Stejskal. 2002. *Field Checklist of the Birds of Arizona.* Arizona Bird Committee.

Rosenberg, Kenneth V, Robert Ohmart, William Hunter, and Bertin Anderson. 1991. *Birds of the Lower Colorado River Valley.* University of Arizona Press.

Stevenson, Mark, editor. 2015. *Tucson Audubon Society's Finding Birds in Southeastern Arizona.* Tucson Audubon Society.

Taylor, Richard Cachor. 2010. *Birds of Southeastern Arizona.* R. W. Morse Company.

_____. 2010. *Location Checklist to the Birds of the Chiricahua Mountains.* Borderland Productions.

_____. 2005. *A Birder's Guide to Southeastern Arizona.* American Birding Association.

_____. 1995. *Location Checklist to the Birds of the Huachuca Mountains and the Upper San Pedro River.* Borderland Productions.

_____. 1994. *Trogons of the Arizona Borderlands.* Treasure Chest Books.

Journals

Western Birds, the quarterly journal of the Western Field

Ornithologists; research papers, records committee reports, distribution and identification analyses, with many contributions from amateurs.

The Vermilion Flycatcher (quarterly magazine). Tucson Audubon Society. 300 E. University Blvd., #120, Tucson, AZ 85705.

ORGANIZATIONS AND BIRD REPORTS

American Birding Association
https://www.aba.org/birding-news

Arizona Field Ornithologists (AZFO)
https://www.azfo.org

Arizona/New Mexico Listserve Archives
http://digest.sialia.com

Audubon Arizona
https://www.audubon.org/news/birding-arizona

eBird
https://ebird.org/home

Facebook Key Word Search
arizonabirding

Southeastern Arizona Bird Observatory (SABO)
http://www.sabo.org

This book would have been less accurate without the enormous archive of records on the Arizona/New Mexico Listserve and the eBird lists managed by Cornell University. Thousands of local and visiting birders have submitted their observations to these two vast data bases. *Birds of Arizona* is an attempt to distill these reservoirs of knowledge and experience into a birder-friendly format. Everyone who has ever participated in either has my sincere thanks.

Range Maps

Range maps show the regular geographic and seasonal occurrence of all species given a full treatment in *Birds of Arizona*. Ordinarily the maximum area of probable occurrence is depicted. **With some exceptions, birds are least common on the periphery of their mapped range.**

"Color dimes"—isolated round points—are meant to draw attention to notable records that are outside a species' normal seasonal distribution, and each may signify single or multiple observations. Usually only the most significant of these records are marked with color dimes. When a species occurs on an island of limited habitat, such as the upper Hualapai Mountains near Kingman, its range is also indicated with a color dime. These spots are *not* to scale. Color dimes are meant to be large enough to be noticeable on the species map, even though an out-of-range record may involve only a single bird that occupied an isolated stock pond—or even a single tree—throughout the duration of its stay. Colors represent the season or seasons of occurrence as shown on the key for the sample map.

Wintering Red-tailed Hawks, Hermit Thrushes, and many other species, are replaced every summer by a wave of new migrants. If a species winters in all or portions of the area where it is present in summer, the region on the map where there is seasonal overlap is shown in purple for resident. Areas where a species is shown as resident—or areas where it occurs in summer, red—are often much larger than the bird's actual breeding range. Although most birds do nest somewhere within the purple or red of their mapped range, neither color is intended to be synonymous with breeding areas. Light purple means a species occurs in every month year-round, but is not known to nest.

Sample Range Map

Range maps for every species should be used in conjunction with the **Habitat** and **Elevation** information provided in the text. Owing to scale considerations, habitat gradients within the range of a bird are frequently too fine to depict on the range maps. Information in the text is essential to understanding the range maps.

<small>COLOR KEY</small>

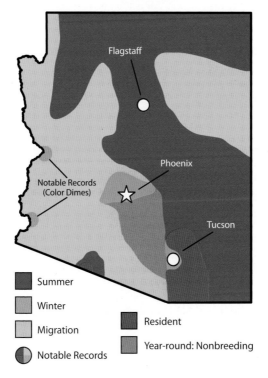

Flagstaff

Phoenix

Notable Records (Color Dimes)

Tucson

■ Summer

■ Winter

■ Migration

◐ Notable Records

■ Resident

■ Year-round: Nonbreeding

17

Species Accounts

Standardized terms are used to describe "Status"—the relative abundance of each species—and the likelihood of finding it in a particular season. These definitions were developed by the American Birding Association. Please note that the Status of any given species in Arizona may be different in different areas of the state and at different elevations.

- **Common:** Found in moderate to large numbers, and easily seen in appropriate habitat at the correct time of year. This category includes some birds like Mourning Dove that may be locally abundant.

- **Fairly Common:** Occurs as singles up to mid-sized, but scattered, flocks, and usually fairly easy to find in appropriate habitat in the right seasons.

- **Uncommon:** Found in low numbers, and usually—but not always— seen with some effort in appropriate habitat in the correct season.

  It is useful to consult eBird alerts and the AZ/NM Listserv when searching for birds in the following categories.

- **Rare:** Occurs annually in very small numbers. Never expected, but may—or may not—be found with extended effort at the appropriate season(s) in the correct habitat.

- **Casual:** Occurs less than annually, but there tends to be a seasonal pattern of occurrence in appropriate habitat; 4 or more records in the past 10 years.

- **Accidental:** Represents an exceptional occurrence that might not be repeated for years; 3 or fewer records in the past 10 years.

In this book the terms "casual" or "accidental" are sometimes used to describe the Status of birds that have occurred in a season when they are not expected.

Birds shown in the photographs in the Species Accounts are adults unless the captions indicate otherwise.

COMMON NAME OF THE SPECIES, *Its Scientific Name*

Description: Length (and wingspan for larger birds) is given in inches, followed by key field marks. Key field marks pertain to diagnostic structural details and plumage patterns that separate similar species. These often begin with bill and head shapes. Color and pattern are especially useful for distinguishing sexes and ages within a species of bird, and these are described when the differences are discernible in the field. If a juvenile or an immature resembles an adult, usually the female, this plumage is not mentioned. **Boldfaced** words indicate crucial identification features.

Similar Species: Differentiates similar-appearing species with key field marks. Underlined Species are vagrant birds to Arizona which are not given a full treatment with photos and range maps.

Voice: Limited to the main calls or songs that are apt to be heard in Arizona. These may be vital for identification—species of some families, owls and flycatchers, for example, are often best told by their vocalizations. Note that some species may be almost entirely silent in our area.

Status & Habitat: Provides information on the relative abundance, seasonality, and preferred habitats where each species of bird occurs in Arizona. Arizona is large and the abundance of a species will vary throughout the state. In this book a bird's Status reflects its usual numbers where it is most apt to be found. The word "local" means a bird only attains its Status in a small area or areas. There are no breeding records for species described as year-round, mapped in light purple. Major habitats are discussed on pages 7-13, with specific examples of each.

Elevations: Represent the extreme seasonal or yearly elevation ranges. *Ordinarily birds will be most common in the mid-range of elevations.*

Behavior: Highlights behavioral characteristics.

Noteworthy: Provides other interesting facts about the species, often specific to Arizona.

Black-bellied Whistling-Duck

Juvenile

Fulvous Whistling-Duck

BLACK-BELLIED WHISTLING-DUCK, *Dendrocygna autumnalis*

Description: 21". **Richly-colored** whistling-duck. ADULT: Fluorescent **orange-red bill; gray face;** long, bright **pink legs**. JUVENILE: Gray bill; gray legs; subdued colors overall. FLIGHT: Black belly; **broad white stripe on upperwing. Similar Species:** Fulvous Whistling-Duck has tawny face and slaty bill, gray legs, and broken white bar on flanks; in flight shows black upperwings and "U"-shaped white band on tail. **Voice:** Common flight call is high, thin, rapidly repeated series of *pi-hee pi-hee* whistles. **Status:** Irregularly fairly common but local in summer (late Apr-early Nov); uncommon in winter (Dec-Mar); numbers fluctuate from year to year. **Habitat:** Desert oases; flooded fields, and valley ponds, often abutting cottonwood groves. **Elevations:** Summer 200'-5,100'; Winter 800'-4,000'. **Behavior:** Active at night. Arizona nests are usually on islands. **Noteworthy:** The Mexican name *Pijiji* (pronounced *pe-he-he*) is for the sound of its whistles.

FULVOUS WHISTLING-DUCK, *Dendrocygna bicolor*

Description: 20". **Tawny-headed** whistling-duck with white "fingers" forming **broken white stripe on flanks**. ADULT: **Orangish face, slaty bill,** long, **slaty legs**. JUVENILE: Resembles dull-plumaged adult. FLIGHT: **Ochre belly;** blackish wings; bold **white crescent on black tail. Similar Species:** Black-bellied Whistling-Duck has gray face with orange bill, pink legs, and solid white stripe on lower wing; in flight shows broad white stripe on upperwing. **Voice:** Calls include shrill repeated series of *gi-me, I wan-it* whistles. **Status:** Casual year-round. **Habitat:** Desert oases; flooded fields, and valley ponds, often abutting cottonwood groves. **Elevations:** Year-round 950'-4,000'. **Behavior:** Active at night. Eats grasses and shallow water plants. **Noteworthy:** Singles are usually tucked in among Black-bellied Whistlers or other ducks.

Tundra Swan

Trumpeter Swan

TUNDRA SWAN, *Cygnus columbianus*

Description: 52". **Large** swan; **slightly concave** bill usually shows **yellow lore**, diagnostic if present. JUVENILE: Dull pinkish-gray bill; gray plumage changes to white by mid Dec. **Similar Species:** Larger Trumpeter Swan has a subtle "Roman nose", a slightly bulging upper mandilbile, always lacking yellow next to eye. Longer neck usually shows pronounced kink near base. Juvenile retains gray plumage until March; bill is half black, even in youngest birds. **Voice:** Call is a repeated gurgling *Burt*—as if trying to find him, but seldom heard in Arizona. **Status**: Rare in winter (mid Nov-Feb). **Habitat:** Agricultural fields and large ponds and lakes without vegetated banks. **Elevations:** Winter 200'-7,700'. **Behavior:** Grazes in fields during day and spends nights on water. **Noteworthy:** Northernmost of the swans, Tundra Swans breed in tundra on the northern rim of Alaska and Canada.

TRUMPETER SWAN, *Cygnus buccinator*

Description: 60". **Very Large** swan, often with very long **neck kinked near base; slight bulge in center of upper bill.** JUVENILE: Stays gray until mid Mar; basal half of bill solid black. **Similar Species:** Smaller Tundra Swan typically has variably-sized yellow spot in front of eye; upper bill is depressed in center, not slightly raised. **Voice:** Expressive, horn-like notes are seldom heard in Arizona. **Status**: Casual in winter (mid Dec-Feb). **Habitat:** Agricultural fields and large ponds and lakes without vegetated banks. **Elevations:** Winter 500'-7,000'. **Behavior:** Most mate at 3 or 4 years of age and remain with their mate throughout the year, often throughout their life. **Noteworthy:** Males average 26 pounds and can weigh up to 35 pounds, giving them the distinction of heaviest flying bird in North America.

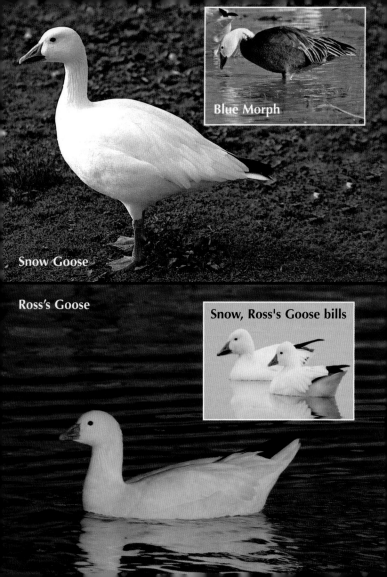

Snow Goose

Blue Morph

Ross's Goose

Snow, Ross's Goose bills

SNOW GOOSE, *Chen caerulescens*

Description: 28". **Medium-sized** white goose with **sloping forehead**; pink bill shows **black "grin patch"** along edges where the mandibles meet. BLUE MORPH: Variably slate-gray on neck, breast, and back. JUVENILE: Dull pinkish-gray bill; gray wash on neck, back, and wings. **Similar Species:** Smaller Ross's Goose (below) lacks "grin patch." Larger swans and white domestic geese do not have black wingtips. **Voice:** Call is raucous, fairly high yelping *wowk* or *wow*. **Status:** Uncommon in winter (mid Oct-mid Mar). **Habitat:** Valley ponds and lakes without vegetated banks. **Elevations:** Winter 100'-4,300'. **Behavior:** Grazes on grasses, grain, and shallow pond vegetation. **Noteworthy:** Blue morphs typically constitute about 1-2 % of Snow Geese in Arizona.

ROSS'S GOOSE, *Chen rossi*

Description: 23". **Small** version of Snow Goose with **steep forehead; stubby, triangular bill**. JUVENILE: Like pale gray adult. **Similar Species:** Snow Goose (above) has black "grin patch" where the mandibles meet, and a proportionately longer bill that merges with sloping forehead. **Voice:** Like Snow Goose but more shrill. **Status:** Rare in winter (late Oct-mid Mar); accidental in summer (mid Mar-late Oct). **Habitat:** Valley ponds and lakes without vegetated banks. **Elevations:** Winter 1,000'-4,300'. **Behavior:** Eats grasses, grain, and marsh vegetation. Often associates with other geese species, especially Snow Geese. **Noteworthy:** "Blue" plumage morph is extremely rare in Arizona. Populations of Ross's Geese in the U.S. have increased from approximately 2,500 in the early 1950s to over a million today.

Canada Goose

Cackling Goose

CANADA GOOSE, *Branta canadensis*

Description: 43". Large, **long-necked** brown goose with **long bill**; white "chin strap", **sloping forehead;** pale or tan breast. **Similar Species:** Much smaller Cackling Goose (below) has a short, stubby bill, vertical forehead, and a short neck. Greater White-fronted Goose (p. 29) has pink bill and orange legs, lacks black neck with contrasting white "chin-strap." **Voice:** Loud, resonant *ha-ronk*. **Status:** Uncommon resident, some withdraw from lowest elevations in summer (mid Mar-mid Oct) and highest elevations in winter (mid Oct-mid Mar). **Habitat:** Summer: High elevation lakes and Phoenix area parks and golf courses; Winter: Valley lakes and ponds. **Elevations:** Summer 100-9,100'; Winter 100-8,300'. **Behavior:** Prefers lakes and large ponds with treeless shores and adjacent grasses or open parks. **Noteworthy:** More numerous and widespread in winter. First successful breeding in 1970 stemmed from introduced Great Basin race, *B. c. moffitti.*

CACKLING GOOSE, *Branta hutchinsii*

Description: 26". Like a mallard-sized Canada Goose with a **vertical forehead; short, stubby bill; short neck**; often lacks white collar; most have **brown underparts. Similar Species:** Much bigger Canada Goose (above) has long bill, long neck, and pale or tan breast. **Voice:** High *huk-huk*, or cackling *w-huk* notes. **Status:** Rare in winter (Nov-Feb); casual in migration (Sep-Oct and Mar-mid Apr); accidental in summer. **Habitat:** Valley lakes and ponds. **Elevations:** Winter 200'-6,800'. **Behavior:** Forages for plants, grains, and invertebrates in lakes, large ponds, and on golf courses. **Noteworthy:** In 2004 the four smallest forms of Canada Goose were reclassified as a separate species called Cackling Goose. All four are possible in Arizona, but "Richardson's" appears to be the most common. Only the very rare "Aleutian" race shows an extensive, contrasting white collar.

Brant

Greater White-fronted Goose

BRANT, *Branta bernicla*

Description: 25". Small, chunky, mostly black saltwater goose with streaked **white forecollar;** short, triangular bill; short neck; white-streaked flanks; **white upper and under tail coverts.** JUVENILE: Wings banded with thin white lines; lacks vertical white lines on flanks. FLIGHT: Usually low over water; black with contrasting white collar and white under tail coverts. **Similar Species:** Black necks of Canada and Cackling Geese contrast with paler backs. **Voice:** Hoarse *k-rronk* notes. **Status:** Casual in winter (mid Nov-Apr). **Habitat:** Valley lakes and ponds. **Elevations:** Winter 300'-3,100'. **Behavior:** Forages for plants, grains, and invertebrates in lakes and large ponds. **Noteworthy:** Drinks salt water. All Arizona records are singles for one day only.

GREATER WHITE-FRONTED GOOSE, *Anser albifrons*

Description: 28". Gray-brown goose with a **pinkish bill;** bright **orange legs.** ADULT: **White foreface surrounds the bill;** irregular black blotches across the belly. JUVENILE: Lacks white foreface and black belly blotches. **Similar Species:** Canada Goose (p. 27) has black head and neck. Domestic <u>Greylag Geese</u> released into urban ponds lack black blotches on their bellies. Juvenile Greater White-fronted Geese stay with adults their first winter. **Voice:** Common flight call is high, yelping *kah-la-luck*. **Status:** Rare in winter (mid Sep-Mar); sporadic (Aug and Apr). **Habitat:** Ponds and lakes without trees. **Elevations:** Winter 100'-9,100'. **Behavior:** Over-wintering birds often associate with other geese species. **Noteworthy:** Breeding in Alaska and Canada and wintering to Mexico, Greater White-fronted Goose has the longest migration route of any North American goose species.

Wood Duck
Male

Wood Duck
Female

Gadwall
Male

Gadwall
Female

WOOD DUCK, *Aix sponsa*

Description: 18.5". Large **drooping hindcrest**. MALE: **Colorful** and elaborate head pattern; **red bill base and eyering**. FEMALE: Tapering **white patch envelopes eye**. FLIGHT: **Long, rectangular tail**. **Similar Species:** Female Hooded Merganser (p. 53) lacks white around eye. Feral male Mandarin Duck has red bill and a coppery "beard" on cheeks; female has long, thin white stripe behind eye. **Voice:** High whistles, squeaks. Female's call a penetrating squeal *ooEEK*. **Status:** Rare in summer (May-Sep); uncommon in winter (Oct-Apr). **Habitat:** Wooded valley ponds, rivers, and streams. **Elevations:** Summer 3,100'-5,200'; Winter 100'-8,000'. **Behavior:** When available, rests under overhanging trees and roots. Feeds on invertebrates, seeds, and fruits in shallow water; does not dive. **Noteworthy:** First detected nesting in Arizona in 1975, Wood Ducks use natural cavities in Arizona sycamore and Fremont cottonwood trees.

GADWALL, *Mareca strepera*

Description: 20". Medium-sized, plain duck with **squarish head**, orange legs, white belly. MALE: Gray with contrasting **buff head and neck**, dark gray bill, **black rear end**. FEMALE: Contrasting paler head and neck and **orange sides to bill**; **white wing patch** often visible at rest. FLIGHT: **Square white wing patch**. **Similar Species:** Female Mallard lacks boxy head shape and has blue wing patch–not white. **Voice:** Female gives high-pitched, nasal *quack*; male quavering *rrep rrep*. **Status:** Uncommon in summer (Jun-Aug); fairly common in winter (Sep-May). **Habitat:** Valley ponds and lakes; requires emergent vegetation for nesting. **Elevations:** Resident 100'-9,200'. **Behavior:** Forages for vegetation in shallow water by tipping up. Often in pairs. **Noteworthy:** Most Arizona Gadwall nests are from elevations above 5,000', but it has nested as low as 200' on the Colorado River; as well as at ponds near Safford, Nogales, and Prescott.

American Wigeon
Female, Male

Eurasian Wigeon
Female

Eurasian Wigeon
Male

AMERICAN WIGEON, *Mareca americana*

Description: 18″. **Gray-headed duck** with short, black-tipped, bluish-gray bill. MALE: Bright green "racing stripe" behind eye; narrow white crown stripe; pinkish breast and flanks. Rarely males may have almost entirely white heads. FEMALE: Mottled grayish head; rusty brown breast and flanks. FLIGHT: Mostly **white wing linings and pointed tail. Similar Species:** Male Eurasian Wigeon (below) has red–not gray–head lacking green stripe; brownish-headed female Eurasian lacks neck-breast contrast of female American Wigeon and black outline at base of bill. In flight Eurasian shows mostly gray–not white–wing linings. **Voice:** Breathy, whistled *will-uh-wew*. **Status:** Common in winter (Sep-Apr); casual in summer (May-Aug). **Habitat:** Valley ponds, especially adjacent to fields of grass, golf courses, or urban parks. **Elevations:** Summer 150′-9,000′; Winter 100′-8,000′. **Behavior:** Grazes in grassy areas. Flocks frequently number in the hundreds. **Noteworthy:** In Arizona, American x Eurasian Wigeon hybrids are less common than pure Eurasian Wigeons. Crosses show reddish on the head patterned like a male American Wigeon.

EURASIAN WIGEON, *Mareca penelope*

Description: 18″. MALE: **Bright rufous head** with yellowish crown stripe; gray back and flanks. FEMALE: Unicolored head, neck, and breast are brown or cinnamon-brown. FLIGHT: Mostly **gray wing linings. Similar Species:** American Wigeon has grayish head and neck that contrasts with breast and white wing linings. **Voice:** Single descending whistle is *wheeel*. **Status:** Rare in winter (Nov-Mar); casual in Apr. and Oct. **Habitat:** Valley ponds adjacent to fields of grass. **Elevations:** Winter 150′-6,800′. **Behavior:** Occurs in our area as singles or twosomes; usually more shy than American Wigeons in the same flock. **Noteworthy:** Eurasian Wigeons in Arizona are unknown away from American Wigeon flocks.

Mallard
Male

Female

Mexican Duck
Male

Female

MALLARD, *Anas platyrhynchos*

Description: 23". Large duck with blue speculum bordered by white; orange legs. MALE: Green head, **bright yellow bill, white neck ring**, reddish breast, curly black central tail feathers. FEMALE: Dark line through eye; orange bill with blotchy black saddle, rarely all black bill. FLIGHT: White underwings. **Similar Species:** Long, spatulate bill of Northern Shoveler (p. 39) apparent. Female Gadwall (p. 31) shows boxy head shape and white wing patch. **Voice:** Male emits rasping *rratt rratt* notes; Female *quacks*. **Status:** Uncommon in summer (mid May-mid Aug); common in winter (mid Aug-mid May). **Habitat:** Lakes, ponds, rivers, and streams. Flocks occasionally descend on alfalfa fields. **Elevations:** Resident 100'-9,500'. **Behavior:** Forages for vegetation by tipping up; grazes on land. **Noteworthy:** Most male Mallards in Arizona migrate too early to breed with hen Mexican Ducks. Hybrids, however, occur; male hybrids often show curly black tail feathers.

MEXICAN DUCK, *Anas diazi*

Description: 23". Like **dark hen Mallard with contrasting paler head and neck**. MALE: **Bill unmarked olive-yellow**. FEMALE: **Brown outer tail feathers**. FLIGHT: Very white underwings. **Similar Species:** Drake Mallard (above) has yellow bill. Hen Mallard has white–not brown– outer tail feathers. **Voice:** Like Mallard. **Status:** Fairly common resident. Most withdraw from higher elevations in winter (Nov-Mar). **Habitat:** Valley lakes, permanent ponds, and rivers. **Elevations:** Summer 1,000'-9,000'; Winter 100'-5,400'. **Behavior:** Usually in pairs year-round. Nests after most Mallards migrate. **Noteworthy:** Recent DNA studies show genetically pure Mexican Ducks are more closely related to American Black Duck of Eastern U.S. than to Mallard. From 1983-2020 Mexican Ducks were classified as a race of Mallard.

Green-winged Teal
Male

Female

Blue-winged Teal
Male

Female

Cinnamon Teal
Male

Cinnamon Teal
Female

GREEN-WINGED TEAL, *Anas crecca*

Description: 14". **Short black bill; bright green speculum**. MALE: Chestnut head with **broad green ear patch; vertical white "shoulder" stripe**. FEMALE: Off-white undertail coverts. **Similar Species:** Female Blue-winged (below) and Cinnamon Teals (below) have larger bills and blue-gray forewings, lack whitish undertail. **Status:** Rare in summer (mid May-mid Aug); common in winter (mid Aug-mid May). **Habitat:** Valley ponds and lakes. **Elevations:** Summer 6,000'-9,300'; Winter 100'-7,000'. **Behavior:** All three teals dabble in shallows. **Noteworthy:** Smallest dabbling duck, weighing about 10 ounces. Rare nester in northern Arizona.

BLUE-WINGED TEAL, *Spatula discors*

Description: 15". Medium-long black bill; **dull orange legs**. MALE: Bluish-gray head with **bold white foreface crescent**. FEMALE: Diffuse, pale foreface. FLIGHT: Pale blue forewing and green speculum. **Similar Species:** Cinnamon Teal (below) has long bill and male usually has red eye. **Status:** Uncommon year-round migration; rare breeder in the White Mountains in summer (Jun-Jul) and rare in winter (Dec-Jan). **Habitat:** Valley ponds and lakes. **Elevations:** Summer 4,200'-9,000'; Winter 100'-8,100'. **Noteworthy:** Some fall juvenile Blue-winged and Cinnamon Teals are probably not safely distinguished.

CINNAMON TEAL, *Spatula cyanoptera*

Description: 16". **Long black bill** slightly spatulate; **yellow legs.** MALE: **Rich cinnamon-red** with red eyes. FEMALE: Uniform plain brown head. FLIGHT: Pale blue forewing and green speculum. **Similar Species:** Female Northern Shoveler (p. 39) has huge bill. **Status:** Uncommon in summer (Jun-Jul); fairly common in winter (Aug-May). **Habitat:** Valley ponds and lakes. **Elevations:** Resident 100'-9,300'. **Noteworthy:** Most Cinnamon Teal nest in NE Arizona marshes, but it has bred in S. Arizona.

Northern Shoveler
Male

Northern Shoveler
Female

Northern Pintail
Male

Northern Pintail
Female

NORTHERN SHOVELER, *Spatula clypeata*

Description: 19". Medium-sized dabbler with **long, spatulate bill**. MALE: Green head with **yellow eyes**, white breast, and cinnamon sides. FEMALE: Nondescript with enormous bill that shows significant orange. FLIGHT: Pale-blue forewing. Loud wingbeats upon take-off. **Similar Species:** Many other female ducks similar, but none have huge bill. Spring males have reverse Mallard (p. 35) underpart pattern with white chest and rusty flanks. **Voice:** Females *quack*, males give soft *thup-tup*. **Status:** Rare in mid summer (May-Aug). Common in fall, winter, and spring (Sep-Apr). **Habitat:** Valley lakes and ponds. **Elevations:** Year-round 100'-9,000'. **Behavior:** Specialized bill enables Shovelers to filter feed on plankton. Groups often circle with their heads underwater, straining food stirred up from below. **Noteworthy:** In winter Northern Shoveler is the most abundant duck in Arizona.

NORTHERN PINTAIL, *Anas acuta*

Description: Male 26", female 20". Slender, **long-necked dabbling duck** with gray bill and **long, pointed tail**. MALE: Brown head with **white neck stripes**. FEMALE: **Long tail.** FLIGHT: Distinctive long neck and tail. **Similar Species:** Other midsized dabbling ducks have shorter, stockier necks and lack the long, pointed tail. **Voice:** Female makes rackety *quacks*. Male gives wheezy whistle. **Status:** Rare breeder in mid summer (May-mid Aug) with a few migrants still present statewide; fairly common in fall, winter, and spring (mid Aug-Apr). **Habitat:** Valley lakes and ponds. Nests are typically in open, grassy highlands. **Elevations:** Summer 200'-9,300'; Winter 100'-8,000'. **Behavior:** Feeds by tipping up, with long tail pointed skyward and head and neck underwater. **Noteworthy:** Northern Pintails have been timed flying over 50 mph in Arizona. Nests are usually located 0.5 mile or farther from open water.

MALE   FEMALE

Ring-necked Duck

Lesser Scaup

Greater Scaup

RING-NECKED DUCK, *Aythya collaris*

Description: **17".** **Gray bill with crisp white ring** and black tip in breeding season (Oct-Jun); peaked hindcrown. MALE: Black with **white "shoulder" wedge**, head glossed purple. FEMALE: White eyering and diffuse, whitish foreface. FLIGHT: Mostly gray underwings. **Similar Species:** Scaups (below) lack white ring on bill. Female scaups lack eyering. **Status:** Uncommon in summer (May-Sep); common in winter (Oct-Apr). **Habitat:** Valley lakes and ponds. **Elevations:** Year-round 100'-9,400'. **Behavior:** Like scaups, forages for aquatic plants and invertebrates; joins flocks of scaups and other ducks. **Noteworthy:** Has bred in central and NE Arizona. Inconspicuous brownish ring at the base of the male's neck gives species its name.

LESSER SCAUP, *Aythya affinis*

Description: **16.5".** **Peaked hindcrown** and bluish-gray bill. MALE: Head usually glossed purple, may look green; body blackish on both ends, whitish in middle. FEMALE: Brownish with crisp white foreface. FLIGHT: **Short white upperwing stripe** extends halfway to wingtip. **Similar Species:** Greater Scaup (below) has rounded head, larger bill, long white upperwing stripes. **Status:** Rare in summer (May-Sep); fairly common in winter (Oct-Apr). **Habitat:** Valley lakes and ponds. **Elevations:** Summer 200'-7,100'; Winter 100'-9,000'.

GREATER SCAUP, *Aythya marila*

Description: **18".** **Rounded head** and bluish-gray bill. MALE: Head usually glossed green, may look purple; body blackish on both ends, whitish in middle. FEMALE: Brownish with crisp white foreface; when present, whitish ear patches are diagnostic. FLIGHT: **Long white upperwing stripe** extends almost to wingtip. **Status:** Fairly common at Lake Havasu but otherwise rare—usually singles—away from Colorado River in winter (Oct-Apr); accidental in summer (May-Sep). **Habitat:** Valley lakes and ponds. **Elevations:** Winter 100'-7,000'. **Noteworthy:** Usually found with Lesser Scaups in Arizona.

41

Canvasback Male

Female

Redhead Male

Female

CANVASBACK, *Aythya valisineria*

Description: 21". Long body; **sloping forehead** slides into **long, black bill**. MALE: Chestnut head, black breast, white body. FEMALE: Tan head, neck, and chest contrast with pale gray body. **Similar Species:** Redhead has rounded head with shorter, white-banded bill. **Voice:** Usually silent. **Status:** Rare visitor in summer (mid Apr-mid Oct); uncommon in winter (mid Oct-mid Apr). **Habitat:** Valley lakes and ponds. **Elevations:** Summer 200'-9,100'; Winter 100-8,400'. **Behavior:** Dives for aquatic plants and invertebrates and strains seeds from bottom mud. Joins large mixed flocks with Redheads and other wintering diving ducks. **Noteworthy:** Arizona flocks seldom number over 100.

REDHEAD, *Aythya americana*

Description: 19". Compact body; **rounded head**; medium-long **tricolored bill** with white band near black tip. MALE: Rich red head with pale blue bill; smoke-gray body. FEMALE: Dull brown overall; slate-gray bill with broad black tip. **Similar Species:** Female Greater and Lesser Scaups (p. 41) have distinct white forefaces. Female Ring-necked Duck (p. 41) has white eyering, peaked hindcrown, and dark upperparts. Long-bodied Canvasback has much longer, all black bill. **Voice:** Usually silent. **Status:** Uncommon in summer (Apr-Aug); fairly common in winter (Sep-Mar). **Habitat:** Usually large and deep ponds and lakes. Nests regularly above 6,000' north of the Mogollon Rim; possible year-round statewide. **Elevations:** Resident 100'-9,300'. **Behavior:** Dives for aquatic plants and invertebrates and strains seeds from bottom mud. Joins large mixed flocks with Canvasbacks and other wintering diving ducks. **Noteworthy:** Hens frequently lays eggs in the nests of other ducks, including other Redheads, and perhaps half of all Redhead ducklings have foster parents.

MALE

FEMALE

Surf Scoter

White-winged Scoter

Black Scoter

SURF SCOTER, *Melanitta perspicillata*

Description: 20". Long bill bulges near forehead; **pale or white nape.** MALE: multicolored bill. FEMALE: Dark cap with **vertical white patch by bill** and white ear patch. FLIGHT: Black wings. **Similar Species:** Immature White-winged Scoter lacks dark cap, has rounded white lore patches, and lacks any white in nape or white in wings. **Status:** Rare in fall and winter (Oct-Mar); accidental in spring (Apr-May). **Habitat:** Deep water lakes and ponds. **Elevations:** Winter 150'-7,450'. **Behavior:** Heavy-bodied sea ducks dive for invertebrate prey on reservoirs with rocky bottoms. **Noteworthy:** Surf is most common Scoter species in Arizona.

WHITE-WINGED SCOTER, *Melanitta deglandi*

Description: 21". **Feathering on top half of bill;** when resting on water often shows small white wing patch. MALE: Orange-tipped bill. FEMALE: Black head with **rounded white patch by bill**; JUVENILE: Also has white ear patches. FLIGHT: Broad white secondary panel on wings. **Similar Species:** Surf Scoter has dark cap, vertical white patch next to bill, whitish or white nape, and entirely black wings. **Status:** Casual in winter (Oct-mid Apr). **Habitat:** Deep water lakes and ponds. **Elevations:** Winter 450'-9,000'.

BLACK SCOTER, *Melanitta americana*

Description: 19". Concave bill bulges near forehead. MALE: Yellow knob on upper bill; entirely black body. FEMALE: Bicolored head with dark cap and whitish cheek and throat. FLIGHT: Wing linings black; flight feathers gray. **Similar Species:** Female and immature Surf Scoter and White-winged Scoters only have small white patches on dark faces; males lack yellow knobs. **Status:** Casual in winter (mid Oct-mid Apr). **Habitat:** Deep water lakes and ponds. **Elevations:** Winter 450'-6,750'. **Noteworthy:** May occur with other scoter species.

Long-tailed Duck
Nonbreeding Male

Breeding pair

Bufflehead
Male

Female

LONG-TAILED DUCK, *Clangula hyemalis*

Description: 16.5". Medium-sized, small-billed sea duck with **mostly white head and neck** and blackish breast in winter. Winter MALE Half-pink bill; white back; **long, black tail.** Winter FEMALE Slaty bill; white face with **dusky cheek patch.** FLIGHT: Black wings contrast with white belly. **Similar Species:** The only wintering Arizona duck with a mostly white head. **Voice:** Single *gut* notes and male sings *ut-o-oawah* with pauses between syllables; also a quavering wail. **Status:** Rare in winter (mid Oct-early May). **Habitat:** Deep water ponds, lakes, and rivers. **Elevations:** Winter 200'-7,000'. **Behavior:** Dives for invertebrate prey on the bottom of ponds, lakes, and rivers. **Noteworthy:** Extraordinarily complex molt results in summer plumage almost the opposite of winter plumage with black and brown replacing white.

BUFFLEHEAD, *Bucephala albeola*

Description: 13". **Small duck** with a small, gray bill. MALE: **Balloon-headed** with white cowl. FEMALE: Rectangular head with an **oval white cheek patch**; dark upperparts with small white speculums. **Similar Species:** Common Goldeneye (p. 49) has bright golden eyes. From a distance, male Common Goldeneye shows round white face spots and extensive white markings on wings. Female Goldeneye lacks the oval cheek patches of female Bufflehead. Winter female Ruddy Duck shows pale lower half of entire face with a diffuse line across the cheek. **Voice:** Usually silent in our area. **Status:** Uncommon in winter (mid Oct-mid May); casual in summer (mid May-mid Oct). **Habitat:** Valley lakes and ponds, usually with surrounding trees and shrubbery. **Elevations:** Winter 100'-9,400'. **Behavior:** Dives for aquatic invertebrates and small fish. Usually found in small, loose flocks. **Noteworthy:** Buffleheads rarely leave the water to walk on the ground.

**Common Goldeneye
Female**

**Common Goldeneye
Male**

**Barrow's Goldeneye
Female, Male**

COMMON GOLDENEYE, *Bucephala clangula*

Description: 18.5″. Chunky, medium-sized diving duck with bright yellow eyes and **sloping forehead peaking over eye**. MALE: **Round white face patch; mostly white wing**. FEMALE: Chocolate-brown head with golden eyes and gray body; in winter its **bill is yellow-tipped. Similar Species:** Bufflehead (p. 47) lacks golden eyes. Male Barrow's Goldeneye (below) has crescent-shaped cheek spots with vertical forehead, and crown peak in front of eyes; female has shorter, mostly orange bill. **Voice:** Usually silent in our area. **Status:** Uncommon in winter (Oct-May). **Habitat:** Valley lakes and ponds, rivers, and canals. **Elevations:** Winter 150′-9,400′. **Behavior:** Has a distinctive, easily heard wing whistle in flight. **Noteworthy:** Common Goldeneyes often associate with Buffleheads in Arizona.

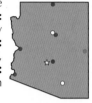

BARROW'S GOLDENEYE, *Bucephala islandica*

Description: 18″. Chunky, medium-sized diving duck with short bill, bright yellow eyes, and **vertical forehead peaking in front of eye**. MALE: **Crescent-shaped white face patch; piano key pattern on wings.** FEMALE: Chocolate-brown head with golden eyes and gray body; in winter **bill mostly yellow-orange. Similar Species:** Male Common Goldeneye (above) has oval cheek spots with sloping forehead, and crown peak above eye; female has longer, yellow-tipped bill. **Voice:** Usually silent in our area. **Status:** Rare in winter (Nov-mid Mar). **Habitat:** Deep lakes and rivers; only regular at reservoirs along the Colorado River. **Elevations:** Winter 150′-7,000′. **Behavior:** Dives for aquatic invertebrates. **Noteworthy:** Barrow's often associate with Common Goldeneyes in Arizona.

Common Merganser
Male

Common Merganser
Female

Red-breasted Merganser
Male

Red-breasted Merganser
Female

COMMON MERGANSER, *Mergus merganser*

Description: 25". Diving duck with **deep-based**, long, slender, red bill. MALE: Green head with short hindcrest; **snow-white breast and flanks**. FEMALE: Rusty head with **crisp white chin spot;** rusty neck contrasts sharply with gray breast. **Similar Species:** Male Red-breasted Merganser (below) has shaggy crest and white collar; female lacks white chin spot. **Voice:** Usually silent. **Status:** Uncommon in summer (Apr-Oct); fairly common but local in winter (Oct-Mar). **Habitat:** Summer: Breeds on clear, cold, fast-running streams within woodlands; disperses to highland lakes; Winter: Usually large lakes. **Elevations:** Summer 2,800'-9,300'; Winter 100'-9,300'. **Behavior:** Dives for small fish, which it catches and holds with "saw-toothed" bill. Typically in flocks. **Noteworthy:** Merganser "teeth", invisible under field conditions, are projections on the horny sheath of the bill. Arizona Common Mergansers are thought to nest on cliff ledges—not inside hollow trees.

RED-BREASTED MERGANSER, *Mergus serrator*

Description: 23". Diving duck with **narrow-based**, long, reddish-orange bill. BREEDING MALE: Dark green head with **shaggy crest**, conspicuous **white neck ring**, mottled reddish breast, and **gray flanks**. NON-BREEDING MALE: Resembles female but shows more white in wing. FEMALE: **Tawny brown head** with thin, shaggy crest; tawny neck blends into gray body. **Similar Species:** Male Common Merganser lacks shaggy crest and white collar; female has bright rusty head with white chin spot. **Voice:** Usually silent. **Status:** Rare in winter (Oct-May); casual in summer (Jun-Sep). **Habitat:** Larger ponds and lakes. **Elevations:** Winter 100'-4,300'. **Behavior:** Dives for fish, which it catches and holds with "saw-toothed" bill. **Noteworthy:** Typically only singles or—rarely—pairs of Red-breasted Merganser occur in Arizona.

MALE

FEMALE

Hooded Merganser

Ruddy Duck

HOODED MERGANSER, *Lophodytes cucullatus*

Description: 18". Small, puffy-headed diving duck with **fan-shaped crest** and short narrow bill. MALE: White crest outlined in black; folded-back crest reduced to thick white stripe; black bill. FEMALE: Tawny-brown crest and bill mostly yellow. JUVENILE MALE: Like female with black bill. **Similar Species:** Male Bufflehead (p. 47) has white sides. Other mergansers much larger with red or orange bills.
Voice: Usually silent. **Status:** Uncommon in winter (mid Oct-mid Apr); casual in summer (mid Apr-mid Oct). **Habitat:** Small, clearwater ponds and lakes. **Elevations:** Winter 100'-7,700'. **Behavior:** Dives for small fish and aquatic invertebrates. **Noteworthy:** Clear nictitating membrane acts like goggles and allows Hooded to hunt underwater.

RUDDY DUCK, *Oxyura jamaicensis*

Description: 15". Small duck with **pale cheeks**; long, **stiff tail, often pointed skyward.** BREEDING MALE: Rich chestnut-red back and sky-blue bill (Apr-Sep, occasionally through Dec). NONBREEDING MALE: Gray with black crown and large white cheek patches. FEMALE: Shows dark lines across pale cheeks. **Similar Species**: Female Bufflehead (p. 47) has an oval white cheek patch. **Voice:** Male uses accelerating series of low, popping notes ending in low croak, *fup fut-fut-fut-fttttp*. **Status:** Uncommon in summer (May-Aug); common in winter (Sep-Apr).
Habitat: Valley lakes and ponds; prefers ponds and lakes with cattails in summer. **Elevations:** Resident 100'-9,400'. **Behavior:** Dives for aquatic plants, as well as small fish and invertebrates. Usually dives when approached; requires a long taxiway for flight. **Noteworthy:** Potentially a breeding species in any county at any elevation in Arizona.

Montezuma Quail
Male

Female

"Masked" Northern Bobwhite
Male

Female

MONTEZUMA QUAIL, *Cyrtonyx montezumae*

Description: 9". Plump, short-tailed, strikingly patterned quail with blob-like **"pony-tail" crest** on hindhead. MALE: **"Clown" face**. FEMALE: Muted facial pattern of male. **Similar Species:** Gambel's Quail (p. 57) has a dark topknot and Scaled Quail (p. 59) has a distinct crest. Masked Bobwhite—confined to Buenos Aires NWR—lacks the "pony-tail" crest of Montezuma Quail. **Voice:** Ventriloquial, airy *vee-urrr* call, like distant falling bomb. **Status:** Fairly common resident. **Habitat:** Foothill and mountain grassy oak woodlands, pine-oak woodland, and open coniferous forests. **Elevations:** Resident 3,800'-10,000'. **Behavior:** Forages for seeds, bulbs, acorns, and insects. Freezes when disturbed, and usually does not run or explode into flight unless danger is within 10'-15'. **Noteworthy:** Montezuma Quail numbers are directly correlated to precipitation the previous summer. Cryptic plumage and habit of freezing makes this species difficult to see.

"MASKED" NORTHERN BOBWHITE, *Colinus virginianus ridgwayi*

Description: 9.75". Plump **reddish** quail. MALE: Black foreface and throat with cinnamon underparts. FEMALE: Buffy eyestripe and throat; lacks chestnut belly. **Similar Species:** Scaled (p. 59) and Gambel's Quail (p. 57) are predominantly blue-gray and crested. Intricately patterned Montezuma Quail (above) has "pony-tail" on hindhead. **Voice**: Explosive *bob-whoit!* **Status:** Eliminated by overgrazing from Arizona by 1897, still largely unsuccessful reintroduction attempts began in 1974 on the Buenos Aires NWR 50 miles southwest of Tucson. **Habitat:** Wide grassy swales in the Altar Valley. **Elevations:** Resident 3,400'-3,800'. **Behavior:** Walks with head held low as it forages for seeds, berries, and insects. Forms flocks in nonbreeding season. **Noteworthy:** Breeding season is timed to take advantage of the summer monsoons, and cocks begin calling after rains commence in July.

Gambel's Quail
Male

Female

California Quail
Male

Female

GAMBEL'S QUAIL, *Callipepla gambelii*

Description: 11". Plump blue-gray quail with dapper black topknot; **chestnut flanks** pin-striped white. MALE: Chestnut cap, long topknot, black face, and **black belly.** FEMALE: Lacks chestnut cap, black face, and black belly. **Similar Species:** Scaled Quail has shorter, tawny crest and scaly neck and breast. Rare Gambel's x Scaled Quail hybrids usually retain Gambel's topknot but show scaly neck and breast. **Voice:** Quavering *wah-h* and loud *chi-CA-go-ga-go*. **Status:** Common resident; rare in NE. **Habitat:** Primarily Sonoran and Chihuahuan desertscrub, but also in NW Great Basin Desert, and may wander into coniferous forest up to 8,000', as well as residential areas within these habitats.

Typically occupies areas with more mesquite and brush than Scaled Quail. **Elevations:** Resident 1,000'-7,000'. **Behavior:** Scatches for seeds, berries, cactus fruits, and insects. Forms flocks in nonbreeding season. **Noteworthy:** Winter precipitation is most important factor determining abundance the following year. Gambel's Quail readily use backyard seed feeders.

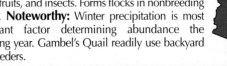

CALIFORNIA QUAIL, *Callipepla californica*

Description: 10". Plump brownish-gray quail with dapper black topknot; **brown flanks** pin-striped white; **scaly underparts.** MALE: Chestnut cap, long topknot, and black face. FEMALE: Lacks chestnut cap and black face. **Similar Species:** Range does not overlap with Gambel's Quail (above). Larger Gambel's never shows scaling on hind neck and belly. **Voice**: Despairing *whah-h* and loud, fast *chic-chic-cool*, both similar to Gambel's Quail. **Status:** Fairly common but local resident. **Habitat:** Agricultural valleys with permanent water and dense thickets within the upper Great Basin Desert. **Elevations:** Resident 5,900'-6,700'. **Behavior:** Forages for seeds, plant buds, and insects. Flocks in nonbreeding season. **Noteworthy:** California Quail were introduced in the valley of the Little Colorado River north of Springerville in 1960.

Scaled Quail
Male

Female

Female

Dusky Grouse
Male

SCALED QUAIL, *Callipepla squamata*

Description: 10". Plump, blue-gray quail with **tawny crest; appears scaly on neck and chest**. MALE: White-tipped crest. FEMALE: Buffy crest. **Similar Species:** Gambel's Quail (p. 57) has dapper black topknot–not tawny crest–chestnut flanks, and unscaled underparts. **Voice:** Sharp *querk!* or *pic-ture pic-ture*. **Status:** Common resident. **Habitat:** Valley grassland and open Chihuahuan Desert scrub, primarily east of the Santa Cruz River. A disjunct high desert population survives in central-eastern Arizona. Prefers flat and gently rolling terrain. **Elevations:** Resident 2,800'-6,700'. **Behavior:** Forages for seeds, plants, and insects. Forms large flocks in non-breeding season. **Noteworthy:** Although shorter overall, on average Scaled Quail outweighs Gambel's Quail by about one ounce.

DUSKY GROUSE, *Dendragapus obscurus*

Description: 20". **Large, gray-brown, square-tailed game bird with feathered legs.** MALE: Bare, inflatable orange combs above eyes; blackish chest. In display shows a raspberry-colored round pouch of bare skin on neck, surrounded by orbit of immaculate white feathers; fans gray-tipped, blackish tail. FEMALE: Mottled neutral gray and soft brown with thin, broken white lines and flecks, primarily on sides. **Similar Species:** Larger, darker Wild Turkeys (p. 63) have entirely bare heads. **Voice:** Male uses very low, soft hoots during courtship that reverberate from nearby like a hollow reed; female cackles. **Status:** Uncommon resident. **Habitat:** Open coniferous forests and aspen glades, especially where interrupted by small clearings and meadows. **Elevations:** Resident 7,800'-11,000'. **Behavior:** Forages for seeds, forbs, fruits, and insects on ground; consumes conifer needles in winter. Freezes when disturbed, and does not fly unless closely approached. Often takes an open, nearby perch when flushed. **Noteworthy:** Population in the San Francisco Peaks north of Flagstaff stems from re-introductions from Arizona's White Mountains in the late 1970s.

Chukar

Ring-necked Pheasant
Female

Ring-necked Pheasant
Male

CHUKAR, *Alectoris chukar*

Description: 14". Fairly large, **red-billed**, red-legged game bird with black and white flank bars. Bold black outline frames pale buff face and throat. Sexes alike. JUVENILE: Lacks black. FLIGHT: **Rusty outer tail feathers.** **Similar Species:** Dusky Grouse (p. 59) lacks red bill and bold black markings. **Voice**: Fast, quacking *chuck-a chuck-a chuck-a*. **Status:** Uncommon resident. **Habitat:** Rocky, sparsely vegetated hillsides and ridges with access to permanent water in seeps, springs, stock tanks, or creeks. **Elevations:** Resident 3,000'-6,700'. **Behavior:** Forages for seeds. Forms flocks from 5-40 in nonbreeding season from July-February. **Noteworthy:** Chukars are native to southern Asia; transplants in Arizona occurred rom 1941-1963. Overgrazing may benefit Chukars by increasing the amount of cheatgrass and other exotic weeds.

RING-NECKED PHEASANT, *Phasianus colchicus*

Description: M 32"; F 21". **Large** game bird with **tapering long tail**. MALE: **Red face**; blue-green head and neck; **molten bronze body**. May have white neck ring or white wings. FEMALE: Buffy, intricately scalloped upperparts. **Similar Species:** Greater Roadrunner (p. 79) resembles female but has long bill and is heavily streaked with white. **Voice:** Descending series of loud, penetrating *kuk-kuk* notes. Thumps wings loudly and cackles when flushed or in display. **Status:** Uncommon resident. **Habitat:** Alfalfa or grain fields with adjacent hedgerows, brushy ditches, or old citrus orchards in river valleys broad enough for farming, primarily in Yuma area. **Elevations:** Resident 100'-3,600'. **Behavior:** Forages for grain, fruits, and insects on ground. Males form small harems of hens in spring. **Noteworthy:** Originally from Asia, pheasants in Arizona are descendants of transplants from 1912-1973. The "White-winged" form originated in Mongolia.

"Mexican"
Male

"Merriam's"
Male

Wild Turkey
Female

Description: Male: 46", female: 37". **Large** game bird with **naked head and neck.** Tail feathers of "Mexican" race birds in SE Arizona are tipped whitish; "Merriam's" race in central and northern Arizona has tail tipped buff. MALE: Head and grotesque, inflatable neck wattles may change color from off-white to pale blue to cherry red within 5 minutes, reflecting the tom's mood; long, black "beard" projects from breast; legs are pink and stout with "fighting" spurs on hind-tarsus. FEMALE: Smaller; head is usually dull pink, sometimes bluish, and wattles are small.

Similar Species: Domestic turkey is usually larger, plumper, often partially or all white.

Voice: Displaying male gives familiar descending *gobble*, and in spring and summer almost any loud noise can prompt gobbling. Females use *tuk* notes and series of *yike* calls; juveniles emit a piping, penetrating series of *peeps*, usually repeated.

Status: Locally fairly common resident.

Habitat: Large mountain canyons, open coniferous forest, and grassy meadows at higher elevations. Less frequently observed in river valley gallery forests of cottonwoods and sycamores, especially adjacent to grassy oak woodlands.

Elevations: Resident 3,800'-10,000'.

Behavior: Terrestrial. Forages by scratching for seeds, nuts, fruits, and insects. Although capable of flights of 200 or more yards, seldom flies except to roost in trees at night. In breeding display, male puffs out feathers, spreads tail, swells facial wattles, droops wings to ground and rattles them, struts, and gobbles. Nomadic and gregarious, turkeys are usually in flocks. Males may form "bachelor" groups in summer while hens tend poults.

Noteworthy: Since 1983, "Mexican" Wild Turkey (also known as "Gould's") has been reintroduced into all of the major ranges of SE Arizona. Arizona fall gobblers weigh up to 26 pounds and average about 18 pounds; hens usually weigh about 12 pounds.

Least Grebe
Breeding

Nest

Pied-billed Grebe
Nonbreeding

Pied-billed Grebe
Breeding and Young

LEAST GREBE, *Tachybaptus dominicus*

Description: 9.5". Tiny diving bird with short **thin neck**, short black bill, and **golden-yellow eyes**. NONBREEDING: White throat. **Similar Species:** Larger Pied-billed Grebe (below) has dark eyes and thicker—often banded—bill. Larger Eared and Horned Grebes (next page) have red eyes, and bold head patterns. **Voice:** Rattling, drawn-out nasal scold. **Status:** Casual year-round; may be present at the same location from several weeks to several years. **Habitat:** Lakes and ponds, especially with cattails and reeds. **Elevations:** Year-round 1,500'-5,600'. **Behavior:** Dives for and also chases aquatic insects and small fish. **Noteworthy:** Often rides high in the water like a "toy duck." In Arizona breeds sporadically, infrequently in consecutive years.

PIED-BILLED GREBE, *Podilymbus podiceps*

Description: 13". Small, **dark-eyed** diver with short **thick neck** and short **thick bill**. BREEDING: Silvery bill with **black ring**; black throat. NONBREEDING: Unmarked horn-colored bill. JUVENILE: Striped face. **Similar Species:** Eared and Horned Grebes (p. 67) have longer, slimmer necks and thin bills; smaller Least Grebe (above) has golden-yellow eyes. **Voice:** Vocal in summer. Male's song is loud *kuh kuh kuh kow kow kow kow-ah kow-ah* and *huzza-huzza-huzza*. **Status:** Uncommon in summer (Jun-Aug); except at highest elevations, fairly common migrant and winter visitor (Sep-May). **Habitat:** Lakes and ponds, especially with cattails and reeds. **Elevations:** Resident 100'-9,200'. **Behavior:** Dives for fish and aquatic invertebrates. Nest is well-concealed floating platform attached to emergent vegetation. **Noteworthy:** When disturbed Pied-billed Grebes slowly submerge and then swim away underwater.

Horned Grebe
Nonbreeding

Breeding

Eared Grebe
Nonbreeding

Breeding

HORNED GREBE, *Podiceps auritus*

Description: 14". Small, big-headed diver with relatively **flat crown, straight bill with ivory tip**. BREEDING: **Thick yellow "horns"** behind red eyes and **rufous neck**. NONBREEDING: Bicolored head with white lower half; **white throat and foreneck**. **Similar Species:** Nonbreeding Eared Grebe (below) has dusky foreneck, peaked crown, grayish cheek outlined with paler rear crescent, and subtly upcurved bill. **Voice:** Usually silent in our area. **Status:** Rare in winter (Oct-mid Apr). **Habitat:** Large ponds and lakes. **Elevations:** Winter 200'-9,000'. **Behavior:** Dives for small fish and aquatic invertebrates. **Noteworthy:** In Arizona only rarely seen in full breeding plumage and only in spring (Apr).

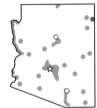

EARED GREBE, *Podiceps nigricollis*

Description: 13". Dainty diver with **peaked crown**; subtly-**upcurved, thin bill**. BREEDING: **Wispy golden fan** behind red eyes and **black neck**. NONBREEDING: Peaked crown; gray cheek outlined with whitish rear crescent; neck variably washed with gray. May have dull yellow eyes in winter. **Similar Species:** Horned Grebe (above) has a flatter crown, white lower face, clean white foreneck, and straight, pale-tipped bill. **Voice:** Burry repeated whistle of *wheat* or *wooh-eat*. **Status:** Uncommon and local summer resident (Jun-Aug), especially in N. Arizona; widespread and fairly common in winter (Sep-May). **Habitat:** Large ponds and lakes, primarily with open or grassy shorelines. **Elevations:** Summer 100'-9,200'; Winter 100'-7,100'. **Behavior:** Dives for aquatic invertebrates. Winter rafts of over 50 birds, occasionally hundreds, may occur on large reservoirs. **Noteworthy:** Most breeding birds in Arizona are in the shallows of lakes and ponds north of the Mogollon Rim, but has bred at Prescott and Willcox.

WESTERN GREBE

Breeding

Nonbreeding

CLARK'S GREBE

Breeding

Nonbreeding

RED-NECKED GREBE

Breeding

Nonbreeding

WESTERN GREBE, *Aechmophorus occidentalis*

Description: 25″. Large grebe with long slender neck; **dull yellow-olive bill;** bright red eyes. Summer: **Black crown envelopes eyes.** Winter: Patch surrounding eye fades to gray. **Similar Species:** Clark's Grebe (below) has bright orange bill; during summer white extends above eye. **Voice:** Loud, grating *kree-kreeek*. **Status:** Uncommon in summer (Jun-Aug); common along Colorado River in winter (Sep-May), uncommon elsewhere. **Habitat:** Large ponds and lakes with both open expanses of water and cattail and bulrush stands. **Elevations:** Winter 100′-7,100′; Summer 150′-9,200′. **Behavior:** Dives for fish in lakes and ponds. **Noteworthy:** Famous for elaborate courtship dance where pairs race across water in unison. Nests year-round in Colorado River lakes.

CLARK'S GREBE, *Aechmophorus clarkii*

Description: 25″. Large grebe with long slender neck; **distinctly orange bill;** bright red eyes. Summer: **Eyes surrounded by white**. Winter: White lores. **Status:** Uncommon in summer (Jun-Aug); common along Colorado River in winter (mid Sep-May), rare elsewhere. **Habitat:** Same as Western Grebe. **Elevations:** Winter 200′-7,100′; Summer 200′-9,000′. **Noteworthy:** Usually found with Western Grebes. Until 1985, Clark's was considered a plumage morph of Western Grebe.

RED-NECKED GREBE, *Podiceps grisegena*

Description: 20″. Large grebe with fairly heavy, **down-angled bill.** BREEDING: **Red neck**. NONBREEDING: Yellowish bill; diffuse grayish neck. **Similar Species:** Larger Western and Clark's Grebes (above) have much thinner bills and proportionately longer necks that are sharply demarcated black and white. **Status:** Rare and irregular winter resident (mid Aug-May). **Habitat:** Large ponds and lakes, primarily reservoirs on the Colorado River. **Elevations:** Winter 450′-4,300′. **Noteworthy:** Often consumes its own feathers while preening, perhaps to aid digestion.

Rock Pigeon

Band-tailed Pigeon

ROCK PIGEON, *Columba livia*

Description: 13″. Introduced pigeon with **black bill** and white cere; iridescent neck; **pink legs**. TYPICAL: **Pale gray body** with **two black wingbars**; gray tail with black terminal band. **Many other plumages,** ranging from entirely white to rusty to all black. FLIGHT: Birds with typical plumage have **white underwings. Similar Species:** Band-tailed Pigeon (below) has yellow bill and feet, white hindneck crescent and lacks black wingbars. **Voice:** Gruff cooing notes and gurgles. Wings clap on take-off. **Status:** Common resident. **Habitat:** Cities, towns, and farms. Flocks often roost under highway overpasses. **Elevations:** Resident 100′-8,000′. **Behavior:** Eats seeds, fruits, and a wide variety of discarded human foods. **Noteworthy:** Rock Pigeons first colonized Arizona towns about 1900.

BAND-TAILED PIGEON, *Patagioenas fasciata*

Description: 14″. Native pigeon with **yellow bill; white crescent on hindneck; dark body** and dark-banded gray tail; **yellow legs**. JUVENILE: Lacks white collar. FLIGHT: **Gray underwings. Similar Species:** Rock Pigeon (above) has black bill and pink legs, usually pale gray body with two bold black wingbars. **Voice:** Owl-like hooting *to-who? to-who? who-o-o?* Wings clap on take-off. **Status:** Usually fairly common but irregular in summer (late Mar-Oct); rare in winter (Nov-late Mar). **Habitat:** Mountain forests and canyon groves. Casual to valley river groves and suburbia. **Elevations:** Summer 4,000′-11,300′; Winter 1,000′-7,100′. **Behavior:** Flocks in Arizona roam up to 20 miles per day in search of acorns, pinyon nuts, mulberries, manzanita berries, and seeds. **Noteworthy:** Possible anywhere in Arizona, Band-tailed Pigeons have been reported from an elevation of 150′ on the lower Colorado River to timberline on the San Francisco Peaks.

Eurasian Collared-Dove

White-winged Dove

Mourning Dove

EURASIAN COLLARED-DOVE, *Streptopelia decaocto*

Description: 12.5". **Large, pale dove** with **black hind-collar** and dark flight feathers. **Similar Species:** Smaller, darker White-winged Dove (below) has white wing crescents. **Voice:** Trisyllabic cooing *coo-coo coop*. **Status:** Common resident, most withdraw from elevations above 7,100' in winter (Nov-Feb). **Habitat:** Valley farms and suburbia; summer wanderers enter mountain openings at high elevations. **Elevations:** Summer 100'-9,500'; Winter 100'-7,100'. **Behavior:** Doves often forage on the ground and use elevated perches. **Noteworthy:** First detected in Arizona in 2000, its population is still expanding.

WHITE-WINGED DOVE, *Zenaida asiatica*

Description: 12". Bulky dove with **bold white wing crescents; square tail with white corners**. **Similar Species:** Similar-sized Mourning Dove (below) has black spots on wings and long, pointed tail. **Voice:** Usually rendered *who cooks for you?* **Status:** Common in summer (Mar-Sep); uncommon in winter (Oct-Feb), most below 5,500'. **Habitat:** Deserts, valleys, foothills, and lower mountain canyons. Common in towns and cities. High elevation birds occur primarily in urban settings or farms. **Elevations:** Summer 100'-8,400'; Winter 100'-5,500'. **Behavior:** Diet in most of its Arizona range includes saguaro nectar and fruits. **Noteworthy:** Arrival of Sonoran Desert population coincides with flowering of saguaros.

MOURNING DOVE, *Zenaida macroura*

Description: 12". Slender dove with **black-spotted wings** and **long, pointed tail**. **Similar Species:** Heavier-set White-winged Dove (above) has white crescents in the wings and white corners on its square tail. **Voice:** Mournful *oah-oo-oo-ooo*. **Status:** Common resident; most withdraw from higher elevations in winter (Nov-Mar). **Habitat:** Deserts, valleys, foothills, and lower mountain canyons. Common in towns and cities. **Elevations:** Summer 100-9,500'; Winter 100'-5,500'. **Noteworthy:** Often considered the most abundant breeding bird in Arizona.

73

Inca Dove

COMMON GROUND DOVE

Male

Female

RUDDY GROUND DOVE

Pair

Female

INCA DOVE, *Columbina inca*

Description: 8.5". Little, **long-tailed** town dove; head and **upperparts entirely "scaled."** FLIGHT: Chestnut wings; **white outer tail feathers**. **Similar Species:** Smaller Common Ground Dove (below) has short tail with black outer tail feathers. **Voice:** Blowy *no hope*. **Status:** Fairly common resident. **Habitat:** Desert and valley farms and towns. **Elevations:** Resident 100'-5,800'. **Noteworthy:** Inca Dove is almost never found far from human habitations. This species nests throughout the year.

COMMON GROUND DOVE, *Columbina passerina*

Description: 6.5". Little, **short-tailed** dove; only head and breast appear scaly; **bill red or pink.** MALE: Blue-gray crown; rosy breast. FEMALE: Uniform gray. FLIGHT: Chestnut wings; **black outer tail feathers**. **Similar Species:** Inca Dove (above) has longer tail and its upperparts appear scaly. Both Inca and Ruddy Ground Doves have slaty bills—not red. **Voice**: Deliberate *wu-u wu-u wuoop*. **Status:** Uncommon resident. **Habitat:** Desert and valley openings and fields adjacent to brush and permanent water. **Elevations:** Resident 100'-5,800'. **Noteworthy:** Usually does not associate with Ruddy Ground Dove.

RUDDY GROUND DOVE, *Columbina talpacoti*

Description: 6.75". Little dove with **medium-length tail; bill slaty**. MALE: Bluish-gray head; ruddy upperparts. FEMALE: Rump tinged reddish. FLIGHT: Chestnut wings; **black outer tail feathers**. **Similar Species:** Common Ground Dove (above) has scaly head and breast and red-based bill. **Voice:** Almost identical to Common Ground Dove but *whoop whoop* notes are delivered at much faster tempo. **Status:** Rare and irregular resident, most common in winter (late Sep-early Apr). **Habitat:** Desert and valley farms and feedlots adjacent to brush and permanent water. **Elevations:** Resident 100'-5,200'. **Noteworthy:** First recorded in Arizona in 1981, Ruddy's often associate with Inca Doves.

Groove-billed Ani

Yellow-billed Cuckoo

GROOVE-BILLED ANI, *Crotophaga sulcirostris*

Description: 13.5". Awkward, disheveled-looking, entirely black bird with a long, floppy tail. Cleaver-like **bill shows lateral grooving. Similar Species:** Male Great-tailed Grackle (p. 423) has much thinner bill and yellow eyes. **Voice:** Whiny, repeated calls of *treach-e-ry*. **Status:** Rare, primarily in summer (mid Jun-Aug) and fall (mid Oct-Nov) but records span year. **Habitat:** Valley areas with thick, rank brush and vines. **Elevations:** Year-round 850'-6,000'. **Behavior:** Eats mostly big, slow-moving insects. In Mexico adults from several pairs known to share communal nest. **Noteworthy:** In Arizona shows a tendency to arrive during the summer rainy season. Only a few records from northern Arizona, including 1 at an elevation of 6,000' at Lyman Lake. Most records are of singles, but a typical flock of a dozen or more birds occurred once near the Mexican border at Arivaca.

YELLOW-BILLED CUCKOO, *Coccyzus americanus*

Description: 12". Sleek brown bird with arched, mostly **yellow bill;** long, **black and white tail.** JUVENILE: Bill lacks yellow. FLIGHT: Like small falcon with **chestnut flight feathers. Similar Species:** Black-billed Cuckoo (accidental Aug-Oct) has black bill, red eyering, mostly gray undertail, and lacks red in the flight feathers. **Voice:** Staccato *cuk-cuk-cuk* ending in *kowlp kowlp*. **Status:** Fairly common summer resident (Jun-Sep); rare earlier or later (Apr-May and Oct). **Habitat:** Valley river and broad foothill canyon stream groves, especially with permanent water, cottonwoods, and willows; strays occur in any grove of trees in arid landscapes and up to lowest pines in mountains. **Elevations:** Summer 100'-6,000'. **Behavior:** Dines on larvae, helping control tent caterpillar outbreaks. Yellow-billed typically does not lay eggs in other bird's nests. **Noteworthy:** Recorded infrequently in May, most arrive after mid June, giving Yellow-billed Cuckoo the distinction of being the last breeding bird to arrive in Arizona.

Bushy crest erected

GREATER ROADRUNNER, *Geococcyx californianus*

Description: 23". Big, **bushy-crested, heavily-streaked ground cuckoo** with long, expressive tail. The crest can be elevated or lowered at will. An inch-long patch of bare, mostly blue skin extends behind the eye. When agitated or in courtship the rear-most end of this skin may turn bright orange.

Similar Species: Distinctive; similarly shaped thrashers are much smaller birds, never streaked on their upperparts.

Voice: Piteous series of *wuah wuah wuah* moans like a sorry puppy, fading at end; male's call is an evenly spaced, fast series of 8-10 *whoop* notes. Both sexes produce a castanet-like bill clatter.

Status: Fairly common resident.

Habitat: Deserts, valley grasslands, and open foothill woodlands and chaparral. Common around lowland urban areas, especially near parks or golf courses, vacant lots, or where homes are widely spaced and retain some native plants. Rarely wanders into open Ponderosa pine forest; sparse in Great Basin Desert sagebrush areas.

Elevations: Resident 100'-7,300'.

Behavior: Although famous for occasionally dining on rattlesnake, staples are primarily smaller snakes and lizards. Hunts prey on the ground with bursts of speed and opportunistically catches young quail or doves, other birds, small rodents, and large insects. Has been timed running parallel to roads at 15 mph. Also eats some cactus fruit. Courting Roadrunners present potential mates with a stick or lizard. Displaying birds may fly 50 feet or higher to the tops of trees or utility poles. On sunny days in cold weather a Roadrunner often spreads its back feathers to reveal black skin, and positions itself to absorb maximum warmth.

Noteworthy: In southern Arizona Greater Roadrunners typically nest twice: once in spring and again during the midsummer monsoons.

Lesser Nighthawk

Common Nighthawk

LESSER NIGHTHAWK, *Chordeiles acutipennis*

Description: 9″. Slim, falconate nightbird; when perched shows **white wing patch below rump**; long, notched tail. MALE: White throat. FEMALE: Buff throat. FLIGHT: White (male) or buff (female) **bar close to wingtip**, midway out in primaries; **rounded wingtips**. **Similar Species:** In flight Common Nighthawk (below) has pointed wingtips. **Voice:** Very long purring trill. **Status:** Common in summer (Mar-Oct); rare in winter (Nov-Feb). **Habitat:** Desert and valley grasslands, especially over stock tanks, sewage ponds, irrigated fields, rivers, dirt roads, and parking lots illuminated by mercury vapor lights. **Elevations:** Summer 100′-7,000′; Winter 100′-2,300′. **Behavior:** Performs intricate ballets while capturing flying insects on the wing; often active well into morning or in late afternoon. **Noteworthy:** At strategic watering areas, over 100 birds may gather in late afternoon before dispersing to forage.

COMMON NIGHTHAWK, *Chordeiles minor*

Description: 9.5″. Slim, falconate nightbird; when perched shows **white wing patch below back**; long, notched tail. MALE: White throat. FEMALE: Buff throat. FLIGHT: White (male) or buff (female) **bar 2/3s of the way to wingtip,** at base of primaries; **pointed wingtips**. **Similar Species:** In flight Lesser Nighthawk (above) has rounded wingtips. **Voice:** Nasal bleat: *peeent*. Males produce a loud bellow with wings in display dives. **Status:** Uncommon in summer (mid May-mid Sep); casual earlier in May or later in September. **Habitat:** Great Basin desertscapes; higher valley grasslands and oak, juniper, and pinyon-juniper savannas; open mountain steppes, large meadows, and burns. **Elevations:** Summer 4,200′-9,000′. **Behavior:** Captures flying insects, often higher above ground than Lesser Nighthawks. **Noteworthy:** Migrating flocks in August may number 100 or more birds.

Common Poorwill

Buff-collared Nightjar

Mexican Whip-poor-will

COMMON POORWILL, *Phalaenoptilus nuttallii*

Description: 7.75". **Small** nightjar with **short tail**. MALE: White tail corners. FEMALE: Buffy tail tips. **Similar Species:** Larger Buff-collared Nightjar (below) has longer tail extending beyond wingtips. **Voice:** Evocative *poor-will!* **Status:** Fairly common in summer (mid Feb-Oct); rarely detected in winter (Nov-mid-Feb). **Habitat:** Deserts and arid grasslands, usually with broken terrain; foothills with open woodland, often in canyons. **Elevations:** Summer 100'-8,500'; Winter 300'-5,100'. **Behavior:** Usually captures flying insects from ground perches. **Noteworthy:** Winter status is unknown, but Common Poorwill is the only species of bird known to hibernate. Early migrants or awakening birds begin appearing after mid-Feb.

BUFF-COLLARED NIGHTJAR, *Antrostomus ridgwayi*

Description: 8.75". Nightjar with **cinnamon hindcollar**. MALE: Extensive white tail corners. FEMALE: Buffy tail tips. **Similar Species:** Larger Whip-poor-will (below) has longer tail and lacks crisp cinnamon hindcollar. **Voice:** Piano-like up-scale notes often rendered *presta-me-tu-cuchillo* in Spanish. **Status:** Rare in summer (Apr-mid Sep). **Habitat:** Foothill thornscrub. **Elevations:** Summer 2,400'-4,700'. **Behavior:** Captures flying insects from short treetops. **Noteworthy:** Its discovery in Guadalupe Canyon in extreme SE Arizona in 1960 was a first U.S. record.

MEXICAN WHIP-POOR-WILL, *Antrostomus arizonae*

Description: 9.75". Nightjar with dark **median crown stripe**. MALE: Bold white tail corners. FEMALE: Buffy tail tips. **Similar Species:** Smaller Buff-collared Nightjar (above) has shorter tail and lacks median crown stripe. **Voice:** Burry *uh-purple-whip! purple-whip! purple-whip!* **Status:** Fairly common in summer (mid Apr-mid Oct). **Habitat:** Mountain pine-oak woodland and coniferous forest, especially in canyon groves. **Elevations:** Summer 3,700'-9,500'. **Behavior:** Usually captures flying insects from tree perches. **Noteworthy:** Occurs to the summit of all borders ranges in SE Arizona, but seldom found north of the Mogollon Rim in central Arizona.

Vaux's Swift

White-throated Swift

VAUX'S SWIFT, *Chaetura vauxi*

Description: 4.75". Small aerialist often described as a "cigar with wings." **Dusky overall**, with paler gray throat, breast, and rump; **short, squared tail**. **Similar Species:** Long-tailed White-throated Swift (below) has contrasting black and white plumage. Larger counterpart in eastern U.S. <u>Chimney Swift</u> (accidental in May and Jul-mid Sep), shows bulging inner primaries. Swallows have shorter, broader-based wings. **Voice:** Thin chittering usually not heard in our area. **Status:** Rare spring (Apr-mid May) and uncommon fall (late Aug-mid Oct) migrant; casual in fall earlier in Aug and later in Oct. **Habitat:** Deserts and valleys to mountain canyons and crests. **Elevations:** Migration 100'-10,000'. **Behavior:** Forages for flying insects. In Arizona often occurs singly, rarely in large loose flocks. **Noteworthy:** SE Arizona represents the easternmost limits of Vaux's Swift regular occurrence.

WHITE-THROATED SWIFT, *Aeronautes saxatalis*

Description: 6.5". **Black and white** aerialist with white "V" on breast and white sides of rump; **long, notched tail** often appears pointed. **Similar Species:** Smaller Vaux's Swift (above) has a stubby tail and lacks white markings. Larger, stockier <u>Black Swift</u> (casual migrant mid May and mid July-mid Aug) shows no white markings. **Voice:** Scratchy, shrill, and rapid series of *jee-jee-jee* notes delivered in flight. **Status:** Common in summer (Mar-Oct); uncommon in winter (Nov-Feb), but sometimes in flocks of 100 or more birds. **Habitat:** Summer: Near mountain cliffs, ridge lines, and canyons. Winter: Primarily SW Arizona lowland areas, including broad agricultural valleys. **Elevations:** Summer 350'-10,000'; Winter 100'-7,500'. **Behavior:** Flocks forage for flying insects. Visits water holes in spring and summer. Nests colonially in cliff crevices. **Noteworthy:** Among North America's fastest fliers, easily zooming to speeds over 100 mph; nonetheless in Arizona frequently taken by Peregrine Falcons.

Broad-billed Hummingbird
Male

Female

White-eared
Hummingbird Male

Female

BROAD-BILLED HUMMINGBIRD, *Cynanthus latirostris*

Description: 4". Lanky **red-billed** hummingbird with notched **blue-black tail** that it wags in flight. MALE: Rich blue throat and breast; deep green back. FEMALE: "Bandito mask" behind eyes; red-based bill; gray underparts; blackish tail with small white corners. **Similar Species:** Female White-eared Hummingbird (below) has broad white eyestripe, green dots on throat and flanks, and large white tail corners on a green upper tail. **Voice:** Dry chattering *t-dik* notes. **Status:** Common in summer (mid Mar-mid Sep); uncommon in winter (mid Sep-mid Mar). **Habitat:** Upper river valleys, foothills and lower mountain canyon groves, and adjacent human communities. **Elevations:** Summer 1,500'-7,000'; Winter 100'-5,200'. **Behavior:** Feeds on nectar and small, soft-bodied insects. May nest twice during spring and summer. **Noteworthy:** Broad-billed Hummingbirds live up to their name with very wide-based bills.

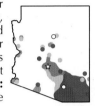

WHITE-EARED HUMMINGBIRD, *Basilinna leucotis*

Description: 3.75". Stout hummingbird with **broad white eyestripe; long wings reach tip of long, green central tail.** MALE: Purple foreface; forest green throat. FEMALE: Usually red-based bill (but may appear all black); green-dotted throat and flanks; white belly; green central tail with white corners. IMMATURE FEMALE: Black bill. **Similar Species:** Female Broad-billed Hummingbird (above) has clean white eyebrow, unblemished gray throat, uniform gray underparts, small white tail corners; wags its tail in flight. **Voice**: Doubled, thin *tsk-tsk* chips; hard chatter. **Status:** Rare in summer (May-Sep); casual earlier in spring and later in fall. **Habitat:** Mountain canyon groves and coniferous forest slopes mixed with some oaks. **Elevations:** Summer 4,800'-9,150'. **Behavior:** Feeds on nectar and gnats. Nests are low in oak or other deciduous tree between 4 and 10' above the ground. **Noteworthy:** Known Arizona nests have been between 6,100'-7,600' in elevation.

Cinnamon Hummingbird

Berylline Hummingbird
Male

Violet-crowned
Hummingbird

BERYLLINE HUMMINGBIRD, *Saucerottia beryllina*

Description: 4". **Red-billed** hummingbird with red primarily on lower mandible, rarely bill may appear black; glittering green throat and breast; **rufous wings and rump; purplish-bronze tail.** MALE: Buffy belly. FEMALE: Gray belly. **Similar Species:** Larger <u>Cinnamon Hummingbird</u> (accidental: 1 record July 1992 in Patagonia) has bright red, black-tipped bill, entirely cinnamon-buff underparts, and lacks rufous wing panels. **Voice:** Toy trumpet *ta-do-ta-tee-ta-teet*; harsh chatter. **Status:** Rare in summer (late Apr-Sep). **Habitat:** Mountain canyon groves. **Elevations:** Summer 4,800'-7,300'. **Behavior:** Feeds on nectar and gnats. May nest twice during spring and summer. **Noteworthy:** The first U.S. record of Berylline Hummingbird came from Madera Canyon in 1964.

VIOLET-CROWNED HUMMINGBIRD, *Leucolia violiceps*

Description: 4.5". **Red-billed** hummingbird with **immaculate white underparts**; back is olive-brown. ADULT: Purple crown. Intensity of crown color does not indicate sex. JUVENILE: May lack purple crown. **Similar Species:** Smaller female Black-chinned Hummingbird (p. 95) lacks red bill, violet crown, and snow-white underparts. **Voice:** Popping *tchk* notes, given singly or in staccato bursts. **Status:** Uncommon in summer (Mar-Sep); rare in winter (Oct-Mar); casual year-round in urban centers. **Habitat:** Foothill and lower mountain canyon groves. **Elevations:** Summer 2,200'-5,800'; Winter 1,250'-5,500'. **Behavior:** Feeds on nectar and gnats. Nests are ordinarily in sycamore trees, rarely in other broadleaf trees. **Noteworthy:** Peak Violet-crowned Hummingbird nesting activity in July seems timed to coincide with the summer rainy season when both flower nectar and tiny insects are most available. The first Arizona nest was in Guadalupe Canyon in 1958.

Blue-throated Mountain-gem
Male

Female

Rivoli's Hummingbird
Male

Female

BLUE-THROATED MOUNTAIN-GEM, *Lampornis clemenciae*

Description: 5.25″. Big, **husky** hummingbird with **medium-length bill**; gray rump; uniform gray underparts; **broad blue-black tail** with **bold white corners**. MALE: Blue throat. FEMALE: Gray throat. **Similar Species:** Female Rivoli's Hummingbird (below) has much longer bill, scaly green sides, and green tail. **Voice:** Piercing, high thin *seep* notes, especially when it flies. **Status:** Fairly common in summer (Apr-Oct); rare in winter (Nov-Mar). **Habitat:** Mountain canyon groves with perennial water. Casual down to 2,000′, up to 9,300′, and accidental in N. Arizona. **Elevations:** Summer 4,800′-7,000′; Winter 2,400′-5,600′. **Behavior:** Feeds on nectar and gnats. Low nests are located under overhanging protection, including cliffs, stream banks, and the eaves of buildings. Successful nests are re-used twice or thrice in the same summer and usually for years, or even decades. **Noteworthy:** Blue-throated is the largest U.S. hummingbird.

RIVOLI'S HUMMINGBIRD, *Eugenes fulgens*

Description: 5.1″. Large, **dark** hummingbird with **long bill**; oily green back. MALE: Iridescent purple cap; white dot behind eye; iridescent green throat; black velvet below. FEMALE: Scaly green sides. JUVENILE MALE: Uniform green scaling below. **Similar Species:** Female Blue-throated Mountain-gem (above) has smooth gray underparts. **Voice:** Imperious *chik!* or *tchik!* chips. **Status:** Common in S. Arizona and rare in N. Arizona--except for Oak Creek Canyon--in summer (Apr-Oct); uncommon and local in winter (Nov-Mar). **Habitat:** Summer: Mountain canyon groves; openings within coniferous forest. Winter: Lower mountain canyons. **Elevations:** Summer 4,800′-9,600′; Winter 3,000′-5,800′. **Behavior:** Feeds on nectar and gnats. Well-concealed nests are high in conifers and broadleaf trees. **Noteworthy:** Subordinate only to Blue-throats, at feeders dominates all smaller hummingbirds.

Plain-capped Starthroat

Flight

Lucifer Hummingbird Male

Female

PLAIN-CAPPED STARTHROAT, *Heliomaster constantii*

Description: 4.9". Large, **olive-brown** hummingbird with **very long straight bill**; thick white facial stripes; long, narrow gorget with red-flecked bottom edge; **white ovals on back and flanks**. **Similar Species:** Green female Rivoli's Hummingbird (page 91) lacks white flank and back ovals. **Voice:** Juicy *wheeck* and *whick* chips. **Status:** Rare in summer (late Apr-Oct, primarily Jul-Sep). **Habitat:** Foothill canyons and hillside agave stands. **Elevations:** Summer 2,750'-5,300'. **Behavior:** Feeds on nectar and gnats. Often takes conspicuous perches on agave stalks and dead tree tops. **Noteworthy:** First U.S. record at Nogales was in 1969. At 1.5", Starthroat has the longest bill of any U.S. hummingbird.

LUCIFER HUMMINGBIRD, *Calothorax lucifer*

Description: 3.75". Slim, green-backed hummer with relatively **long, deeply-arched bill.** MALE: Elongated, pointed purple gorget; long, thin tail. FEMALE: Broad apricot stripe behind eye; apricot and cream underparts; extensively rufous tail base. **Similar Species:** Female Black-chinned Hummingbird (p. 95) lacks broad, apricot stripe behind eye and never shows rufous at base of tail. **Voice:** Lightly smacking *cheat cheat* notes, sometimes run together into a thin stutter. **Status:** Uncommon and local in summer (Apr-mid Oct). **Habitat:** Foothill canyons; hillside agave and ocotillo stands. **Elevations:** Summer 3,000'-5,800'. **Behavior:** Male performs courtship display over the head of female as she sits on nest. Lucifers are seemingly subordinate to almost all other hummingbird species at feeding stations, and may not visit feeders until dusk. **Noteworthy:** It was 89 years from Arizona's first Lucifer Hummingbird sighting in 1874, until the next sighting in 1963. In Latin the name "Lucifer" mean "Light bearer".

93

Ruby-throated Hummingbird
Male

Ruby-throated Hummingbird
Female

Male

Female

Black-chinned Hummingbird

RUBY-THROATED HUMMINGBIRD, *Archilochus colubris*

Description: 3.75". **Lanky**, green-backed hummer with proportionately short bill; **tail projects well beyond wingtips**. MALE: **Narrow black chin strap**; glowing red throat; white spot behind eye; broad white collar; black tail deeply notched. FEMALE: Green crown; flanks tinged buff; longest primary has sharp tip; holds green-based tail steady while feeding. **Similar Species:** Male Broad-tailed Hummingbird has ragged eyering, lacks black chin and deeply cleft tail. Tail-wagging female Black-chinned Hummingbird (below) has longer bill, dull, somewhat grayish crown, and narrow primaries ending in a blunt point. **Voice:** Identical to Black-chinned Hummingbird. **Status:** Casual most of year (June-mid Apr). **Habitat:** Feeding stations in valleys, canyons, and urban areas. **Elevations:** Year-round 1,900'-7,000'. **Behavior:** Consumes twice its body weight in nectar and gnats during daylight hours. **Noteworthy:** When found in Tucson in Dec 2004, Arizona became the last state in the Lower 48 to record this species.

BLACK-CHINNED HUMMINGBIRD, *Archilochus alexandri*

Description: 3.75". **Lanky**, green-backed hummer with medium-long bill; **tail barely projects beyond wingtips**. MALE: **Wide black chin**; violet throat band (often looks black); white spot behind eye; broad white collar below throat. FEMALE: Crown dull grayish-green; throat finely stippled; pale gray underparts; longest primary has blunt tip; wags green-based tail while feeding. **Similar Species:** Female Anna's (p. 97) has diffuse stripe behind eye, heavily dotted throat, dark gray breast with iridescent green flank spotting. **Voice:** Soft *tchup* notes, sometimes doubled or repeated in a series. **Status:** Common summer resident (Mar-mid Oct); casual (Feb and mid Oct-mid Nov). **Habitat:** Deserts, valleys, foothills, and mountains, especially urban areas, oases, river and stream groves. **Elevations:** Summer 100'-8,000'. **Behavior:** Nests near Cooper's Hawks may discourage predation from jays. **Noteworthy:** Arizona's most abundant summering hummingbird.

Anna's Hummingbird
Displaying Male

Female

Costa's Hummingbird
Displaying Male

Female

ANNA'S HUMMINGBIRD, *Calypte anna*

Description: 3.75". **Stocky** hummingbird with **short bill**. MALE: Rose-red, square-cut hood. FEMALE: Diffuse stripe behind eye; spotted throat often with central "beard"; iridescent green flank discs. **Similar Species:** Lanky female Black-chinned Hummingbird (p. 95) has white spot–not stripe– behind eye, finely stippled throat, and lacks green flank discs. **Voice:** Scratchy *zzzt-zzt-zz-zzt* song; call is emphatic *tsik*. **Status:** Common resident; withdraws from higher elevations in winter (Oct-Mar). **Habitat:** Deserts, valleys, foothills, and mountains, especially in urban areas, desert oases, and river and stream groves. **Elevations:** Summer 100'-9,100'; Winter 100'- 5,500'. **Behavior:** Feeds on nectar and gnats without obvious tail-wagging. **Noteworthy:** Anna's is Arizona's most abundant wintering hummingbird. Numbers peak at feeding stations in the Huachuca and Chiricahua Mountains in autumn (Aug-Oct).

COSTA'S HUMMINGBIRD, *Calypte costae*

Description: 3.5". **Chubby**, no-neck hummingbird with **short bill and tail**. MALE: Purple hood with flaring purple gorget. FEMALE: Tiny dots on throat; whitish underparts. **Similar Species:** Larger, darker female Anna's Hummingbird (above) often has "bearded" throat and green flank spots; larger, lankier female Black-chinned Hummingbird (p. 95) has obvious neck. **Voice:** Tiny, tinny *sit* chips; very high, thin, continuous *iiiii* song, rising and fading in volume. **Status:** Uncommon in summer-fall (Jun-Nov) and fairly common in winter-spring (Dec- May). **Habitat:** Desert, valley groves, and foothill  canyons, especially west of San Pedro River. **Elevations:** Summer 100'-5,800'; Winter 100'- 4,900'. **Behavior:** Wags tail as it feeds on nectar and gnats. **Noteworthy:** During May, after the spring wildflower season ends, some Costa's may migrate to California, Baja, and Sonora, while others follow blossoming ocotillos to higher elevations.

Calliope Hummingbird
Male

Female

Broad-tailed Hummingbird
Male

Female

CALLIOPE HUMMINGBIRD, *Selasphorus calliope*

Description: 3.1". **Tiny; very short bill** and **very short tail**. When perched wings extend beyond tail. MALE: Rays of magenta radiate from chin. FEMALE: Loose rows of green flecks radiate from chin; apricot wash below; tail tipped snow white. **Similar Species:** Larger female Costa's Hummingbird (p. 97) has whitish underparts. **Voice:** Usually silent in our area. **Status:** Rare spring (late Mar-mid May) and uncommon fall (mid Jul-Oct) migrant. **Habitat:** Urban areas; valley groves and oases; foothill canyons; hillside agave and ocotillo stands, and mountain canyons and meadows. **Elevations:** Migration 100'-9,300'. **Behavior:** Feeds on nectar and gnats. Adult males precede females and immatures in fall migration and almost all are gone by the end of Aug. **Noteworthy:** Calliope Hummingbird is the smallest bird in the United States and Canada.

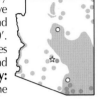

BROAD-TAILED HUMMINGBIRD, *Selasphorus platycercus*

Description: 3.75". **Long-tailed** with irregular **white eyering**. MALE: Deep red, square-cut gorget; white collar; narrow rufous tail edgings. FEMALE: Throat spotted green; buffy flanks; green rump; limited red at base of outer tail. **Similar Species:** Female Rufous and Allen's Hummingbirds (p. 101) have rufous edges on rump coverts and solid red at the base of their tails. **Voice:** Sibilant *ch-dip ch-dip ch-dip*. Wingtips of male Broad-tail produce trill. **Status:** Common in summer (Mar-Sep); uncommon migrant (mid Feb-May and mid Jul-Oct); rare in winter (Nov-mid Feb). **Habitat:** Summer: Mountain canyons and meadows. Migration: Deserts and valleys to mountain tops. Winter: Primarily feeding stations in urban areas and mountain canyons. **Elevations:** Summer 4,900'-11,400'; Migration 400'-11,400'; Winter 100'-5300'. **Behavior:** Feeds on nectar and gnats. **Noteworthy:** Broad-tails are the most common high-elevation hummingbird breeding in Arizona.

Rufous Hummingbird
Male

Female

Allen's Hummingbird
Male

RUFOUS HUMMINGBIRD, *Selasphorus rufus*

Description: 3.5". **Small** hummingbird with **orange flanks** and **rufous tail**. MALE: Fiery orange-red gorget; mostly **copper-red upperparts**. FEMALE: Iridescent blotch in central throat; rusty edging on rump feathers. IMMATURE: Evenly spotted throat. **Similar Species:** Adult male Allen's Hummingbird (below) has green back and its outermost two tail feathers are toothpick-thin. Male Rufous in Arizona have 50% or less of back green; nape and back of male Allen's is green. Without examining photos, female and immature Rufous/Allen's should not be separated in the field. **Voice:** Angry *tzchk tzchk* and *tzchup* chips; male's wing trill higher than male Broad-tailed's. **Status:** Uncommon in spring (Mar-early May.); common in fall (Jul-Oct); rare in winter (Nov-Feb). **Habitat:** Spring: Primarily in lowland valleys and urban areas. Fall: Valleys and urban areas, foothill canyons, hillside agave stands, and mountain canyons and meadows. Winter: Feeding stations. **Elevations:** Migration 100-10,700'; Winter 100'-5,300'. **Behavior:** Often dominates larger hummingbird species at feeders. **Noteworthy:** If migration distance is divided by body length, the 2,000-mile journey of Rufous Hummingbirds is among the longest in the animal kingdom.

ALLEN'S HUMMINGBIRD, *Selasphorus sasin*

Description: 3.35". Like fractionally larger Rufous Hummingbird (above), but adult male has almost solid **green back**. **Similar Species:** See Rufous Hummingbird (above). **Voice:** See Rufous Hummingbird (above). **Status:** Uncommon in summer and fall (late Jun-mid Oct); accidental in late Feb. **Habitat:** Foothill canyons, hillside agave stands, and mountain canyons and meadows. Adult males depart by mid-August. **Elevations:** Migration 1,500'-7,000'. **Behavior:** Feeds on nectar and gnats. **Noteworthy:** Banding studies have shown that Allen's constitutes about five percent of migrant summer and fall Rufous/Allen's in the Santa Rita and Huachuca Mountains, and only about one percent in the Chiricahua Mountains.

Virginia Rail

Sora

VIRGINIA RAIL, *Rallus limicola*

Description: 9.5". Small marsh bird with **long, thin, slightly downcurved bill**; red legs. ADULT: Red bill; cinnamon underparts. JUVENILE: Blackish bill; sooty breast. **Similar Species:** Sora (below) has short, thick yellow bill and olive legs. **Voice:** Song is metallic *t-dik t-dik t-ik t'dik t'dik t'dik*; call is accelerating series of grunts *wunk wunk wuk wuk wuk-uk-krrr*. **Status:** Uncommon in summer (May-Aug); fairly common in winter (Sep-Apr). **Habitat:** Marshes; ponds and lakes with reeds and cattails. **Elevations:** Summer 100'-9000'; Winter 100'-5,900'.

Behavior: Eats aquatic invertebrates, small fish, and seeds. May feed on open mudflats, but usually shy and hidden. Slinks through reeds when disturbed; seldom flies. **Noteworthy:** Aside from the principal nest, Virginia Rails may construct up to five additional nests. These may be backups if the first nest is destroyed, or serve as safe havens after the young fledge.

SORA, *Porzana carolina*

Description: 8.75". Plump little marsh bird with **stubby yellow bill**; olive legs. ADULT: Black foreface surrounding bill; gray breast. JUVENILE: Dull buffy breast. **Similar Species:** Virginia Rail (above) has long, curved bill and red legs. **Voice:** Inquisitive *kuh-wee?* notes; also an initial *squeeah* followed by a long squealing whinny *tk-d-d-d-d-d-d-d-d-dah*. **Status:** Fairly common fall, winter, and spring (Aug-mid May); uncommon in summer (mid May-Jul). **Habitat:** Marshes, as well as ponds and lakes with reeds and cattails. **Elevations:** Summer 700'-9,400'; Winter 100'-5,000'. **Behavior:** Feeds primarily on seeds. May feed on mudflats and open shorelines, but usually shy and hidden. Slinks through reeds when disturbed; seldom flies. **Noteworthy:** Soras are the most widespread rails in North America; Arizona is the southernmost breeding range for the species.

Black Rail

Ridgway's Rail

BLACK RAIL, *Laterallus jamaicensis*

Description: 6". Sparrow-sized, very secretive marsh bird with **short, black bill**; black head; chestnut nape; black **upperparts speckled white. Similar Species:** The blackish juveniles of Virginia Rails and Soras lack white dots above and both have colors on their uniquely-shaped bills. **Voice**: Squeaky *kee-kee-derrr* territorial calls occur primarily from mid Feb-June. California subspecies found in Arizona usually does not call at night. **Status:** Rare resident. **Habitat:** Shallow marshes dominated by threesquare bulrush with stable water depths of less than 2". **Elevations:** Resident 150'-600'. **Behavior:** Eats seeds and small aquatic invertebrates. Extremely shy, it is usually heard and seldom seen. **Noteworthy:** Limited by narrow habitat parameters, the Arizona population probably numbers less than 100 birds.

RIDGWAY'S RAIL, *Rallus obsoletus*

Description: 14.5". Large marsh bird with **long orange bill**; olive legs. ADULT: Buff orange neck and chest. JUVENILE: Mostly gray. **Similar Species:** Much smaller, brighter orange Virginia Rail (p. 103) has more curved red bill and red legs. **Voice:** Loud, long, mechanical series of *kdick* calls which gradually speed-up and slow down. **Status:** Rare resident. **Habitat:** Marshes and reservoirs with extensive reedbeds, cattails, and bulrushes. **Elevations:** Resident 100'-1,000'. **Behavior:** Feeds primarily on crayfish and freshwater clams. Occasionally seen on mudflats and open shorelines, but usually stays concealed. Slinks through reeds when disturbed; seldom flies. **Noteworthy:** Clapper Rails were split into three species in 2014 and the Pacific coast and Colorado River basin birds became Ridgway's Rail. Recent censuses have found about 300 "Yuma" race Ridgway's Rails in Arizona.

ADULTS   IMMATURES

Purple Gallinule

Common Gallinule

American Coot

PURPLE GALLINULE, *Porphyrio martinicus*

Description: 12.5". Glossy purple and green marsh bird with **baby-blue frontal shield**; white undertail coverts; yellow legs. JUVENILE: Thick olive bill; buffy overall with bluish-green tinge on wings. **Similar Species:** Larger Common Gallinule (below) has white flank line and bright red frontal shield. **Status:** Casual in summer (mid Jun-early Oct). **Habitat:** Marshes and ponds with reedy edges, primarily in the vicinity of Tucson. **Elevations:** Summer 1,000'-5,600'.

COMMON GALLINULE, *Gallinula galeata*

Description: 14". Brown-backed marsh bird with **bright red frontal shield** and mostly red bill; **broken white line on flank**. JUVENILE: Frontal shield reduced; dusky bill becomes yellow in immature. **Similar Species:** American Coot (below) lacks white flank line and bright red frontal shield. **Status:** Fairly common but local resident; casual up to 7,000'. **Habitat:** Marshes and ponds with reeds and cattails. **Elevations:** Resident 100'-4,300'. **Behavior:** Forages in water and on mudflats, and grazes on land adjacent to water. **Noteworthy:** Unlike Coots, Gallinules spend most of their time under cover.

AMERICAN COOT, *Fulica americana*

Description: 15". Stocky, dull **black** aquatic bird with stout **white bill**. ADULT: Small, diamond-shaped, maroon frontal shield. JUVENILE: Pale gray below; downy young have blood-red head markings. **Similar Species:** Plain-colored Pied-billed Grebe (p. 65) is tawny-brown. **Status:** Common resident; abundant in winter (Sep-Apr). **Habitat:** Lakes, ponds, and sluggish rivers with permanent water, often next to pastures and golf courses. **Elevations:** Resident 100'-9,400'. **Behavior:** Forages in water, on mudflats, and grazes on land adjacent to water. Nests in marshes. **Noteworthy:** Often the most abundant wetland species observed in winter on Arizona ponds and lakes, numbers may run into the thousands.

Sandhill Crane

**Northern Jacana
Adult**

Juvenile

SANDHILL CRANE, *Antigone canadensis*

Description: 41-46", wingspan 72-84". **Very tall** wading bird with **long tertials on lower back forming a "bustle."** ADULT: Entirely gray with red crown; most variably stained rusty on body. JUVENILE: Lacks red crown and whitish cheeks. FLIGHT: Neck and legs fully extended. **Similar Species:** Smaller Great Blue Heron (p. 177) lacks red crown, lacks tertial "bustle," flies with neck folded back on body. In 2017, 2019, and 2020 a vagrant <u>Common Crane</u> from Europe—distinguished by its white-striped black head and neck—summered south of Flagstaff, and in Nov., 2020 one was at Willcox. This or another was near Duncan in Feb., 2021. **Voice:** Loud, gurgling *hgarrrr hgarrr* bugles may carry for several miles. **Status:** Common in winter (Oct-Mar); casual above 7,000' in summer (Jun-Sep). **Habitat:** Valley fields and pastures with nearby shallow ponds. **Elevations:** Winter 100'-4,300'. **Behavior:** Wintering Sandhills primarily forage for waste corn in stubble. Daily routine includes loafing from mid-day to late afternoon, usually at the same shallow ponds used for evening roosts. Migrating flocks occasionally soar above 10,000' over mountains. **Noteworthy:** Even in midwinter Sandhill Cranes perform elaborate courtship displays. First Sulphur Springs Valley census in 1970 showed approximately 850 birds; in January 2021 the population had grown to 47,000 Sandhills.

NORTHERN JACANA, *Jacana spinosa*

Description: 9.5". Yellow-billed tropical shorebird; spindly-legged with **extremely long toes**. ADULT: Black and chestnut. JUVENILE: White eyebrows and underparts; dull brown back. FLIGHT: **Lime-yellow flight feathers.** Usually lifts both wings upon landing. **Similar Species:** Other shorebirds lack juvenile's extremely long toes. **Voice:** Screechy *eep* notes. Calls if startled. **Status:** Casual; records for every month. **Habitat:** Reservoirs and sluggish streams with aquatic plants and weedy banks. **Elevations:** Year-round 1,400'-4,000'. **Noteworthy:** Once found, may stay for weeks or even half a year.

Black-necked Stilt
Female

Male

American Avocet
Breeding Female

Nonbreeding Male

BLACK-NECKED STILT, *Himantopus mexicanus*

Description: 14". Black and white shorebird with **needle bill and very long red legs**. MALE: Black back. FEMALE: Back tinged brown. JUVENILE: Brown back. **Similar Species:** American Avocet (below) has upturned bill and blue-gray legs. **Voice:** Long series of querulous *wik wik wik* calls; scratchy *pleunk* notes. **Status:** Common in summer (Apr-Sep); fairly common in winter (Oct-Mar), withdrawing from higher elevations. **Habitat:** Valley rivers, ponds and lakes with sandy, muddy, or barren shorelines. **Elevations:** Summer 100'-9,000'; Winter 100'-4,200'. **Behavior:** Feeds by picking and probing along open muddy edges of ponds and lakes. Prefers to nest on islands. **Noteworthy:** Populations of Stilts in Arizona are growing, seemingly in response to an increase of man-made ponds, lakes, and wastewater recharge basins.

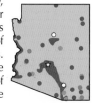

AMERICAN AVOCET, *Recurvirostra americana*

Description: 18". Black and white shorebird with long, thin **up-turned bill** and **long, blue-gray legs**. MALE: Gently upturned bill. FEMALE: Bill tip is sharply kinked upwards. BREEDING: Head and neck rich tawny. NONBREEDING: Head and neck pale gray. **Similar Species:** Black-necked Stilt (above) has straight bill and red legs. **Voice:** Protests intruders with sharp, loud *wheep* or *wheek* notes. **Status:** Common but local in summer (Mar-mid Nov); uncommon in winter (mid Nov-Feb), withdrawing from higher elevations. **Habitat:** Valley rivers, ponds and lakes with sandy, muddy, or barren shorelines. **Elevations:** Summer 100'-9,000'; Winter 100'-4,250'. **Behavior:** Filter feeds by sweeping curved bill back and forth underwater. Nests colonially. **Noteworthy:** The first known Arizona nest of American Avocet was at Lake Cochise, Willcox in 1965, where the present late summer population sometimes exceeds 250 birds.

Black-bellied Plover
Nonbreeding

Breeding
Male

American Golden-Plover
Nonbreeding

Breeding
Male

BLACK-BELLIED PLOVER, *Pluvialis squatarola*

Description: 11.5". Largest plover; big head, thick bill, and **white tail**.
BREEDING: Ermine cape divides frosted white back from coal black face
and underparts. NONBREEDING: Neutral gray upperparts, white belly.
FLIGHT: **Bold white wingstripe, black "armpits,"** white rump and tail.
Similar Species: In flight smaller American Golden-Plover (below)
lacks strong white wingstripe, black "armpits," and pure white rump.
Voice: High, plaintive whistle *whooo-ee*. **Status:** Uncommon migrant
(Apr-May, Aug-Oct); casual in summer (Jun-Jul).
Usually occurs alone or in twosomes. **Habitat:**
Valley ponds and lakes with sandy or muddy
shorelines. **Elevations:** Migration 100'-7,100'.
Behavior: Feeds by sight; sprints, stops, and stabs for
food. **Noteworthy:** Usually seen in Arizona in drab
nonbreeding plumage, Black-bellied Plovers are
known as Grey Plovers in the eastern hemisphere.

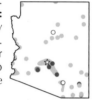

AMERICAN GOLDEN-PLOVER, *Pluvialis dominica*

Description: 10.25". Large plover but structurally delicate with small head,
thin bill, and **dark tail**. BREEDING: White "question marks" on face end
in blobs on chest; golden-shingled back. NONBREEDING: Pale fringes
on brown back feathers. FLIGHT: Faint white wingstripe, **smoky-gray
underwings, dark rump and tail**. **Similar Species:** Black-bellied Plover
(above) has white tail; in flight shows black "armpits" and white
wingstripe. Pacific Golden-Plover (accidental in S. Arizona from Phoenix
to Willcox late Jun-mid Sep) shows three–not four–primary tips. **Voice:**
Sharp *h-wheee?* queries. **Status:** Rare migrant (late
Mar-Jun and mid Sep-Nov), usually seen as singles.
Habitat: Valley ponds and lakes with sandy or
muddy shorelines. **Elevations:** Migration 100'-
6,000'. **Behavior:** Feeds by sight; sprints, stops, and
stabs for food. **Noteworthy:** Arizona birds are
usually in nonbreeding plumage.

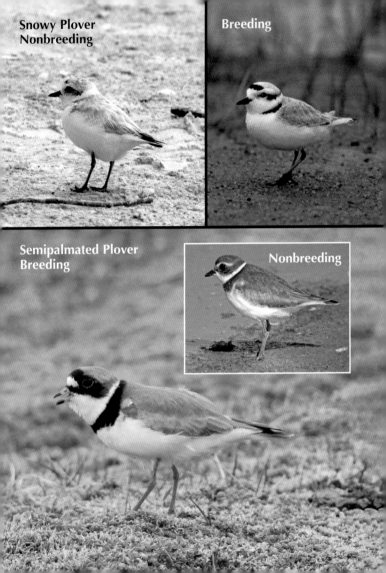

Snowy Plover
Nonbreeding

Breeding

Semipalmated Plover
Breeding

Nonbreeding

SNOWY PLOVER, *Charadrius nivosus*

Description: 6.5". Small **pale** plover with **thin black bill; incomplete breast band; dark legs**. BREEDING: Black forehead, ear patches, and black "lapels." NONBREEDING: Lacks black accents. **Similar Species:** Stubby-billed Semipalmated Plover (below) has brown upperparts, complete dark breast band, and orange legs. **Voice:** Clear *peep* notes and soft *chew-y* calls. **Status:** Rare and irregular in summer (Apr-mid Oct), casual in winter. **Habitat:** Valley ponds and lakes with sandy, muddy, or barren shorelines. **Elevations:** Summer 100'-7,100'. **Behavior:** Uses run-and-stop technique to catch insects. **Noteworthy:** Snowy Plovers are most apt to breed in Arizona after a very wet winter. Has bred near Willcox at Lake Cochise and near Gila Bend.

SEMIPALMATED PLOVER, *Charadrius semipalmatus*

Description: 7.25". Small **brown** plover with stubby, **orange-based bill; complete breast band; orange legs**. BREEDING: Black headband envelops eye; black-tipped, bright orange bill. NONBREEDING: White eyebrow; dull orange-based bill. **Similar Species:** Snowy Plover (above) has gray upperparts, incomplete breast band, black bill, and dark legs. Young Killdeer (p. 117) with a single breast band has very long bill and bluish legs. **Voice:** Silent in our area. **Status:** Uncommon migrant (Apr-mid May and mid Jul-Sep). Rare in late fall (Oct-Nov) and accidental in winter (Dec-Mar). **Habitat:** Valley ponds and lakes with sandy, muddy, or barren shorelines. **Elevations:** Migration 100'-7,100'. **Behavior:** Uses run-and-stop technique to catch insects. **Noteworthy:** Arizona migrants breed in Alaska and Canada, and winter south along the Pacific coast from Mexico to southern South America.

Killdeer
Adult

Juvenile

Mountain Plover
Nonbreeding

KILLDEER, *Charadrius vociferus*

Description: 10.5″. Dark brown plover with long bill; **two black breast bands**; long tail. JUVENILE: one breast band. FLIGHT: White stripe full length of long wing; **orange rump**. **Similar Species:** Smaller, stubby-billed Semipalmated Plover (p. 115) has only one breast band. **Voice:** Often heard, strident *kee-e* or *kil-lee* calls. **Status:** Common but nomadic resident, many withdraw from elevations above 5,500′ in winter (mid-Sep–mid Apr). Winter population is augmented by northern migrants. **Habitat:** Valley fields and pastures, golf courses, ponds and lakes, and broad, sandy riverbeds with water. **Elevations:** Resident 100′–9,400′. **Behavior:** Eats insects it catches on the ground. Nests in gravel, even on Tucson and Phoenix rooftops. Feigns broken wing to distract intruders from nest. **Noteworthy:** Buff and blackish-brown Killdeer eggs are often invisible against background pebbles.

MOUNTAIN PLOVER, *Charadrius montanus*

Description: 9″. **Plain, tan**, dry-country plover; **long white eyebrows** join on white forehead. BREEDING: Black forecrown. FLIGHT: White underwings. **Similar Species:** Larger, browner Killdeer (above) has longer tail, double chest bands, and shows orange rump in flight. **Voice:** Usually silent in winter; harsh, high-pitched rattling display calls. **Status:** Uncommon in winter (Nov–mid Mar); rare migrant (mid Mar–early Apr and Sep–Oct); accidental in summer (early Apr–Aug). Winter flocks usually range from a few to over 200. **Habitat:** Barren desert flats, tilled fields, and dry pastures with low, new growth. **Elevations:** Migration and Winter 100′–5,600′. **Behavior:** Feeds by sight; sprints, stops, and stabs for insects. May associate with cattle. **Noteworthy:** An Arizona Mountain Plover nest at 6,860′ was discovered in 1996. This is the only North American shorebird that typically never forages, roosts, or breeds on any shore.

BREEDING   NONBREEDING

Spotted Sandpiper

Solitary Sandpiper

SPOTTED SANDPIPER, *Actitis macularius*

Description: 7.5". Shorebird with **white eyebrows** and **white shoulder bar** that bobs as it walks. BREEDING: Heavy black spotting below; orange bill. NONBREEDING: Unspotted underparts. FLIGHT: Stiff, bowed wingbeats; white wingstripe. **Similar Species:** Larger, darker Solitary Sandpiper has longer legs and bold white eyering; in flight lacks wingstripe and shows barred outer tail. **Voice:** Call is whistled *puip*. **Status:** Common migrant (Apr-May and Jul-Oct) and uncommon breeder in mid summer (Jun); uncommon in winter (Nov-Mar), when most withdraw from high elevations. **Habitat:** Desert, valley, foothill, and mountain canyon ponds, lakes, streams, and rivers. **Elevations:** Summer 100'-9,000'; Winter 100'-5,400'.

Behavior: Patrols shorelines searching for insect prey, bobbing almost constantly. Females are sometimes polyandrous, with multiple male partners over a breeding season. **Noteworthy:** Spotted Sandpipers in breeding plumage are seen Apr-Aug; for the majority of the year in Arizona-- from Sep-Mar--they are typically unspotted.

SOLITARY SANDPIPER, *Tringa solitaria*

Description: 8.5". Shorebird with **white eyering**; dark **back dotted white**. FLIGHT: Black and white **barred outer tail feathers**; lacks wingstripe. **Similar Species:** Smaller, paler Spotted Sandpiper has shorter legs, white shoulder bar, white eyestripe; in flight shows white wingstripe and lacks barred outer tail. **Voice:** Call is shrill *pee-weet*. **Status:** Uncommon migrant in spring (mid Mar-mid May) and fairly common in fall (Jul-mid Oct); rare in winter (mid Oct-mid Mar); accidental in summer (mid May-Jun). **Habitat:** Valley ponds, small lakes, seasonally flooded puddles, and marshes. **Elevations:** Migration 100'-8,500'; Winter 700'-5,200'. **Behavior:** Wades in shallows and stirs mud to bring insects to surface. Bobs, but less than a Spotted Sandpiper. **Noteworthy:** Usually seen in ones or twos, but aggregations of ten or more may appear in the limited habitat available in Arizona.

119

Greater Yellowlegs
Juvenile

Nonbreeding

Greater Yellowlegs
In Flight

Lesser Yellowlegs
Breeding

Nonbreeding

GREATER YELLOWLEGS, *Tringa melanoleuca*

Description: 14″. Large, long-necked shorebird with **medium-long, thick-based, subtly upturned bill**; long, yellow legs. FLIGHT: Mostly white rump and tail. **Similar Species:** Smaller Lesser Yellowlegs (below) has short, thin, very straight bill. **Voice:** Emphatic, descending three-noted whistle *TEW-Tew-tew*. **Status:** Uncommon spring (late Feb-May) and fairly common fall migrant (Jul-Nov); uncommon in winter (Dec-late Feb). **Habitat:** Valley ponds, lakes, and rivers with sandy, muddy, or barren shorelines; flooded fields. **Elevations:** Migration 100′-9,000′; Winter 100′-5,000′. **Behavior:** Active feeder, chases small fish and aquatic invertebrates in shallows. **Noteworthy:** Migrating Greater Yellowlegs flocks, rarely over 20 birds, occasionally congregate at the few ponds, lakes, and wetlands in Arizona's water-poor valleys.

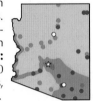

LESSER YELLOWLEGS, *Tringa flavipes*

Description: 10.5″. Midsized, long-necked shorebird with **short, thin, very straight bill**; long, yellow legs. FLIGHT: Mostly white rump and tail. **Similar Species:** Larger Greater Yellowlegs (above) has longer, slightly upturned bill, usually gray at the base. Smaller Solitary Sandpiper (p. 119) has bold white eyering, shorter, greenish legs; in flight has a dark rump and central tail. **Voice:** Fluting two-note whistles *tu-tu*, often strung together in a series. **Status:** Uncommon spring (Mar-May) and fairly common fall migrant (Jul-Nov); rare in summer (Jun) and in winter (Dec-Feb). **Habitat:** Valley ponds, lakes, and rivers with sandy, muddy, or barren shorelines. **Elevations:** Migration 100′-7,000′; Winter 100′-4,100′. **Behavior:** Although less active than Greater Yellowlegs, often chases small fish and aquatic invertebrates in shallows. **Noteworthy:** During migration in Arizona, flocks of Lessers—rarely over 25 birds—are almost as apt to occur as flocks of Greater Yellowlegs.

Willet
Nonbreeding Adult

Marbled Godwit
Nonbreeding

WILLET, *Tringa semipalmata inornata*

Description: 15″. Stocky gray shorebird with **stout, straight gray bill** and gray legs. BREEDING: Barred, spotted, and mottled pattern. FLIGHT: **Striking black and white wings**. **Similar Species:** Greater Yellowlegs (p. 121) has bright yellow legs. **Voice:** Excited *pa-whee-whee-whee! pa-whee-whee-whee!* **Status:** Uncommon migrant (Apr-May and Jul-Sep); rare outside of migration periods and at elevations above 5,000′. **Habitat:** Valley ponds, lakes, and rivers with sandy, muddy, or barren shorelines. **Elevations:** Migration 100′-4,300′. **Behavior:** Forages for aquatic insects and other invertebrates on sandy shores and mudflats. **Noteworthy:** Arizona has the larger "Western" subspecies of Willet that differs from the "Eastern" subspecies (*T. s. semipalmata*) in having much less patterned breeding plumage.

MARBLED GODWIT, *Limosa fedoa*

Description: 18″. Large shorebird with pale eyestripe and **long, bicolored, upcurved bill**. BREEDING: Heavily barred below. NONBREEDING: Pale buff below. FLIGHT: **Cinnamon underwings** and orange inner flight feathers on upperwings. **Similar Species:** Gray-faced Hudsonian Godwit, casual at Willcox and near Phoenix in late May and late July, has small black-diamond patterns on back feathers, orange-banded or chestnut belly, and in flight shows a white band at base of black tail. Larger Long-billed Curlew (p. 125) has very long, downcurved bill. Similar-sized Whimbrel (p. 125) is much grayer, has bold head stripes, and a downcurved bill. **Voice:** Repeated *ka-wheck* notes. **Status:** Rare spring (mid Apr-Jun) and uncommon fall migrant (mid Jul-Oct); casual in winter. **Habitat:** Valley ponds and lakes with sandy, muddy, or barren shorelines; marshes and flooded fields. **Elevations:** Migration 100′-7,100′. **Behavior:** Probes so deeply in shallow water for aquatic insects and other invertebrates that it occasionally submerges its head. **Noteworthy:** In Arizona typically occurs singly or in twosomes; very rarely in groups of more than 10.

123

Whimbrel

Long-billed Curlew

WHIMBREL, *Numenius phaeopus*

Description: 17". **Large** shorebird with **boldly striped crown** and dusky eyestripe; **long, downcurved bill.** JUVENILE: Shorter bill. FLIGHT: Underwings dark. **Similar Species:** Long-billed Curlew (below) has diffuse head markings, longer bill, and cinnamon underwings in flight. Similar-sized Marbled Godwit (p. 123) lacks head stripes and has long, slightly upcurved bill. **Voice:** Vibrato whistle *whi-pi-pi-pi-pi-pi-pi.* **Status:** Rare spring (Apr-mid Jun) and casual fall (mid Jul-Sep) migrant. **Habitat:** Valley ponds and lakes with sandy, muddy, or barren shorelines; flooded fields, primarily below 4,200'. **Elevations:** Migration 100'-7,100'. **Behavior:** Forages along shorelines and in open, flat areas for insects and small invertebrates on the surface. Does not use long bill for probing. **Noteworthy:** Extremely widespread, Whimbrels are known from all continents except Antarctica.

LONG-BILLED CURLEW, *Numenius americanus*

Description: 23". North America's largest shorebird. **Very large**, mostly plain-faced sandpiper with a **very long, downcurved bill** and long legs. JUVENILE: Shorter bill. FLIGHT: **Underwings bright cinnamon. Similar Species:** Smaller Whimbrel has bold crown stripes and shorter bill; lacks any buff in the plumage and Long-bill's cinnamon underwings in flight. **Voice:** Call is loud *cur-lee.* **Status:** Uncommon and nomadic most of year (Jul-mid May); rare in early summer (mid May-Jun). **Habitat:** Valley ponds and lakes with sandy, muddy, or barren shorelines. Also feeds in bare desert pastures, newly plowed fields, and short grass prairies. **Elevations:** Summer 100'-9,000'; Winter 100'-4,200'. **Behavior:** Walks briskly, poking well in front of its shadow with its extraordinary bill; may probe mud or clods of soft earth. **Noteworthy:** Female curlews are noticeably larger and longer-billed than males. Has nested in grasslands near Eagar at an elevation of about 7,150'.

BREEDING	NONBREEDING
Western Sandpiper	
Semipalmated Sandpiper	
Least Sandpiper	

WESTERN SANDPIPER, *Calidris mauri*

Description: 6.5". Small sandpiper with **blackish legs; relatively long bill with slight droop toward fine tip**. BREEDING: Red tints on crown, ears, and base of scapular feathers. **Similar Species:** Semipalmated Sandpiper (below) has short, straight bill; lacks red tints. **Voice:** Tinkling calls or high, scratchy *djeeet*. **Status:** Fairly common spring (Apr-mid May) and common fall (Jul-Oct) migrant; uncommon in winter (Nov-Mar). **Habitat:** Valley ponds, lakes, and rivers with barren shorelines. **Elevations:** Migration 100'-7,100'; Winter 750'-4,200'. **Behavior:** All small Calidrids feed along shorelines probing for small invertebrates. **Noteworthy:** Small *Calidris* sandpipers are collectively known as "Peeps".

SEMIPALMATED SANDPIPER, *Calidris pusilla*

Description: 6.25". Small sandpiper with **blackish legs; short, straight bill with blunt tip**. **Similar Species:** Western Sandpiper (above) has long, tapering bill with slight droop; when they overlap, most Westerns show red tints in plumage. **Voice:** Rough *churt*. **Status:** Rare migrant (late Apr-May and Jul-mid Sep); accidental in June. **Habitat:** Valley ponds and lakes with barren shorelines, usually below 4,200'. **Elevations:** Migration 100'-8,700'. **Noteworthy:** Arizona records usually involve 1-2 birds found within mixed flocks of Western and Least Sandpipers.

LEAST SANDPIPER, *Calidris minutilla*

Description: 6". Small sandpiper with **yellowish legs;** short and thin, slightly arched bill; brownish breast. **Similar Species:** Larger Western (above) and Semipalmated Sandpipers (above) both have black legs. **Voice:** Shrill *jeeet*. **Status:** Very common migrant and common winter visitor (Jul-mid May). **Habitat:** Valley ponds, lakes, and rivers with barren shorelines. **Elevations:** Migration 100'-9,400'; Winter 100'-7,100'. **Noteworthy:** Least is the world's smallest sandpiper.

Baird's Sandpiper
Adult

Juvenile

White-rumped Sandpiper
Breeding

Showing white rump

BAIRD'S SANDPIPER, *Calidris bairdii*

Description: 7.5" Midsized sandpiper with very long wings extending beyond tail; **scaly back; buffy wash across chest;** dark legs. BREEDING: Big black spots on pale back. JUVENILE: White fringes on scaly back more contrasty than adult; breast washed cinnamon. **Similar Species:** Smaller Semipalmated and Western Sandpipers (p. 127) lack Baird's scaly upperparts, buffy breast, and very long wings. White-rumped Sandpiper (rare in May), similar in size and structure, has red fringes on back feathers, white rump, and streaked flanks. **Voice:** Squealing *kreeeel*. **Status:** Rare spring (mid Apr-May) and fairly common fall (Jul-mid Oct) migrant. Casual Mar-mid Apr and mid Oct-mid Nov. **Habitat:** Valley ponds and lakes with barren shorelines. Spring migrants use wetlands above 1,000'. **Elevations:** Migration 100'-9,000'. **Behavior:** Feeds slowly and deliberately on mudflats and in shallow water. **Noteworthy:** Baird's Sandpipers breed in the high Arctic and winter in southern South America, placing them among the world's longest-distance migrants.

WHITE-RUMPED SANDPIPER, *Calidris fuscicollis*

Description: 7.5" Midsized sandpiper with very long wings extending beyond tail; **tiny red mark at base of bill;** dark legs. BREEDING: **Rows of well-defined spots extend to flanks; rusty-fringed back feathers.** NONBREEDING: Whitish eyebrow; gray-fringed back feathers; grayish chest with faint streaks. FLIGHT: **Broad white rump band. Similar Species:** Baird's Sandpipers (above) have buffy breast and lack any flank streaking. **Voice:** High, thin, reedy *zeeet* or *teeter*. **Status:** Rare spring migrant (May), primarily final two weeks; accidental in summer (Jun-Jul). **Habitat:** Valley ponds and lakes with barren shorelines. **Elevations:** Migration 1,500'-4,200'. **Behavior:** Probes shallows and mud for tiny invertebrates. **Noteworthy:** In migration may cover 2,600 miles in a single flight. Records usually involve 1-3 birds, but a flock of 11 were at Willcox in 2009.

Red Knot Breeding

Nonbreeding

Pectoral Sandpiper Adult

Juvenile

Dunlin Breeding

Nonbreeding

RED KNOT, *Calidris canutus*

Description: 10.5". Chunky, midsized sandpiper with **short neck**; short, black bill; long wings; dusky olive legs. BREEDING: **Orange face, neck, and underparts.** NONBREEDING: Scaled and streaked gray breast; barred flanks. JUVENILE: Finely scaled upperparts. FLIGHT: **Unmarked gray rump and tail. Similar Species:** Nonbreeding Dowitchers have much longer bills. **Voice:** Usually silent in our area. **Status:** Rare fall (mid Jul-mid Sep) migrant; accidental late Oct. **Habitat:** Valley ponds and lakes with barren shorelines. **Elevations:** 700'-4,200'. **Noteworthy:** Although usually gregarious, Arizona records are of single birds. Red Knots transition from orange to gray plumage in August.

PECTORAL SANDPIPER, *Calidris melanotos*

Description: 8.75". Midsized sandpiper with **heavily streaked breast contrasting sharply with white belly**; yellowish legs. **Similar Species:** Least Sandpiper (p. 127) is much smaller. Larger Ruff has unmarked breast. **Voice:** Rolling *churrrk*. **Status:** Rare spring (Apr-mid May) and uncommon fall (mid Aug-Oct) migrant. Casual in summer. **Habitat:** Ponds and lakes, especially with grassy or weedy margins. **Elevations:** 100'-7,100'. **Noteworthy:** Most fall Arizona migrants are juveniles.

DUNLIN, *Calidris alpina*

Description: 8.5". Stocky, midsized sandpiper with long, **stout, drooping bill;** blackish legs. BREEDING: Reddish back; black belly. NONBREEDING: Drab with **brownish breast. Similar Species:** Smaller nonbreeding Western Sandpiper (p. 127) has shorter bill and cleaner white on breast. **Voice:** Flight call is harsh *kreee*. **Status:** Uncommon fall (mid Sep-Nov) migrant; rare in winter and spring (Dec-early May). **Habitat:** Valley ponds, lakes, and rivers with sandy, muddy, or barren shorelines. **Elevations:** Migration 100'-9,000'; Winter 150'-4,200'. **Behavior:** Probes and "stitch-feeds" like a miniature sewing machine.

**Stilt Sandpiper
Breeding**

**Stilt Sandpiper
Juvenile**

**Sanderling
Juvenile**

STILT SANDPIPER, *Calidris himantopus*

Description: 8.5". Stocky, midsized sandpiper with **thin, drooping bill** and **long, yellow-green legs.** BREEDING: Chestnut ear; scaly, blackish back; heavily barred flanks. NONBREEDING: Pale unpatterned gray above. JUVENILE: Like nonbreeding adult, but back scaly black. **Similar Species:** Larger dowitchers (p. 137) have much straighter and longer bills, and proportionately shorter legs. **Voice:** Rising and rough *w-wur-rp.* **Status:** Rare spring (mid Apr-May) and uncommon fall (mid Jul-mid Oct) migrant. **Habitat:** Valley ponds and lakes with barren shorelines. Spring 850'-4,900'; Fall 100'-7,100'. **Behavior:** Feeds like a dowitcher, but longer legs and shorter bill force its head down lower and its tail up higher. **Elevations:** Migration 100-7,100'. **Noteworthy:** Early fall migrants in Arizona are usually adults in breeding plumage, but by September Stilt Sandpipers lack flank bars.

SANDERLING, *Calidris alba*

Description: 8". Midsized, mostly **white sandpiper** with straight black bill, **black shoulder crescent**, and jet black legs. BREEDING: Reddish head and breast. NONBREEDING: Entirely pale gray above. JUVENILE: Like nonbreeding adult, but inky black "snowflake" pattern on white back. FLIGHT: Broad white wing stripe on mostly black wing. **Similar Species:** Smaller nonbreeding Western Sandpiper (p. 127) has longer, drooping bill, and lacks the black shoulder crescent. **Voice:** Chittering *kip* notes. **Status:** Rare spring (Apr-May) and uncommon fall (Jul-mid Oct) migrant. **Habitat:** Valley ponds and lakes with barren shorelines, primarily below 4,300'. **Elevations:** Migration 100'-7,100'. **Behavior:** Famously chases lapping waves in and out, plunging bill into moist sand in search of tiny crustaceans before the sand compacts. **Noteworthy:** Breeding north of the Arctic Circle, Sanderlings are among the most cosmopolitan of all birds, wintering on 6 of the 7 continents. Most of Arizona's fall migrants are juveniles.

Ruddy Turnstone Breeding

Juvenile

Upland Sandpiper

Profile

Ruff Nonbreeding Female

Juvenile

RUDDY TURNSTONE, *Arenaria interpres*

Description: 9.5". Midsized, distinctively marked sandpiper with short black bill, **whorled black breast band,** and **orange legs.** BREEDING: Red back and wing marks. NONBREEDING: Dull brown above. JUVENILE: Like nonbreeding adult, but scaly back. FLIGHT: Strikingly patterned with contrasting white marks and stripes. **Voice:** Chattering *ch-d-d-d-d-dk.* **Status:** Rare fall migrant (Jul-early Oct). **Habitat:** Valley ponds and lakes with barren shorelines. **Elevations:** 100'-4,200'. **Noteworthy:** Arizona migrants retain flame red tints in July, but by August are usually brownish.

UPLAND SANDPIPER, *Bartramia longicauda*

Description: 12". Medium large sandpiper with short, thin, black-tipped **yellow bill; small head with big eye;** long thin neck; long yellow legs. FLIGHT: Dark outer wings; **long** dark **tail. Similar Species:** Lesser and Greater Yellowlegs have black bills; in flight Yellowlegs show mostly white rumps and tails. **Voice:** Flight call is clear, repeated *qui-dip* notes. **Status:** Casual fall migrant (Jul-Sep). **Habitat:** Valley fields—often cut-over alfalfa pastures, and grasslands with short herbaceous cover. **Elevations:** 1,500'-4,500'. **Noteworthy:** Primarily a Great Plains species, it once occurred SE of Tucson in conjunction with Prairie Dogs.

RUFF, *Calidris pugnax*

Description: Male: 12"; Female: 10". Medium large sandpiper with short, thick-based, drooping bill; **back feathers black with pale fringing**; long, variably green, yellow, or orange legs. MALE: Mostly orange bill. FEMALE: Black bill. NONBREEDING: Mostly white underparts. JUVENILE: Buffy neck and breast. FLIGHT: White underwings; **white "U" on rump. Similar Species:** Upland Sandpiper (above) has a thin, mostly yellow bill, big eye, thin neck. **Status:** Casual spring (mid May) and rare fall and winter (mid Jul-mid Feb) migrant. **Habitat:** Valley flooded fields, and ponds and lakes with barren shorelines. **Elevations:** 400'-4,200'. **Noteworthy:** Arizona's first known Ruff was Nov, 1974.

**Short-billed Dowitcher
Juvenile**

Breeding

**Long-billed Dowitcher
Nonbreeding**

Breeding

SHORT-BILLED DOWITCHER, *Limnodromus griseus hendersoni*

Description: 11". Bulky shorebird with **long, straight bill**; flat-backed posture while feeding. BREEDING: Face and underparts largely chestnut, including the lower belly; **unmarked foreneck; breast spotted.** NONBREEDING: Unpatterned gray. JUVENILE: Broad coppery fringes on upperpart feathers; **"tiger" barring on tertials**. FLIGHT: White wedge up lower back; barred tail mostly white. **Similar Species:** Long-billed Dowitchers have rounded backs when feeding; their sharp *keek* notes are much harsher than Short-billed calls. Seen together, female Long-billed (below) has noticeably longer bill than any Short-billed Dowitcher; juvenile Long-billed has plain gray tertials. **Voice:** Rapid series of *tu-tu-tu* calls. **Status:** Casual spring (mid Apr-May) and rare fall (Jul-Oct) migrant. **Habitat:** Valley ponds and lakes with barren shorelines. **Elevations:** 100'-7,100'. **Behavior:** Dowitchers feed with "sewing-machine" probing motion. **Noteworthy:** Most adults pass in the last half of July and juveniles in Aug-Sep.

LONG-BILLED DOWITCHER, *Limnodromus scolopaceus*

Description: 11.5". Bulky shorebird with **very long, straight bill**; protruding chest with round-backed posture while feeding. BREEDING: Face and underparts entirely chestnut; **barred sides of foreneck and breast.** NONBREEDING: Unpatterned gray. JUVENILE: Narrow rusty fringes on upperpart feathers. FLIGHT: White wedge up lower back; barred tail mostly dark. **Similar Species:** See Short-billed Dowitcher (above); best distinguished by call. **Voice:** Sharp *keek* notes, often in rapid series. **Status:** Fairly common migrant (Apr-May and Aug-Oct); uncommon in winter (Nov-Mar); casual in summer (Jun-Jul). **Habitat:** Valley ponds, lakes, and rivers with sandy, muddy, or barren shorelines. **Elevations:** Migration 100'-9,000'; Winter 100'-7,100'. **Noteworthy:** Most juvenile Long-bills arrive in September. From mid October to mid April virtually all Arizona dowitchers are Long-billed.

137

Wilson's Snipe

Red Phalarope
Breeding Female

Red Phalarope
Nonbreeding

WILSON'S SNIPE, *Gallinago delicata*

Description: 10.5". Stocky, heavily-striped, **short-legged** shorebird with a **long, straight bill** and longitudinal **white back stripes**. FLIGHT: Zigzags up, then abruptly drops into cover. **Similar Species:** Dowitchers (p. 137) have a white rump and longer legs; lack back stripes. **Voice:** When flushed, gives raspy *scaaip* call; males make a "winnowing" sound with outspread tail in display dives. **Status:** Rare summer breeder (May-Aug); common in winter (Sep-Apr). **Habitat:** Valley marshes, flooded fields, rivers, streams, ponds, and lakes with grassy or weedy shores. **Elevations:** Summer 6,700'-9,000'; Winter 100'-8,400'. **Behavior:** Secretive, usually motionless within short marshy vegetation; sometimes feeds more openly on mudflats, but rarely far from concealing vegetation. Usually solitary, but in migratory peaks small numbers may occur together. **Noteworthy:** Flexible, sensitive bill-tip enables Snipe to find worms in mud.

RED PHALAROPE, *Phalaropus fulicarius*

Description: 8.5". Phalarope with comparatively **short, thick bill**. BREEDING: Yellow bill; **entirely chestnut neck and underparts**. NONBREEDING: Black bill; white forehead and forecrown; blackish ear; unmarked gray back. **Similar Species:** Larger Wilson's Phalarope (p. 141) has longer bill, gray forehead and forecrown. Smaller Red-necked Phalarope (p. 141) shows strong "V" stripes on back. **Voice:** Trilled *chrrrt!* **Status:** Rare year-round migrant, primarily fall (mid Sep-Nov). **Habitat:** Valley ponds and lakes. **Elevations:** Migration 450'-5,550'. **Behavior:** Like all phalaropes, Red Phalaropes often feed by spinning rapidly in tight circles to create upwellings that bring small food items to the water's surface. **Noteworthy:** In Arizona, Red Phalarope usually occurs singly and typically in nonbreeding plumage.

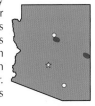

Wilson's Phalarope
Breeding Female

Nonbreeding

Red-necked Phalarope
Breeding Female

Juvenile

WILSON'S PHALAROPE, *Phalaropus tricolor*

Description: 9.25". Long-bodied phalarope with **needle bill**. BREEDING: **Eyestripe widens down sides of neck**. NONBREEDING: **Gray forehead and crown;** pale gray upperparts; yellow legs. **Similar Species:** Smaller Red-necked Phalarope (below) has strong "V" stripes on its back. Lesser Yellowlegs (p. 121) has much longer legs and white dotted wings and back. **Voice:** Guttural *whuh*. **Status:** Common migrant (Apr-mid Jun and mid Jul-mid Oct); irregular visitor in mid summer (mid Jun-mid Jul). **Habitat:** Valley lakes, ponds, and river pools with barren shorelines. **Elevations:** Migrant 100'-9,000'. **Behavior:** Spins in circles to bring tiny food items to surface. More apt to be seen feeding on mudflats than other phalaropes. **Noteworthy:** Female Wilson's Phalaropes are larger and brighter than males.

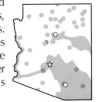

RED-NECKED PHALAROPE, *Phalaropus lobatus*

Description: 7.75". Small phalarope with **bold "V" stripes on its back**. BREEDING: **Red yoke around white throat**. NONBREEDING: White forehead and pale "V" on back. **Similar Species:** Larger Wilson's Phalarope (above) has longer bill, unmarked back, white rump, yellow legs. Breeding Red Phalarope (p. 139) has yellow bill, red underparts; nonbreeding lacks "V" stripes on back. **Voice:** Hard *chit* notes. **Status:** Uncommon spring (mid Apr-May) and fairly common fall (mid Aug-mid Oct) migrant. Casual in summer and winter. **Habitat:** Valley lakes and ponds with barren shorelines. **Elevations:** Migrant 100'-9,000'. **Behavior:** Like all species of phalaropes, Red-necked females court multiple males and may lay eggs in several nests; males provide all care for eggs and young. **Noteworthy:** In Arizona usually 5 or fewer are seen, but during peak migration occasionally more than 50 are observed, and rafts of over 500 have been recorded at Lake Havasu. Red-necked Phalaropes winter on southern seas.

141

Long-tailed Jaeger

Juvenile

**Parasitic Jaeger
Light Morph**

Juvenile

Pomarine Jaeger

**Dark Morph
Adult**

LONG-TAILED JAEGER, *Stercorarius longicaudus*

Description: 15″, wingspan 43″. **Smallest** jaeger with **short, half-black bill; slender wings; relatively long tail**, regardless of age. JUVENILE: All juvenile Jaegers have barred underwings. FLIGHT: Bouyant. **Dark underwings lack pale flash marks;** gray upperwing contrasts with dark primaries. **Similar Species:** Larger Parasitic Jaeger (below) has medium long bill with outer third dark and, in flight, underwing has single white flash mark at base of primaries; all dark upperwing. **Status:** Casual migrant (late Aug-mid Oct). **Habitat:** All jaegers in Arizona use large lakes, esp. Lake Havasu on Colorado River. **Elevations:** Migrant 450′-7,100′.

PARASITIC JAEGER, *Stercorarius parasiticus*

Description: 16.5″, wingspan 46″. Medium-sized jaeger with **small head; medium length bill**, about 1/3rd dark at tip; **central tail feathers always pointed.** Both light and dark morphs occur in Arizona. JUVENILE: Often distinct **rusty tones**. FLIGHT: Falcon-like; **underwings show single bold white flash marks at base of primaries;** black upper wings show white primary shafts. **Similar Species:** Larger Pomarine Jaeger (below) has long, heavy bill; in flight, underwing has two white flash marks, broad at the base of primaries, and a narrow crescent next to the wing linings; central tail feathers always rounded. **Status:** Rare migrant (late Aug-early Nov). **Elevations:** 450′-7,100′. **Behavior:** All rob fish from gulls.

POMARINE JAEGER, *Stercorarius pomarinus*

Description: 18.5″, wingspan 52″. **Largest** Jaeger with **long, heavy bill,** about 1/3rd dark at tip; **central tail feathers always rounded,** even if short. FLIGHT: Direct; **Underwings show two white flash marks at base of primaries, outermost broad and the innermost a thin crescent;** black upper wing shows white shafts of primaries. **Similar Species:** Other jaegers are smaller and lack round central tail feathers; underwings show one or no white flash marks at base of primaries. **Status:** Casual migrant (Sep-early Dec). **Elevations:** Migrant 450′-3,100′.

Heermann's Gull Breeding

1st Winter

Sabine's Gull Juvenile

Juvenile

Breeding

HEERMANN'S GULL, *Larus heermanni*

Description: 19", wingspan 51". **Dark-mantled**, medium-sized gull with **long bill** and long wings. ADULT BREEDING: White head; red bill; gray body. IMMATURE: Sooty black overall. FLIGHT: **Dark wings concolor with back** with narrow white trailing edge. **Similar Species:** Same-sized Ring-billed Gull (p. 149) has pale gray mantle. **Voice:** Silent in our area. **Status:** Rare visitor (Oct-Jun). **Habitat:** Valley ponds and lakes, usually with barren shorelines. **Elevations:** 150'-4,200'. **Behavior:** Primarily eats fish, often robbing them from other birds, especially pelicans. **Noteworthy:** Heermann's Gulls usually arrive singly and only stay part of one day. Approximately 90% of the world population nests on Isla Raza in the Sea of Cortéz, about 200 miles south of Arizona.

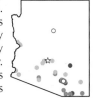

SABINE'S GULL, *Xema sabini*

Description: 13.5", wingspan 33". Small gull with **very short bill** and long wings. BREEDING: **Gray hood; yellow-tipped black bill.** JUVENILE: Brown neck and mantle banded with wavy, white lines. FLIGHT: Striking, **tricolored wings with white inner triangles. Similar Species:** Same-sized Bonaparte's Gull (p. 147) adult has pale gray mantle, longer bill lacking yellow tip. Immature Bonaparte's has dark ear spot; in flight lacks tricolored wings. **Voice:** Silent in our area. **Status:** Rare and irregular fall migrant (late Aug-mid Oct); casual in spring and summer (Apr-Jul). **Habitat:** Valley ponds and lakes, usually with barren shorelines. **Elevations:** Migration 200'-9,000'. **Behavior:** May pick food off the water's surface while swimming or in tern-like flight. **Noteworthy:** Usually migrates from its Arctic breeding grounds well out to sea. Most Arizona records pertain to juveniles.

Bonaparte's Gull

Franklin's Gull

Laughing Gull

BONAPARTE'S GULL, *Croicocephalus philadelphia*

Description: Description: 13.5", wingspan 33". **Small**, tern-like gull with **slender black bill**. BREEDING: Black hood; red legs. NONBREEDING: **Black spot behind eye**. FLIGHT: **White wedge on outer wing**. IMMATURE FLIGHT: Black wing slashes; black-tipped tail. **Similar Species:** Breeding Franklin's Gull (below) has deep red bill and nonbreeding has almost solid black hind-hood. **Status:** Uncommon migrant (late Mar-May and Sep-Nov); rare in winter (Dec-late Mar); casual (Jun-Aug). **Habitat:** Valley ponds and lakes with barren shorelines. **Elevations:** Migration 100'-9,000'. **Behavior:** Plucks food from water surface or dives like tern.

FRANKLIN'S GULL, *Leucophaeus pipixcan*

Description: 14.5", wingspan 36". Small gull with **thick white eye-arcs**. BREEDING: Black hood; red bill; variably pinkish on breast. NONBREEDING: Dark half-hood; black bill. FLIGHT: Pale underwings; narrow **black crescents on white wingtips**. IMMATURE FLIGHT: Black wingtips; incomplete black band on tail. **Similar Species:** Breeding Bonaparte's Gull (above) has black bill and bright red legs; nonbreeding Bonaparte's has black ear spot. **Status:** Uncommon but local in spring (late Mar-May); rare in summer and fall (Jun-mid Nov). **Habitat:** Valley ponds and lakes with barren shorelines, especially Lake Cochise. **Elevations:** Migration 100'-9,000'. **Behavior:** Forages for water insects.

LAUGHING GULL, *Leucophaeus atricilla*

Description: 16.5", wingspan 40". Medium-sized gull with **long bill.** BREEDING: Black hood; narrow white eye-arcs; red bill. NONBREEDING: Sooty hindcrown and nape; black legs. FLIGHT: **Black wingtips**. IMMATURE FLIGHT: Broad black tail band. **Similar Species:** Smaller Franklin's Gull (above) has short bill, broad white eye-arcs, adult shows white wingtips in flight. **Status:** Rare year-round visitor. **Habitat:** Valley ponds and lakes, usually with barren shorelines. **Elevations:** Migration 100'-4,200'. **Behavior:** Eats carrion, insects, eggs, and fish.

First Year

Short-billed Gull
Nonbreeding Adult

First Winter

Ring-billed Gull
Nonbreeding Adult

SHORT-BILLED GULL, *Larus brachyrhynchus*

Description: 16", wingspan 43". Medium-sized gull with quite short, delicate bill; **dove-like head**, and **medium gray mantle**; takes three years to mature. ADULT: **Yellow bill; dark eye; olive-yellow legs**. SECOND-WINTER Pale bill with dark tip; brownish nape. FIRST-WINTER Pink bill with black tip; dark eye; overall brownish body, wings, and tail; pink legs. **Similar Species:** Larger adult Ring-billed Gull (below) has pale eye and black band on its longer bill; paler mantle. First winter birds are more contrasting black, gray, and white, with less brown. Second winter has yellow bill with black tip or ring; looks cleaner overall with less brown on nape; paler gray mantle; yellow legs.
Voice: Pealing *mew-ah*. **Status:** Casual in winter (Nov-mid Mar). **Habitat:** Large valley ponds and lakes, usually with barren shorelines. **Elevations:** Winter 450'-4,200'. **Behavior:** Can flutter over water to glean surface food; may drop mollusks from air to crack shells. **Noteworthy:** Short-billed was split from Old World Mew Gull in 2021.

RING-BILLED GULL, *Larus delawarensis*

Description: 18", wingspan 48". Medium-sized gull with short bill and **pale mantle**; takes three years to mature. ADULT: Black ring on yellow bill; **pale yellowish eye; yellow legs**. SECOND-WINTER Head and neck flecked with brown. FIRST-WINTER Pink bill with black tip; dark eye; gray back with blackish shoulders, flight feathers, and tail; pink legs. **Similar Species:** Larger adult California Gull (p. 151) has dark eye and red spot near tip of its longer bill; mantle is darker. Second year California is very mottled with bluish legs. First winter California lacks Ring-billed Gull's white head and uniform gray mantle. **Voice:** Squealing *wheeah*. **Status:** Common year-round; most withdraw from elevations above 7,000' in winter (Oct-mid Mar) and below 1,500' in summer (Jun-Aug). **Habitat:** Major rivers; valley ponds and lakes, usually with barren shorelines. **Elevations:** Summer 1,500'-9,000'; Winter 100-7,000'.
Noteworthy: Arizona's most numerous gull.

California Gull
Nonbreeding Adult

Juvenile

First Winter

Herring Gull
Nonbreeding Adult

Juvenile

First Winter

CALIFORNIA GULL, *Larus californicus*

Description: 21", wingspan 54". **Large gull** with **dark eye**; takes four years to mature. ADULT: Yellow bill with **red spot** and **black ring** near tip; **medium-gray mantle; yellow-green legs.** NONBREEDING: Head and chest streaked with brown. SECOND-WINTER Black-ringed bluish bill and blue legs; gray back and mottled whitish shoulders. FIRST-WINTER Pink bill with dark tip; Scaly mantle. FLIGHT: Outer primaries black; inner primaries pale. **Similar Species:** Smaller first-winter Ring-billed (p. 149), unlike second-winter California Gull, has pink—not bluish—bill and legs. **Voice:** Shrill, deliberate *wee wee* and *wow-w* calls. **Status:** Uncommon (Aug-mid Dec); otherwise rare (mid Dec-Jul). **Habitat:** Valley ponds and lakes, usually with barren shorelines. **Elevations:** Summer 150'-9,000'; Winter 100'-7,000'. **Behavior:** Scavenges on water and shore. **Noteworthy:** In 1848 California Gulls are credited with saving Mormons in Utah from a plague of grasshoppers.

HERRING GULL, *Larus argentatus*

Description: 25", wingspan 58". **Very large gull** with **pale eye, flat forehead;** and **pink legs**; takes four years to mature. ADULT: **Pale gray mantle.** NONBREEDING Head and chest streaked with brown. SECOND-WINTER Black-tipped pink bill; mottled brown back with limited gray. FIRST-WINTER Pale head with black bill; variably brown body. FLIGHT: Immatures have pale panel on inner flight feathers; adults show black and white wingtips. **Similar Species:** Smaller second-winter California (p. 151) has bluish—not pink—bill and legs; adult has dark eye and darker mantle. **Voice:** Honking *Wuk wuk* calls and excited *kee-a kee-a* screams. **Status:** Uncommon in winter (mid Sep-Jan); rare in spring (Feb-early May); casual in summer. **Habitat:** Valley ponds and lakes, usually with barren shorelines. **Elevations:** Winter 150'-6,000'. **Behavior:** Scavenges on water and shore. **Noteworthy:** Immature Herring Gulls seem to be more apt to wander than adults, and appear more often than older birds in Arizona.

151

Iceland Gull
First Winter

First Winter

First Winter

Lesser Black-backed Gull
Nonbreeding Adult

ICELAND GULL, *Larus glaucoides thayeri*

Description: 22", wingspan 54". Large gull with **dark eye**; four years to mature. ADULT: Medium-gray mantle; **dark pink legs**. NONBREEDING: Head and chest streaked with brown. SECOND-WINTER Black-tipped pink bill and pink legs; gray back; tan-mottled wings. FIRST-WINTER Black bill; patterned brown back with bold white edges; brownish checkered wings with white-edged dark primaries; pink legs. FLIGHT: Pale underwings. Adults show only trace black edgings on wingtips.
Similar Species: Larger first-winter Herring Gull (p. 151) is darker brown with a noticeably paler head; flight feathers are dark with pale panel on inner primaries; tail is brownish-black. Adult has glaring yellow eye and a paler mantle. **Voice:** Usually silent in our area. **Status:** Rare in winter (mid Oct-mid Feb). **Habitat:** Large valley ponds and lakes, usually with barren shorelines. **Elevations:** Winter 400'-7,100'. **Behavior:** Scavenges. **Noteworthy:** Described as a subspecies of Herring Gull until 1973, the former "Thayer's Gull" was lumped with Iceland Gull in 2017. All records are single first winter birds.

LESSER BLACK-BACKED GULL, *Larus fuscus*

Description: 21", wingspan 54". Large gull with hostile **yellow eye accentuated by dark smears**; takes four years to mature. ADULT: **Dark gray mantle; yellow legs**. NONBREEDING: Head and hind-neck heavily streaked with brown. SECOND-WINTER Mostly black bill; dark gray back and dark brown wings; dull yellow legs. FIRST-WINTER Whitish head with black bill; white-speckled dark back; dull pink legs. FLIGHT: Dark underwings. Adults show only small white spots on black wingtips.
Similar Species: Larger, paler Herring Gull (p. 151) lacks blackish smears around eye; legs are pink. **Voice:** Rapid, adenoidal *gaw-gaw-gawk*. **Status:** Casual in fall and winter (early Sep-early Mar). **Habitat:** Large valley ponds and lakes, usually with barren shorelines. **Elevations:** Winter 400'-4,200'. **Noteworthy:** Most Arizona records are first winter birds, but a few adults have also been reported.

153

**Black-legged Kittiwake
Breeding Adult**

**Black-legged Kittiwake
Juvenile**

**Least Tern
Breeding Adult**

BLACK-LEGGED KITTIWAKE, *Rissa tridactyla*

Description: 17", wingspan 36". Small gull with dark eye and medium-gray mantle; takes three years to mature. ADULT: **Unmarked yellow bill; ink black legs.** NONBREEDING: Gray ear muffs. JUVENILE: Black bill; black collar. ADULT FLIGHT: **Solid black wingtips.** JUVENILE FLIGHT: **White flight feathers outlined by inverted black V on inner wings. Similar Species:** Smaller juvenile Sabine's Gull (p. 145) has scaly brown back; adult Sabine's has yellow-tipped black bill; lacks black slash on inner wing in flight. **Voice:** Usually silent in winter. **Status:** Casual in winter (Nov-Feb); accidental in Apr. **Habitat:** Large valley ponds and lakes, usually with barren shorelines. **Elevations:** Winter 400'-6,900'. **Behavior:** Plunge dives for fish like a tern. **Noteworthy:** Most Arizona records pertain to juveniles.

LEAST TERN, *Sternula antillarum*

Description: 8.5". **Smallest tern** in North America. ADULT: Distinctive **yellow bill, yellow legs,** and **white forehead.** JUVENILE: Black bill; white crown; black stripes behind eyes connect with black nape; thick black shoulder bar. FLIGHT: Quick, deep wingbeats reveal ink-black outermost primaries. **Similar Species:** All other Arizona terns are larger and lack yellow legs or adult's yellow bill. **Voice:** Usually silent in our area. **Status:** Rare but annual spring migrant (mid Apr-Jun); casual in fall (Jul-early Sep). **Habitat:** Valley ponds and lakes with barren shorelines. **Elevations:** Migrant 450'-4,200'. **Behavior:** Dives for insects and small fish swimming on or just below the surface. **Noteworthy:** Most Least Tern records in Arizona are of adult-plumaged birds.

Black Skimmer
Adult

Black Tern
Breeding Adult

Nonbreeding

Nonbreeding

BLACK SKIMMER, *Rynchops niger*

Description: 18". Very large tern-like, black and white bird with **huge, black-tipped red bill, upper half shorter than lower half;** red legs. BREEDING: Black neck; NONBREEDING: White collar. JUVENILE: Scaly brown. FLIGHT: Buoyant; long, contrasting white underwings held above body. **Similar Species:** Distinctive; no other bird in Western Hemisphere has an undershot bill. **Voice:** Silent in our area. **Status:** Casual in spring (May) and fall (Sep-Oct). **Habitat:** Valley ponds and lakes with barren shorelines. **Elevations:** Migrant 200'-4,200'. **Behavior:** Snaps up fish it touches while skimming the surface. **Noteworthy:** In Arizona, Black Skimmers are usually only present for a single day.

BLACK TERN, *Chlidonias niger*

Description: 10". Small **short-tailed tern** with thin, black bill. BREEDING: **Black head and body**. NONBREEDING: White head with black crown and ear muffs; upperparts dark gray; dark smudges on sides of breast. FLIGHT: Bouncy and erratic with silvery underwings. **Similar Species:** All other Arizona terns have pale gray upperparts and lack "ear muffs". **Voice:** Quick raspy *cheep chep chep*. **Status:** Rare spring (May-Jun) and uncommon fall (mid Jul-Sep) migrant; casual (Apr and Oct-early Nov). **Habitat:** Valley ponds and lakes with barren shorelines. **Elevations:** Migrant 100'-9,000'. **Behavior:** Seldom dives like other terns; sorties rapidly across lakes chasing insects and snatching prey items from the surface. **Noteworthy:** While Black Terns may appear singly in our area, often they number from a few to more than 20. Most birds seen after mid-August are transitioning from black to white underparts.

Common Tern
Breeding

Juvenile

Forster's Tern
Nonbreeding Adult

COMMON TERN, *Sterna hirundo*

Description: 14". Medium-sized tern with **pale gray underparts, short tail** only extends to end of wing. BREEDING: Black cap; red bill with black tip (may lose black tip in midsummer); red legs. NONBREEDING: **Black half-hood**, black or mostly black bill and legs; most have **black shoulder bar**. FLIGHT: **Dark wedge** in outer flight feathers **on gray upperwing**. **Similar Species:** Forster's Tern (below) has long tail extending well beyond wings and lacks black shoulder bars; in flight shows silvery primaries. <u>Arctic Tern</u>, accidental in Spring (mid May-early June) and Fall (Sep-early Oct) in SE Arizona has a shorter, all-red bill, rounder head, and much shorter legs than either Common or Forster's; in flight has translucent wings like Forster's, but underparts are much darker gray than Forster's. **Voice:** Harsh *kee-rrr*. **Status:** Rare spring (mid Apr-May) and fall (mid Jul-Oct) migrant. **Habitat:** Valley ponds and lakes with barren shorelines. **Elevations:** Migrant 150'-8,000'. **Behavior:** Plunge-dives for small fish and insects. **Noteworthy:** Common Tern in Arizona is usually seen as singles or twosomes, rarely in flocks.

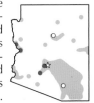

FORSTER'S TERN, *Sterna forsteri*

Description: 14.5". Medium-sized tern with **white underparts; long tail** extends well beyond wings. BREEDING: Black cap; orange-red bill with black tip; long orange legs. NONBREEDING: **Jet black ear** on white face; black bill and legs. FLIGHT: **Silvery primaries on snowy upperwings are edged black on the underwings**. **Similar Species:** Common Tern (above) has short tail not extending beyond wings; in flight shows blackish wedge on upper side of gray outer wings. **Voice:** Burry *yurrrh*. **Status:** Rare spring (Apr-early Jun) and uncommon fall (Aug-mid Nov) migrant; casual in summer and winter. **Habitat:** Valley ponds and lakes with barren shorelines. **Elevations:** Migrant 100'-9,000'. **Behavior:** Plunge-dives for small fish and insects. **Noteworthy:** Forster's Tern is more common than Common Tern in Arizona, and flocks of over 25 migrants are occasional on Colorado River reservoirs.

Elegant Tern
Breeding

Elegant Tern
Nonbreeding

Caspian Tern
Adult

Caspian Tern
Nonbreeding Adult

ELEGANT TERN, *Thalasseus elegans*

Description: 17". Large, **shaggy-crested** tern with thin, slightly decurved, **orange bill; black legs.** BREEDING: **Black cap encompasses eye.** NONBREEDING: Black half-hood touches eye. FLIGHT: Outer feathers of **white underwing** outlined in black. **Similar Species:** Larger Caspian Tern (below) has black-tipped red bill; in flight underwing shows black primaries. Non-breeding birds always have streaked forehead and crown. Slightly larger <u>Royal Tern</u>, accidental in late July in the greater Phoenix area, has a stouter straight bill, and its black hind crown is barely connected to rear edge of its eyes. **Voice:** Grating *brr-rick*. **Status:** Casual in summer (May-mid Aug). **Habitat:** Valley ponds and lakes. **Elevations:** Summer 150'-4,100'. **Behavior:** Plunge-dives for small fish. **Noteworthy:** About 95% of the world population—about 50,000 birds—breeds on Isla Rasa in the Sea of Cortéz, approximately 200 miles south of the Sonora-Arizona border. Migration carries some Elegant Terns 5,000 miles south to Chile.

CASPIAN TERN, *Hydroprogne caspia*

Description: 21". Very large tern with **thick red bill** with black tip; black legs. BREEDING: Black cap; NONBREEDING: **Obvious black streaks on forehead and crown.** FLIGHT: Broad white underwings with **black primaries.** **Similar Species:** Smaller Elegant Tern (above) has thin orange bill; in flight shows largely white underwings. Nonbreeding Elegant always has unstreaked white forehead. **Voice:** Rolling, harsh *Mix-it-up*; whistled, burry *swee-a* in flight. **Status:** Rare year-round visitor, most common in spring (mid Mar-May) and fall (Aug-mid Nov). **Habitat:** Valley ponds and lakes with barren shorelines. **Elevations:** Summer and Migration 100'-9,000'; Winter 100'-450'. **Behavior:** Plunge-dives for small fish and insects. **Noteworthy:** Caspian is the largest tern in the world. In Arizona it is most common along the Colorado River, the only area where Caspian Terns occur in winter.

Red-throated Loon
Nonbreeding

Red-throated Loon
Juvenile

Pacific Loon
Breeding

Pacific Loon
Nonbreeding

RED-THROATED LOON, *Gavia stellata*

Description: 25". By weight, **smallest** of the loons; **thin bill angled up**. NONBREEDING: Mostly white face and throat with narrow gray hindneck; **white-spotted** dark back. JUVENILE: Dusky throat. FLIGHT: Head held lower than back. **Similar Species:** Larger Pacific Loon (below) has straight tapering bill, usually held horizontally. In winter has crisp black-white contrast on sides of neck and an unmarked dark back. **Voice:** Usually silent in our area. **Status:** Rare in winter (Nov-mid Apr). **Habitat:** Large lakes and reservoirs, fairly regular at Lake Havasu. **Elevations:** Winter 150'-7,100'. **Behavior:** Dives for fish. **Noteworthy:** Other loons need an open stretch of water of about 100 feet to get airborne, but Red-throated Loons can fly without a runway.

PACIFIC LOON, *Gavia pacifica*

Description: 26". **Small loon** with rounded crown and straight **tapering bill.** BREEDING: Blackish face contrasts with pale gray crown, nape, and hindneck; black back with white piano keys. NON-BREEDING: Dark brown upperparts and crown; **dark sides of neck contrast sharply with white throat**. Most show thin, dark "chinstrap." **Similar Species:** Larger Common Loon (p. 165) has heavy, chisel-shaped bill; lacks crisp black-white contrast on sides of neck; and—in close view—lacks the Pacific's black chinstrap. **Voice:** Usually silent in our area. **Status:** Uncommon on Colorado River reservoirs, rare elsewhere in winter (late Oct-Mar); casual migrant (Apr-May and mid Sep-late Oct). **Habitat:** Large ponds and lakes. **Elevations:** Winter 100'-9,000'. **Behavior:** Dives for fish. **Noteworthy:** Pacific is the most common species of loon in the world.

Common Loon Juvenile

Breeding

Yellow-billed Loon Juvenile

COMMON LOON, *Gavia immer*

Description: 32". **Large loon** with a blocky head shape and **heavy, silver-gray, chisel-tipped bill.** BREEDING: Black head and bill; black back checkered with white squares. NONBREEDING: Gray-brown above; **partial white collar** with diffuse edges; thick white arcs around eyes. JUVENILE: Diffusely scaled back. **Similar Species:** Smaller Pacific Loon (p. 163) has sharp black-white contrast between hindneck and throat; smaller, thinner, more tapering bill; and—in close view—usually a dark chinstrap. **Voice:** Distinctive, poignant wailing seldom heard in our area. **Status:** Uncommon on Colorado River reservoirs, rare elsewhere in migration and in winter; rare in Arizona in summer (mid May-mid Oct). **Habitat:** Large ponds and lakes. **Elevations:** Migration and Winter 100'-9,000'. **Behavior:** Makes long dives for fish. **Noteworthy:** Typically only single Common Loons occur away from Colorado River reservoirs. Some birds may begin to molt into breeding plumage before departing in late March or April.

YELLOW-BILLED LOON, *Gavia adamsii*

Description: 34". **Largest** loon with a "double-peaked" head shape and **heavy, ivory-colored, subtly upturned bill.** NONBREEDING: Gray-brown above; **partial white collar** with diffuse edges; thick white arcs around eyes. JUVENILE: Obvious pale barring on back. **Similar Species:** Smaller Common Loon (above) holds symmetrical silver-gray bill angled downwards or horizontally. **Voice:** Distinctive deep yodels seldom heard in our area. **Status:** Casual in winter (Nov-Mar); accidental in other months and away from Colorado River. **Habitat:** Large ponds and lakes. **Elevations:** Winter 450'-1,150'. **Behavior:** Circumpolar breeder in the high Arctic. **Noteworthy:** Only single Yellow-billed Loons have been found in Arizona.

Wood Stork

Adult

Magnificent Frigatebird
Juvenile

Adult Male

WOOD STORK, *Mycteria americana*

Description: 40", wingspan 60". **Tall, white wader** with **bare, blackish head and neck; long, thick, down-curved bill.** JUVENILE: Feathered head. FLIGHT: Outstretched head and neck; **broad white wings with entirely black flight feathers;** long legs extend well beyond short tail. **Similar Species:** No other large, white, bald-headed bird occurs in Arizona. In flight American White Pelican tucks in its head and legs. **Voice:** Generally silent in our area. **Status:** Casual in summer (Jul-early Oct). **Habitat:** Marshes, swamps, ponds, and large lakes. **Elevations:** Summer 100'-3,000'. **Behavior:** Nabs fish and amphibians in shallows. **Noteworthy:** Storks are apparently pushed into our area by *chubascos*, ferocious summer storms in the Gulf of California.

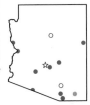

MAGNIFICENT FRIGATEBIRD, *Fregata magnificens*

Description: 40", wingspan 90". **Large brown or black seabird** with long, thin, hook-tipped bill; very long, forked tail. MALE: Entirely black with red chin pouch. FEMALE: All brownish-black with white vest. IMMATURE: Brown with white head and belly. Immature plumage held 4 or more years. FLIGHT: Angular shape with long tail usually held closed, somewhat like a giant mosquito. **Similar Species:** White and Brown Pelicans, Wood Storks, Great Blue Heron, and Sandhill Cranes all have broad wings and comparatively short tails. **Voice:** Generally silent in our area. **Status:** Casual in summer (Jun-Oct); accidental in mid Mar. **Habitat:** Broad desert valleys. **Elevations:** Summer 100'-3,700'. **Behavior:** Robs fish from other sea birds and skims ocean surface for offal. **Noteworthy:** Only seen soaring over Arizona after major storms in the Gulf of California. Weighing slightly more than three pounds, Frigatebirds have the lightest wing-loading compared to wingspread of any species of bird.

Blue-footed Booby
Immature

Adult

Immature

Brown Booby
Immature

Adult

BLUE-FOOTED BOOBY, *Sula nebouxii*

Description: 32″, wingspan 62″. Large seabird with long, bluish-gray, conical bill; **white patches on upper and lower back**. ADULT: Finely-streaked white head; white barred back; entirely white underparts, turquoise blue legs and feet. IMMATURE: "Dirty" head, neck, and breast fade into white belly; gray legs and feet. FLIGHT: Long, tapering tail. **Similar Species:** Regardless of age, shorter-tailed Brown Booby (below) lacks any white patches on back. **Voice:** Generally silent in our area. **Status:** Rare late summer (late Aug-early Nov) and winter (mid Dec-mid Feb) visitor. **Habitat:** Large lakes and reservoirs, primarily Lake Havasu on the Colorado River. **Elevations:** Year-round 100′-3,800′. **Behavior:** Plunge-dives for fish. **Noteworthy:** Most records pertain to single birds, but up to 4 immatures have been observed together. The bright blue legs and feet of adult birds seldom seen in Arizona.

BROWN BOOBY, *Sula leucogaster*

Description: 30″, wingspan 57″. Large seabird with entirely **brown upperparts**; long, conical bill; **yellow feet**. ADULT: Brown chest sharply divided from pure white belly. MALE: Whitish head. FEMALE: Yellowish face and bill. IMMATURE: Brown belly and gray legs and feet. FLIGHT: Comparatively short tail. Immature has dark underwings. **Similar Species:** Larger, longer-tailed Blue-footed Booby (above) has white patches on back, and lacks yellow feet. **Voice:** Generally silent in our area. **Status:** Rare late summer (Aug-mid Oct; casual through mid Feb) visitor. **Habitat:** Large lakes and reservoirs, primarily Lake Havasu on the Colorado River. **Elevations:** Summer 100′-1,100′. **Behavior:** Plunge-dives for fish. **Noteworthy:** Most records pertain to single immatures. Occasionally loafs with Blue-footed Boobies when both species are present.

Neotropic Cormorant
Immature

Nonbreeding

Double-crested Cormorant
Immature

Nonbreeding Adult

NEOTROPIC CORMORANT, *Nannopterum brasilianum*

Description: 26″. **Pointed, triangular-shaped, bare yellowish to orange skin behind the bill, feathered lores,** relatively thin neck, relatively **long tail.** ADULT: Black overall. Breeding birds have white outlining gular pouch. IMMATURE: Mostly brown with mottled neck. FLIGHT: Head-and-neck appear same length as long tail. **Similar Species:** Double-crested Cormorant (below) is larger with rounded gular patch, bare orange lores, thick neck, and short tail. Immature has pale underparts. **Voice:** Generally silent. **Status:** Common in central Arizona; otherwise usually uncommon resident, rare north of Mogollon Rim. **Habitat:** Large ponds and lakes. **Elevations:** Summer 100′-9,000′; Winter 100′-7,000′. **Behavior:** Pursues fish underwater. Often seen out of water with wings spread to dry. **Noteworthy:** Neotropic Cormorant only officially entered the ranks of Arizona's avifauna in 1961.

DOUBLE-CRESTED CORMORANT, *Nannopterum auritum*

Description: 33″. **Rounded, bare orange skin behind the bill, bare orange lores,** relatively thick neck, relatively **short tail.** ADULT: Black overall. Breeding birds have wispy white plumes behind eyes. IMMATURE: Varies from brown to almost whitish on neck and breast. FLIGHT: Head-and-neck appear longer than short tail. **Similar Species:** Neotropic Cormorant (above) is smaller with triangular gular patch, thin neck, and tail about as long as neck. Immatures have feathered, usually dark lores; mottled brownish throat and breast. **Voice:** Generally silent. **Status:** Common in central Arizona; otherwise fairly common resident; numbers at low elevations peak in winter (Oct-Apr) and numbers at high elevations peak in summer (May-Sep). **Habitat:** Large ponds and lakes. **Elevations:** Summer 100′-9,400′; Winter 100′-7,100′. **Behavior:** Pursues fish underwater; rides low with bill angled upward. **Noteworthy:** Often nests in Great Blue Heron rookeries.

American White Pelican
Nonbreeding

Brown Pelican
Adult

Immature

Description: 60", wingspan 108". **Enormous white water bird** with huge, scoop-shaped **yellowish-orange bill**. FLIGHT: White forewing and black hindwing; head folded back to body. **Similar Species:** Smaller Brown Pelican (below) never has an entirely orange bill nor entirely white body; soaring Brown Pelican shows entirely dark wings. Smaller Wood Stork (p. 167) with similar wing pattern soars with head and legs fully extended. **Voice:** Generally silent. **Status:** Uncommon transient year-round. **Habitat:** Large ponds and lakes. **Elevations**: Year-round 100'-9,200'. **Behavior:** Forages for fish in shallows. Eats between 20-40% of its weight in fish each day. American White Pelicans often feed cooperatively by encircling fish, then simultaneously dipping their heads. **Noteworthy:** Banding studies show that some of Arizona's passage White Pelicans are hatched in Great Salt Lake and in Idaho.

Description: 48", wingspan 84". **Large gray or brown water bird** with big, scoop-shaped **greenish-gray bill**. ADULT: Whitish head and silvery-gray body. IMMATURE: Brown overall. FLIGHT: Entirely dark wings. **Similar Species:** American White Pelican (above) at rest is all white and substantially larger than Brown Pelican. Soaring White Pelican has all-white forewing and all-black hindwing. **Voice:** Generally silent. **Status:** Rare transient year-round, especially in late summer (Jul-Aug), primarily south of Mogollon Rim and below 4,200'. **Habitat:** Large ponds and lakes. **Elevations**: Year-round 100'-8,000'. **Behavior:** Plunge-dives for fish in shallows. **Noteworthy:** Most Arizona records pertain to sub-adults. Some summers 100 or more immature Brown Pelicans are found in southern Arizona, apparently pushed into our area by ferocious tropical storms in the Gulf of California.

American Bittern

Least Bittern

AMERICAN BITTERN, *Botaurus lentiginosus*

Description: 28″. Heavy-set, **heavily-striped** heron with **prominent black malar stripe** continuing down sides of long neck. FLIGHT: Blackish flight feathers contrast with the brown upperparts. **Similar Species:** Immature Black-crowned Night-Heron (p. 183) lacks black stripes on sides of neck; in flight has unicolored wings. **Voice:** Flight call is nasal *squark*; Deep, hollow *LOONK-aloonk* song is almost never heard in Arizona. **Status:** Rare in winter (Sep-May); casual in summer (Jun-Aug). **Habitat:** Lake and pond margins, especially with tall reeds and cattails. **Elevations:** Winter 100′-7,000′. **Behavior:** Captures prey by standing motionless. If disturbed, points bill skywards and imperceptibly sinks into reeds. **Noteworthy:** Most records of American Bittern in Arizona occur in migration periods from mid January-March and late September-December.

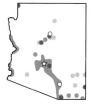

LEAST BITTERN, *Ixobrychus exilis*

Description: 13″. Miniature heron with **burnished-buff shoulders**. MALE: Black cap and back. FEMALE: Sooty cap and brown back. FLIGHT: Bright buff shoulders contrast with dark wings. **Similar Species:** Larger Green Heron (p. 183) lacks buff shoulders and a cinnamon face. **Voice:** Males advertise for mates using a series of rapid *kuh* notes, dying away at end. Females deliver a series of rapid, rail-like *keks*. **Status:** Uncommon in summer (mid Mar-Oct); rare in winter (Nov-mid Mar). **Habitat:** Lake and pond margins, especially with tall reeds and cattails. **Elevations:** Resident 100′-4,300′. **Behavior:** Stalks prey in shallow water. If disturbed slinks away or flushes in a short flight into deep reeds. **Noteworthy:** This is the smallest member of the heron and egret family in the U.S.

Red-winged
Blackbird

Immature

Great Blue Heron
Adult

Description: 46", wingspan 72". **Very large, blue-gray heron** with long, dagger-like bill; cinnamon thighs; long, dark legs. ADULT: White stripe divides black crown; long black plumes on head when breeding; black shoulders. JUVENILE: Solid dark crown; heavily streaked foreneck and breast. FLIGHT: Ponderous and deliberate wingbeats with its long neck folded back into a collapsed letter "S".

Similar Species: Sandhill Crane (p. 109) has solid gray plumage with a red crown; flies with shallow wingbeats and an outstretched neck.

Voice: Loud, guttural *ruhh*, sometimes repeated.

Status: Fairly common resident; most withdraw from high elevations in winter (Dec-Feb).

Habitat: Lakes and ponds, permanent rivers and streams; concentrated near nesting colonies while breeding from early spring to early fall. Wanders widely, primarily in valleys, after the breeding season.

Elevations: Summer 100'-9,000'; Winter 100'-6,900'.

Behavior: Patiently stalks shoreline or shallows for fish, crayfish, frogs, and other prey. Hunts for rodents and reptiles in flooded fields. After spearing a large food item, repositions it head downwards to swallow. Occasionally catches fish too big to ingest. Often perches in trees. Nests colonially; builds large stick nests as high as possible, usually in cottonwoods, sycamores, Ponderosa pines—or introduced eucalyptus, palms, or on man-made towers. Nests are frequently re-used and nest trees may harbor other species of herons and egrets, or cormorants. May change mates from one year to the next.

Noteworthy: Great Blue is the largest and most widespread member of the heron and egret family in North America.

177

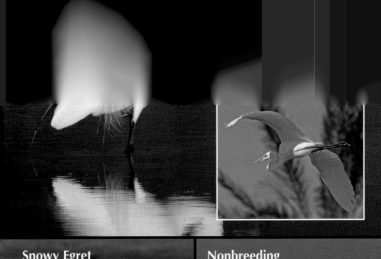

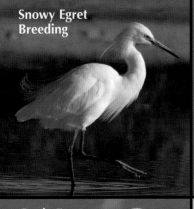

Snowy Egret Breeding

Nonbreeding

Cattle Egret Breeding

Nonbreeding

GREAT EGRET, *Ardea alba*

Description: 39". **Large egret with yellow bill; black legs and feet.** BREEDING: Nuptial plumes on back. **Similar Species:** Much smaller Snowy Egret (below) has black stiletto bill and yellow feet. **Voice:** All egrets give harsh, grating calls. **Status:** Uncommon resident; numbers at low elevations peak in winter (Nov-Mar) and numbers at high elevations peak in summer (Apr-Oct). **Habitat:** Lakes, ponds, rivers, and streams. **Elevations:** Summer 100'-9,000'; Winter 100'-5,400'. **Behavior:** Spears fish and small terrestrial vertebrates. **Noteworthy:** Slaughter of Great and Snowy Egrets by plume hunters in the late 1800s led to formation of the National Audubon Society in 1905.

SNOWY EGRET, *Egretta thula*

Description: 24". **Slender black bill;** mostly **black legs** that contrast with **yellow feet.** BREEDING: Nuptial plumes on head, neck, and back. JUVENILE: Legs mostly yellow. **Similar Species:** Cattle Egret (below) has short neck, short yellow bill, and short legs. **Status:** Uncommon resident in lower river valleys; more widespread in summer and migration (mid Mar-Oct). **Habitat:** Lakes and ponds, rivers and streams. **Elevations:** Summer 100'-9,000'; Winter 100'-4,100'. **Behavior:** Spears fish, other small aquatic vertebrates, and insects.

CATTLE EGRET, *Bubulcus ibis*

Description: 19". **Short, thick neck;** short, thick, **yellow bill; short legs pastel-colored in summer and dusky in winter.** BREEDING: Buffy crown, foreneck, and back. **Similar Species:** Snowy Egret (above) has thin neck, black stiletto bill, and yellow feet. **Status:** Uncommon resident; numbers peak in summer (mid Apr-Sep). **Habitat:** Valley fields, pastures, lakes, and ponds. Has bred from the lower Colorado River up the Gila River to Safford. **Elevations:** Summer 100'-7,100'; Winter 100'-4,200'. **Behavior:** May follow livestock and tractors to catch insects. **Noteworthy:** Discovered in Arizona near Phoenix in 1966.

179

Little Blue Heron
Nonbreeding

Immature

Tricolored Heron
Breeding

Immature

Reddish Egret
Immature dancing

Nonbreeding

LITTLE BLUE HERON, *Egretta caerulea*

Description: 24". Bluish body with maroon head and neck; **blue bill with black tip**; greenish legs. ADULT: Orange eye. IMMATURE: White or blue-mottled plumage with yellow eye. **Similar Species:** Much larger red morph Reddish Egret (below), the expected morph in Arizona, has pale yellow eyes, and usually feeds more actively. **Voice:** Usually silent in our area. **Status:** Casual in summer (late Sep); accidental in winter (Oct-Jan). **Habitat:** Valley lakes and ponds. **Elevations:** Summer 200'-6,450'. **Behavior:** Spears fish, small aquatic vertebrates, and insects. Hunts slowly and deliberately. **Noteworthy:** In Arizona blue adults outnumber immature white or "calico" Little Blue Herons.

TRICOLORED HERON, *Egretta tricolor*

Description: 26". White belly and foreneck; very long bill. BREEDING: Base of bill intense cobalt blue; long, straw-yellow nuptial plumes on nape. NONBREEDING: Yellow bill. IMMATURE: Rufous neck. **Similar Species:** Little Blue Heron (above) and much larger Reddish Egret (below) lack white belly and foreneck. **Status:** Casual in summer and early fall (Apr-Oct); accidental in winter (Oct-Jun). **Habitat:** Valley lakes and ponds. **Elevations:** Summer 450'-4,300'. **Behavior:** Spears fish, small aquatic vertebrates, and insects.

REDDISH EGRET, *Egretta rufescens*

Description: 30". ADULT: **Pink-based bill** and shaggy red neck. IMMATURE: Gray overall with **blackish bill, pale yellow eye**, and **dark legs**. **Similar Species:** Much smaller Little Blue Heron (above) has bicolored bill and greenish legs. **Status:** Rare in summer and fall (late Jun-late Nov); accidental (Dec-Jan and Apr). **Habitat:** Valley lakes and ponds. **Elevations:** Summer 300'-6,450'. **Behavior:** Active feeder that startles prey into open water with vigorous "dancing," while holding its wings widespread. **Noteworthy:** Since the first record in 1996, only red morph immatures have been substantiated in Arizona.

181

Green Heron
Adult

Immature

Black-crowned Night-Heron
Adult

Immature

GREEN HERON, *Butorides virescens*

Description: 18". Small, **thick-necked**, and short-legged heron. ADULT: **Rich chestnut neck**. Slate upperparts may have greenish gloss. IMMATURE: Streaked neck and breast. **Similar Species:** Smaller Least Bittern (p. 175) has bright buff shoulders and a cinnamon face. **Voice:** Squawking *queowk!* alarm; also series of guttural *cuk-cuk-cuk-uh-uh-uh* calls. **Status:** Uncommon resident; withdraws from higher elevations in winter (Dec-Feb). **Habitat:** Valley ponds and lakes, and rivers and streams, especially with reeds, cattails, brush, and adjacent trees. **Elevations:** Summer 100'-8,000'; Winter 100'-5,400'. **Behavior:** Perches motionlessly at water's edge for long periods before striking fish, frogs, insects, mice, or other prey. **Noteworthy:** Green Herons may drop food into water to attract small fish and other aquatic delicacies.

BLACK-CROWNED NIGHT-HERON, *Nycticorax nycticorax*

Description: 25". Medium-sized, **stocky** heron with **short, thick neck** and red eyes. ADULT: **Black bill, crown, and back**. IMMATURE: Heavily spotted white above and heavily streaked brown below; olive-yellow bill takes three years to turn black. FLIGHT: Broad, pale underwings. **Similar Species:** Long-necked <u>Yellow-crowned Night-Heron</u>, is accidental May-Aug below 2,100'. Gray adult has off-white crown; juvenile has blackish bill. **Voice:** Quizzical *quock?* **Status:** Uncommon but nomadic resident; withdraws from higher elevations in winter (Nov-Mar). **Habitat:** Valley ponds and lakes, especially with reeds and trees. **Elevations:** Summer 100'-9,400'; Winter 100'-7,000'. **Behavior:** Sit-and-wait hunter striking unwary fish, frogs, snakes, or other aquatic prey. Primarily nocturnal. During the day typically roosts in dense cover near water. **Noteworthy:** Occurs on all continents except Antarctica. In midsummer roving flocks in Arizona may number more than 20.

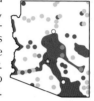

White-faced Ibis
Adult

White-faced Ibis
Immature

Glossy Ibis
Adult

WHITE-FACED IBIS, *Plegadis chihi*

Description: 23". Dark wading bird with a long, decurved bill and **red eyes**. BREEDING: Purple overall with glossy green back and wings; bare **red face outlined by white; legs red**. NONBREEDING: Duller with finely streaked neck; pink facial skin. **Similar Species:** Breeding adult Glossy Ibis (casual) has slaty facial skin and dark eyes; short bluish-white lines above and below eyes do not meet; gray legs with red confined to knees. Immatures probably not separable in field. **Voice:** Alarm call is low, quacking *waarr, waarr*. **Status:** Common in summer (Apr-Oct); uncommon in winter (Nov-Mar). **Habitat:** Barren pond shores, flooded fields, and short grass pastures. **Elevations:** Summer 100'-9,000'; Winter 100'-5,100'. **Behavior:** Probes with sickle bill for insects and invertebrates. **Noteworthy:** During peak migration periods in April, August-September, and Dec-Jan, flocks may number over 100, rarely over 1,000. In the summer of 2000, Breeding Bird Atlasers found over 1500 White-faced Ibis and many active nests in Cibola NWR.

GLOSSY IBIS, *Plegadis falcinellus*

Description: 23". Dark wading bird with a long, decurved bill; **dark eyes; pale blue lines above and below eyes do not meet**. BREEDING: Purple overall with glossy green back and wings; **knees are red**. NONBREEDING: Duller; slaty facial skin; retains short, pale lines above and below the eyes. **Similar Species:** Breeding adult White-faced Ibis (above) has red facial skin and white lines encircling the eyes; red legs. **Voice:** Identical to White-faced Ibis. **Status:** Casual summer visitor (mid Mar-Aug); recently casual in mid winter (mid Dec-mid Jan). **Habitat:** Barren pond shores, flooded fields, and short grass pastures. **Elevations:** Summer 100'-4,300'; Winter 900'-1,000'. **Noteworthy:** First recorded in Arizona in 2001, Glossies ordinarily occur as 1-2 birds in a flock of White-faced Ibis.

White Ibis
Adult

Immature

Roseate Spoonbill
Adult

Immature

WHITE IBIS, *Eudocimus albus*

Description: 24". Medium-large wading bird with a long, decurved **red bill** and **red legs**. ADULT: White: IMMATURE: Dusky head and neck; solid brown back becomes blotchy white by first spring. FLIGHT: Adult has **white wings with black wingtips**; immature has wings with black trailing edge. **Similar Species:** White belly eliminates other ibis species. Snowy Egret (p. 179) lacks red bill or legs; wings never have black markings. **Voice:** Resonant honking *hunnck* notes. **Status:** Casual year-round visitor. **Habitat:** Barren pond shores, flooded fields, and short grass pastures. **Elevations:** Year-round 100'-3,800'. **Behavior:** Probes mud and shallows for crustaceans and insects. **Noteworthy:** Usually occurs as a single in Arizona, where it often associates with Snowy and Great Egrets.

ROSEATE SPOONBILL, *Platalea ajaja*

Description: 32". **Pink wading bird** with a **long, spatulate bill**. ADULT: Deep pink with bald head. BREEDING: Black-banded hindcrown; crimson red shoulders; orange tail. IMMATURE: White feathered head; pale pink overall. **Similar Species:** The only large pink bird in Arizona. **Voice:** Deep, gutteral *ruhh, ruhh*. **Status:** Casual year-round, but primarily in summer (late Jul-mid Oct). **Habitat:** Muddy seasonal ponds, flooded fields with emergent grasses and tall weeds. **Elevations:** Year-round 100'-4,200'. **Behavior:** Forages by filtering muddy water, rhythmically swinging its specialized bill back and forth. Crustaceans in diet impart pink color. **Noteworthy:** Usually occurs as singles or twosomes in Arizona, rarely in groups more than 5, and it often associates with Snowy and Great Egrets. Most records are of sub-adults.

Description: 50", wingspan 110". **Huge**, black, raptor-like bird **with bare head and neck**. ADULT: Head is orange and yellow. JUVENILE: Head is gray. FLIGHT: **Enormous wingspread approaching 10 feet; long primaries splayed like fingers; long white triangles on underwings;** irregular thin white lines on upperwings; infrequently flaps and—in silhouette—resembles a small glider plane.

Similar Species: Much smaller juvenile Golden Eagle (p. 195) has white-based tail in flight; soaring adult Golden Eagle lacks long white triangles under the wings.

Status: Uncommon resident.

Habitat: Cliffs; primarily forages over open terrain.

Elevations: Resident 2,000'-10,000'.

Behavior: Locates carrion by sight; prefers medium-sized animals, such as deer or calves. Arizona nests are in shallow caves and grottos in the Grand Canyon.

Noteworthy: With a weight of almost 20 pounds, the California Condor is the heaviest raptor in North America, twice the weight of a Golden Eagle, and it also has the longest wingspan of any North American bird. Last recorded near Williams in 1924, the reintroduction of Condors in Arizona began with 6 birds released at the Vermilion Cliffs in 1996. In 2018 the Peregrine Fund recorded 85 wild Condors in the Arizona population. Through the end of 2021, the most reliable site to see free-flying California Condors is from the pedestrian walkway on the Highway 89A Navajo Bridge across the Colorado River. Since Condors can forage up to 125 miles in a day, it is not surprising that they have been observed throughout the Grand Canyon, north as far as Zion National Park in Utah, west of Las Vegas, Nevada, east to Los Alamos, New Mexico, and south as far as Oak Creek Canyon near Sedona, Arizona. Life span potentially exceeds 60 years. Ingesting lead shot from deer, elk, and other carcasses is the principal cause of Condor mortality.

Black Vulture
Adult

Turkey Vulture
Juvenile

Turkey Vulture
Adult

BLACK VULTURE, *Coragyps atratus*

Description: 25", wingspan 59". Large, chunky, raptor-like bird with **bare black head; black** overall with **short tail**. FLIGHT: **Outermost wingtips silvery**, contrasting with black inner wings; soars with wings in a flattened "M." Snappy wingbeats, unique among raptors. **Similar Species:** Turkey Vulture (below) has smaller-headed, slimmer silhouette; adult has red head. In flight Turkey Vulture has longer, narrower two-toned wings, and longer tail. Soars with wings held in shallow "V." **Voice:** Usually silent. **Status:** Uncommon resident, but flock size decreases in summer (May-Sep). **Habitat:** Southern valleys from lower Gila River east through the San Bernadino NWR in extreme SE corner of Arizona. **Elevations:** Resident 500'-5,400'. **Behavior:** Locates carrion by sight. **Noteworthy:** Black Vultures often cue on Turkey Vultures to find carrion. They were not recorded in Arizona until 1920.

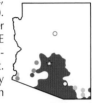

TURKEY VULTURE, *Cathartes aura*

Description: 26", wingspan 66". Large **blackish-brown** raptor-like bird with **long tail**. ADULT: **Bare red head**. JUVENILE: Bare dark head. FLIGHT: **Two-toned wings** with pale flight feathers that contrast with black wing-linings; **"teeter-totters"** as it soars. **Similar Species:** Stockier Black Vulture (above) has black head, broad wings with silvery circles at the tips. Soaring Golden Eagle lacks bicolored wings. **Voice:** Low, breathy *whuh whuh* calls occasionally audible from close range. **Status:** Common in summer (mid Mar-mid Oct); uncommon in winter (mid Oct-mid Mar). **Habitat:** Summer: All habitats. Winter: Primarily in low elevation, agricultural western valleys; also winters in Douglas, SE Arizona. **Elevations:** Summer 100'-12,600'; Winter 100'-4,100'. **Behavior:** Locates carrion by smell and by sight. May form huge roosts with over 100 birds. **Noteworthy:** Summering Arizona Turkey Vultures migrate south of the U.S.; wintering birds probably originate from near the Canadian border.

Osprey
Adult

Northern Harrier
Adult Female

Adult Male

Female

OSPREY, *Pandion haliaetus*

Description: 23", wingspan 63". Large, fish-eating hawk with **white head** and **dark eyestripe**. MALE: Unstreaked, clean white breast. FEMALE: Often shows a necklace of dark streaks across breast. JUVENILE: Scaled buff on the back and wings; buffy wash on the breast. FLIGHT: **Leading edge of wings sharply crooked at wrist** and down-bowed. **Similar Species:** Larger Bald Eagle (p. 195) lacks dark eyestripe; has dark—not white—underparts. **Voice:** Short, chirping whistles. **Status:** Uncommon resident. Wandering birds occur throughout the year, with an increase in spring (Mar-Apr) and fall (Aug-Oct). **Habitat:** Lakes, ponds, rivers, and streams with fish; transients occur in all habitats. Except for a few Sonoran Desert River nests, especially near Phoenix, breeding habitat for most Arizona Ospreys is above 5,500'. **Elevations:** Summer 100'-9,400'; Winter 100'-5,500'. **Noteworthy:** In 2000 Arizona's breeding population was estimated between 100-120.

NORTHERN HARRIER, *Circus hudsonius*

Description: 18", wingspan 43". Small head with **owl-like facial disk**. MALE: Gull-like pattern of gray above and white below. FEMALE: Brown, with streaked underparts. JUVENILE: Pale rusty underparts. FLIGHT: **Long wings held slightly above horizontal; white band across rump. Similar Species:** Large-headed Short-eared Owl (p. 227) lacks conspicuous white rump band; in flight wider wings sweep high above horizontal. **Voice:** Female's call is shrill *eeea*. **Status:** Rare—sometimes absent—in summer (mid May-mid Jul); common in winter and migration (mid Jul-mid May). **Habitat:** Valley grasslands, pastures, fields, marshes, shallow ponds, large vacant lots and airports within cities. **Elevations:** Summer 3,000'-7,000'; Winter 100'-7,200'. **Behavior:** Quarters low and buoyantly over the ground, hunting with acute hearing, as well as sight. Takes low perches. Nomadic, population density is relative to prey abundance. **Noteworthy:** Male Northern Harriers are often polygynous and may attend more than one nest.

193

Bald Eagle
Adult

Juvenile

Golden Eagle
Adult

Juvenile

BALD EAGLE, *Haliaeetus leucocephalus*

Description: 31", wingspan 80". **Very large raptor** with big head and big bill. ADULT: **White head and tail**. IMMATURE: Blotchy plumage lacks pattern. FLIGHT: Long, rectangular wings held on horizontal plane. JUVENILE FLIGHT: Blotchy white underwings and white wingpits. **Similar Species:** Immature Golden Eagle (below) shows sharp black and white tail pattern and often sharp white wing patches. **Voice:** Usually silent. **Status:** Uncommon resident; migrants augment population in winter (Oct-Mar). **Habitat:** Summer: Large lakes and rivers, often with adjacent cliffs; Winter: Lakes and broad valleys. **Elevations:** Summer 900'-9,400'; Winter 100'-7,100'. **Behavior:** Arizona birds may nest on cliffs, as well as tall trees. Breeding birds specialize on fish. In winter also eats carrion and hunts waterfowl. **Noteworthy:** After breeding some eagles move to high elevation trout lakes and range as far north as Canada. About 140 Bald Eagles breed in Arizona; the winter population is probably over 300.

GOLDEN EAGLE, *Aquila chrysaetos*

Description: 30", wingspan 80". **Very large raptor** with relatively small head; **golden crown and nape**. ADULT FLIGHT: Long, all-dark wings held slightly above level. JUVENILE FLIGHT: White tail with broad black band at tip; usually large white wing "diamonds." **Similar Species:** Immature Bald Eagle (above) lacks crisp black terminal band on white tail and has mottled white wings. **Voice:** Usually silent. **Status:** Uncommon resident; withdraws from high elevations in winter (Nov-Feb) **Habitat:** Deserts and valleys to mountain coniferous forest. Territories include cliffs and canyon walls suitable for nests and open terrain for hunting. **Elevations:** Summer 1,500'-10,500'; Winter 100'-7,200'. **Behavior:** Hunts open country for rabbits and other small mammals, as well as birds as large as Sandhill Cranes. Builds and reuses large, bulky nests, primarily on cliff ledges, rarely trees. **Noteworthy:** Golden Eagles usually do not breed in drought years with limited rabbit availability.

White-tailed Kite
Adult

Mississippi Kite
Juvenile

Mississippi Kite
Adult

WHITE-TAILED KITE, *Elanus leucurus*

Description: 15", wingspan 39". Elegant gray and white raptor with **black shoulders**; long pointed wings; **long white tail**. JUVENILE: Buffy wash on neck and breast. FLIGHT: Buoyant, wings held high above body; frequently hovers. **Similar Species:** Adult Mississippi Kite (below) is gray overall with a black tail. **Voice:** Whistled *pity pity*. **Status:** Usually uncommon in summer (Apr-Sep) and rare in winter (Oct-Mar), but numbers fluctuate from year to year. **Habitat:** Flat or gently rolling valley grasslands, pastures, and fields with scattered trees. **Elevations:** Resident 100'-4,600'. **Behavior:** Forages over open country for rodents, and less often snakes and lizards. Unlike most other raptors, usually produces two broods per year. **Noteworthy:** White-tailed Kite was not substantiated in Arizona until 1972.

MISSISSIPPI KITE, *Ictinia mississippiensis*

Description: 14", wingspan 31". Gray raptor with **pearly head** and **long black tail**. JUVENILE: Thick brown streaks below; banded tail. FLIGHT: Graduated wingtips; long, black, rectangular tail. Does not hover. **Similar Species:** White-tailed Kite (above) is mostly white with white tail. **Voice:** Whistled *kweer* notes. **Status:** Uncommon in summer (late Apr-Sep). **Habitat:** Tall cottonwood groves in river valleys. **Elevations:** Summer 100'-7,000'. **Behavior:** Plucks insects, especially Apache cicadas, off the canopy of cottonwood trees. Small colonies of these kites nest high in cottonwood groves, and often forage together. **Noteworthy:** Mississippi Kite was not recorded in Arizona until 1970. Although possible from Yuma to Flagstaff, they are only known to regularly breed on the lower San Pedro River from St. David north to the area of its confluence with the Gila River near Winkelman.

Sharp-shinned Hawk
Adult

Juvenile

Cooper's Hawk
Adult

Juvenile

SHARP-SHINNED HAWK, *Accipiter striatus*

Description: Male: 10", female: 14", wingspan 20-28". Small-headed bird-hawk, **straw-thin legs, square-ended tail**. ADULT: Black cap scarcely contrasts with slate-gray upperparts. JUVENILE: Coarse, reddish-brown streaks below. FLIGHT: Head barely projects beyond elbows when soaring. **Similar Species:** Cooper's Hawk (below) has proportionately larger head, thicker legs, and rounded tail tip. Immature Cooper's has narrow streaks on breast. **Voice:** Series of *kew* notes. **Status:** Rare in summer (Apr-Sep); uncommon in winter (Oct-Mar). **Habitat:** Summer: Mountain coniferous forest and upper stream groves. Winter: Valley groves and wooded lower mountain canyons. **Elevations:** Summer 5,600'-10,400'; Winter 100'-7,000'. **Behavior:** Cat-like when it hunts small birds, approaching stealthily, then capturing its prey with a burst of speed. **Noteworthy:** Female Sharp-shins weigh nearly twice as much as males.

COOPER'S HAWK, *Accipiter cooperii*

Description: Male: 14", female: 20", wingspan 29-37". Medium-sized bird-hawk with **rounded tail-tip**. ADULT: Black cap contrasts with blue-gray upperparts. JUVENILE: Thin dark streaks on white underparts. FLIGHT: Distinctive flap-flap-glide flight style. Head projects well beyond elbows when soaring. **Similar Species:** Immature Sharp-shinned is coarsely streaked. Larger juvenile Northern Goshawk (p. 201) usually has obvious white eyebrows. **Voice:** Series of *kek kek kek kek* notes. Juvenile begs with quavering *wee-h* calls. **Status:** Fairly common resident; most withdraw from upper elevations in winter (Oct-Mar). **Habitat:** Urban areas; valley, foothill, and mountain canyon groves; pinyon-juniper and Ponderosa pine forest. **Elevations:** Summer 100'-9,000'; Winter 100'-5,500'. **Behavior:** Small mammals constitute about 30 percent of its diet in Arizona. **Noteworthy:** About 300 Cooper's Hawks live in Tucson. Eye color, yellow in juveniles, becomes deep red as the bird ages.

Adult

Juvenile

NORTHERN GOSHAWK, *Accipiter gentilis*

Description: Male: 21", female: 26", wingspan 41-46". **Large**, long-tailed bird-hawk with **obvious white eyebrow**. ADULT: Thick white eyebrow bordered by dark crown and broad, dark gray eyestripe; gray upperparts; finely gray-barred breast; long, indistinctly banded gray tail. JUVENILE: Pale brown head, typically with bold white eyebrows; speckled brown upperparts; underparts white to buffy with dense, dark brown streaking; heavily streaked undertail coverts. FLIGHT: Broad wings and long, narrow tail with wedge-shaped tip.

Similar Species: Smaller Cooper's Hawk (p. 199) lacks bold white eyebrow. Adult Cooper's is rusty-barred below, more lightly streaked juveniles show mostly white under tail coverts; in flight Cooper's has more narrow wings and rounded tail corners. Similar-sized immature Red-tailed Hawk has much boxier profile, shorter tail, and lacks the white eyebrow.

Voice: Call at nest is deliberate, strident *gii gii gii gii gii* notes.

Status: Rare resident; withdraws from upper elevations in winter (mid Oct-mid Mar).

Habitat: Mountain forests and canyon groves with tall timber. May hunt in the desert and grassland surrounding the mountains, even in summer. Casual migrant through valleys.

Elevations: Summer 4,800'-10,700'; Winter 2,600'-9,000'.

Behavior: Hunts large birds and mammals, including Band-tailed Pigeons, Mourning Doves, Steller's Jays, Northern Flickers, squirrels, and cottontails. Prefers mature forests with large trees and open understories for nesting. Aggressively defends nest and has injured humans who approached too near.

Noteworthy: By weight Northern Goshawk is the largest accipiter in the world. Not officially listed by federal agencies, the declining "Apache" race of Northern Goshawk, confined to the mountains of SE Arizona, is slightly larger and darker than any other subspecies of this holarctic raptor.

Common Black Hawk
Adult

Adult

Juvenile

Zone-tailed Hawk
Adult

Adult

Juvenile

COMMON BLACK HAWK, *Buteogallus anthracinus*

Description: 21", wingspan 50". Bulky with **long yellow legs**. ADULT: Black with **one broad white tail band**. JUVENILE: Thick black moustache; striped underparts; multi-banded tail. FLIGHT: "Flying umbrella"; broad wings with pale crescents at base of primaries; short, fan-shaped tail. **Similar Species:** Much lankier adult Zone-tailed Hawk (below) has multiple white tail bands. **Voice:** Whistled, complaining *wink wink wink oo-wink wink*, end notes fading in intensity. **Status**: Uncommon summer resident (Mar-Oct). **Habitat:** Cottonwood and sycamore groves along permanent streams and rivers in valley, foothill, and mountain canyons. **Elevations:** Summer 450'-9,000'. **Behavior:** Hunts frogs and small fish from stream banks. **Noteworthy:** Flight pattern is reminiscent of Black Vulture. An estimated 160-180 pairs nest in Arizona. In mid March, waves of Black Hawks move north along the Santa Cruz River through Tubac.

ZONE-TAILED HAWK, *Buteo albonotatus*

Description: 20", wingspan 51". Slim and black with **multiple white tail bands**. ADULT: Two or three white tail bands. JUVENILE: Black with inconspicuous, small white speckles; many thin tail bands. FLIGHT: Heavily checkered flight feathers. **Similar Species:** Juvenile Common Black Hawk (above) has patterned face, very broad wings; underparts heavily striped black-and-white. **Voice:** Long *kreeeeeah* scream. **Status:** Uncommon in summer (mid Mar-mid Sep); rare in winter (mid Sep-mid Mar). **Habitat:** Desert washes to mountain coniferous forest, especially riparian groves. **Elevations:** Summer 100'-10,000'; Winter 100'-7,000'. **Behavior:** Similarity to Turkey Vulture in flight seemingly lulls lizards, birds, and small mammals into complacency. Nests high in one of the tallest trees in its territory. **Noteworthy:** Occasionally soars with Turkey Vultures. With an estimated 200-300 pairs of breeding Zone-tails, Arizona has the majority of the U.S. population.

Harris's Hawk
Adult

Adult

Juvenile

Gray Hawk
Adult

Juvenile

Adult

HARRIS'S HAWK, *Parabuteo unicinctus*

Description: 21", wingspan 46". Chocolate-brown hawk with rufous wings and thighs; **white at base and tip of tail.** JUVENILE: Mottled chest and belly. FLIGHT: White base of tail; chestnut wing-linings. **Similar Species:** Zone-tailed Hawk (p. 203) is black and has multiple white tail bands. **Voice:** Sore-throated *kaarrrh* and *ayeh* notes. **Status:** Fairly common resident; peak abundance is in central Arizona. **Habitat:** Sonoran and Chihuahuan Desert scrub and valley grasslands. Found in large city parks, on golf courses, and at wastewater recycling basins in Tucson and Phoenix. **Elevations:** Resident 400'-5,400'. **Behavior:** Hunts reptiles, birds, and small mammals. Two or more Harris's often hunt cooperatively and use relays to run down rabbits. **Noteworthy:** Harris's Hawks form social aggregations in fall and winter that may number up to 18 birds.

GRAY HAWK, *Buteo plagiatus*

Description: 17", wingspan 36". Small hawk with large, **dark eye** and striking **black and white tail bands**. ADULT: Entirely gray. JUVENILE: White face with bold black eyestripe and moustache. FLIGHT: Several flaps then a glide like a Cooper's Hawk. **Similar Species:** Immature Cooper's Hawk (p. 199) has lemon or orange-colored eyes and low contrast tail bands. **Voice:** Piercing whistle *wee-ah, wee-ah* and shrill, drawn-out *kreeeeeh*. **Status:** Fairly common in summer (Mar-mid Oct); rare in winter (mid Oct-Feb). **Habitat:** River valley and foothill canyon cottonwood groves; mountain canyon sycamore riparian. **Elevations:** Summer 900'-6,000'; Winter 900'-5,200'. **Behavior:** Ambushes lizards and birds in trees. **Noteworthy:** There were approximately 200 pairs of Gray Hawks in Arizona in 2018. Formerly confined to river bottom cottonwoods, since 2000 Gray Hawks have colonized some major canyons in mountains near the Mexican border.

RED-SHOULDERED HAWK

Red-shouldered Hawk Adult

Adult

Juvenile

BROAD-WINGED HAWK

Adult

Adult

Juvenile

RED-SHOULDERED HAWK, *Buteo lineatus elegans*

Description: 17", wingspan 40". Plain face; **red shoulders; short, polka-dotted wings; long, black-and-white banded tail.** ADULT: **bright, rusty chest and shoulders.** JUVENILE: Dull red shoulders; dark streaks on chest and belly. FLIGHT: Like a Cooper's Hawk but with rufous wing-linings; checkered black-and-white underwing; pale crescents at base of primaries. **Similar Species:** Smaller Broad-winged Hawk (below) has dark malar stripes framing pale throat; chest is streaked brown; in flight shows mostly white wings outlined with black. **Voice:** Steady, squealing *qeee-ah* notes. **Status:** Rare local resident; rare year-round visitor. **Habitat:** River valley woodland. **Elevations:** Summer 100'-1,950'; Winter 100'-7,000. **Behavior:** Ambush predator. Hunts reptiles, birds, and small mammals within woodlands, often from low perches. **Noteworthy:** The first Arizona nest was on the Colorado River in 1981; since 2000 has regularly attempted to nest near Wickenburg.

BROAD-WINGED HAWK, *Buteo platypterus*

Description: 15", wingspan 34". **Smallest** of the Arizona Buteo hawks; brown above; brown face with dull amber eyes and pale eyebrows; **dark malar stripes frame pale throat**. ADULT: Heavily streaked chest; barred belly. JUVENILE: brown-streaked chest. FLIGHT: **Broad but pointed white underwings with black trailing edge**; black-and-white banded tail, **bands widening noticeably towards tip**. **Similar Species:** Immature Cooper's Hawk (p. 199) has bright lemon or orange eyes; much longer tail with low contrast tail bands. **Voice:** Piercing whistle *p-wee*. **Status:** Rare spring (Apr-mid May) and fall (Sep-mid Oct) migrant. Casual in summer and winter. **Habitat:** Rests during migration in river valley and canyon groves; often migrates high above ridgelines. **Elevations:** Migrant 150'-9,000'. **Behavior:** Hunts insects, lizards, and birds from concealment. **Noteworthy:** Every fall small numbers of Broad-winged Hawks are reliably seen from the South Rim of the Grand Canyon, with peak passage during the last week of September.

SHORT-TAILED HAWK

Adult light morph

dark morph

light morph

SWAINSON'S HAWK

Adult light morph

Juvenile

Adult light morph

SHORT-TAILED HAWK, *Buteo brachyurus*

Description: 17", wingspan 38". Small hawk with **big head**; white forehead and lores. Wingtips reach to tail tip. LIGHT MORPH: **Dark helmet**. DARK MORPH: Blackish overall. FLIGHT: Often soars at great altitude on broad, black-trimmed wings with bulging secondaries and pale ovals at base of primaries; low contrast tail-barring with noticeable broad, dark subterminal band. **Similar Species:** Larger, light morph Swainson's Hawk (below) has dark bib across chest. **Voice:** High, thin, dying *keee-h*. **Status:** Rare in summer (Apr-Oct); casual in winter (Sep-Mar) and migration (mid Mar-mid May and Sep-Oct). **Habitat:** Summer: mountains, primarily coniferous forest. Winter: river valley groves; wooded urban areas. Migration: River valleys and mountain canyons. **Elevations:** Summer 4,000'-9,500'; Winter 2,300'-3,300'. **Behavior:** Stoops from great heights on treetop birds. **Noteworthy:** Most Arizona birds are light morphs. Short-tails were first recorded from the Chiricahua Mountains in 1985.

SWAINSON'S HAWK, *Buteo swainsoni*

Description: 21", wingspan 52". Hawk with **long, narrow, pointed wings**. LIGHT or RUFOUS MORPH: **broad dark bib**. DARK MORPH: white chin; **white under tail coverts**. JUVENILE: Thick moustache extends to sides of chest. FLIGHT: Light and rufous morphs exhibit **"reversed" wing pattern** with dark flight feathers and ivory or cinnamon wing linings. Dark morph has all dark wings. Long tapering wings are held in a shallow "V". **Similar Species:** Smaller Short-tailed Hawk (above) has compact shape, and rounded—not pointed—wings. **Voice:** Shrill *weee-a*. **Status:** Fairly common in summer (mid May-Aug); common migrant (mid Mar-mid May and mid Aug-mid Oct). **Habitat:** Summer: Grassy desertscrub, large fields and pastures; valley grasslands, and large mountain meadows; Migration: Primarily open country from low desert to high mountains. **Elevations:** Summer-1,900'-9,500'; Migration 100'-9,500'. **Behavior:** Insectivorous; rarely takes vertebrates. **Noteworthy:** Dark morphs are rare in Arizona. Flocks of 50-500 may occur in fall.

"Western"
Light Adult

"Western"
Light Juvenile

"Harlan's"
Adult

"Fuerte's"
Adult

"Western"
Rufous Adult

Description: 20", wingspan 50". Common, bulky, broad-winged hawk with **broad tail, usually--except for "Harlan's"--coppery-red in adults. Mottled upperparts** and **belly band** diagnostic when present. Many color morphs exist. "WESTERN" ADULT: Dark throat; breast colors include white, buffy, rufous, and black morphs. Belly is usually heavily streaked, producing a "banded" effect. Rufous morph "Western" has a solid black belly and dark morph "Western" has entire underparts uniform black. "FUERTE'S" ADULT: Underparts and underwings whitish with belly streaking fine, faint, or absent. "HARLAN'S" ADULT: Black with white streaks on chest; whitish tail with diffuse dusky tip. JUVENILE: Yellow eyes; finely-barred tail. FLIGHT: All but blackest dark morph show **dark shoulder bars** on the underwings.

Similar Species: Light morph Ferruginous Hawk (p. 213) has rufous shoulders and back, and fully feathered reddish leggings. Dark morph Ferruginous lacks white-streaked chest of "Harlan's" Red-tails.

Voice: Typical call is harsh, drawn-out scream *kreeeahh*.

Status: Common resident, most common in winter (Sep-Apr), when migrants augment resident population. "Harlan's" race is rare in winter. Most Red-tails withdraw from Lower Colorado River Valley in summer (May-Aug).

Habitat: Especially abundant in valleys, but widespread in all habitats from the desert floor to open mountain forests.

Elevations: Resident 100'-11,000'.

Behavior: Opportunistic; hunts either by pouncing on prey from an elevated perch or stooping from flight. Courting birds may fly in tandem with legs outstretched, lock talons, and perform acrobatic dives and rolls. Nests in trees, saguaros, utility poles, or on cliffs.

Noteworthy: During winter it is estimated that four Red-tails per mile occur along valley highways in Arizona.

Ferruginous Hawk Adult

light morph

dark morph

Rough-legged Hawk Adult Male

Adult female

FERRUGINOUS HAWK, *Buteo regalis*

Description: 23", wingspan 56". **Largest buteo; large bill; feathered legs.** Two color morphs. LIGHT ADULT: Gray head; **rufous back** and shoulders; **reddish leggings**; pale tail with reddish tinge. DARK ADULT: Entirely gray tail. IMMATURE: Like adult, but reduced red highlights. FLIGHT: Feathered red legs form contrasting "V" against pale tail. **Similar Species:** Smaller Red-tailed Hawk (p. 211) usually has dark head, dark belly band, rufous tail–or finely banded tail in immatures, and lacks dark leggings. **Voice:** Shrill *keeerrrr*. **Status:** Rare in summer (May-Sep); uncommon in winter (Oct-Apr). **Habitat:** Summer: Prairie grasslands. Winter: Grasslands, farm fields, and pastures; mountain clearings. **Elevations:** Summer 4,700'-8,800'; Migration and Winter 100'-9,500'. **Behavior:** Eats rodents and other small mammals; historically specialized on prairie dogs. May use utility poles and fence posts, but often perches on the ground. **Noteworthy:** About 5% of Arizona Ferruginous Hawks are dark morph.

ROUGH-LEGGED HAWK, *Buteo lagopus*

Description: 21", wingspan 53". **Large buteo**; small bill; **feathered legs; white tail with wide black subterminal band.** ADULT: Pale head; variably streaked pale breast; often a dark "cumberbund." JUVENILE: Like adult but subterminal tail band dusky. FLIGHT: Underwings white with square black wrist. **Similar Species:** "Harlan's" Red-tailed Hawk (p. 211) and dark morph Ferruginous Hawk (above) lack large black wrist marks and broad black tail band. **Voice:** Usually silent in winter. **Status:** Rare in winter (Nov-Mar); casual in spring (Apr) and fall (Oct). **Habitat:** Desertscrub; valley grasslands and fields. **Elevations:** Winter 100'-9,200'. **Behavior:** Primarily feeds on small rodents; will eat carrion. **Noteworthy:** Arizona is the southernmost limit of the Rough-legged's usual winter range. Entirely black dark morph with the same tail pattern as light morph is accidental here.

Female

Male

BARN OWL, *Tyto alba*

Description: 16″. Medium-large **gold and white owl** with **dark eyes** and **heart-shaped face**. MALE: Underparts white. FEMALE: Underparts usually buff. FLIGHT: Both sexes appear ghostly white at night.

Similar Species: Pale—but not white—Short-eared owl (p. 227) is mostly active at dawn and dusk, has yellow—not deep brown—eyes, and a striped breast.

Voice: Rasping, hair-raising screech, often given in flight.

Status: Uncommon in summer (Mar-Oct); Numbers vary annually, but usually fairly common in winter (Nov-Feb). Winter population is probably augmented by migrants from the north.

Habitat: Open deserts and valleys with suitable dark roosting and nesting sites. Casual in mountain Ponderosa pine forests or above 7,200′.

Elevations: Resident 100′-5,700′.

Behavior: Nocturnal; hunts rodents with long, coursing flights. Arizona Barn Owls spend the daylight hours sequestered under palm fronds, inside dense trees, abandoned buildings, old wells, mine shafts, under highway bridges, within crevices in stacks of baled hay, and on shaded cliff ledges. Barn Owls often nest in the same places they roost. They are also known to excavate three- to six-foot-long burrows into the sides of steep arroyo banks. More than 10 percent of male Barn Owls in the Southwest are thought to be polygamous, with two or even three mates. Winter communal roosts may contain more than 20 Barn Owls.

Noteworthy: Barn Owls occur on every continent except Antarctica, and are often considered the most widely distributed land birds in the world.

215

NORTHERN SAW-WHET OWL

Adult

Juvenile

FLAMMULATED OWL

NORTHERN SAW-WHET OWL, *Aegolius acadicus*

Description: 8". **Big-headed**, little mountain owl with **whitish goggles**; short tail. JUVENILE: Unmarked buffy belly. **Similar Species:** Flammulated Owl (below) has ear tufts and dark eyes. **Voice:** Long rhythmic series of mellow toots, about 2 per second, much faster than Rocky Mountain form of Northern Pygmy-Owl. Calls infrequently after June. **Status:** Rare resident. **Habitat:** Mountain coniferous forest, especially mixed with some Gambel's oak or aspen; in winter (Nov-Mar) small numbers may descend to desert and valley towns and oases. **Elevations:** Summer 5,100'-10,800'; Winter 150'-8,200'. **Behavior:** Nocturnal; hunts rodents at night from low perches. Some probably migrate southward or move down-slope in the fall. If detected but left undisturbed in the daytime, usually just snoozes. **Noteworthy:** May cache excess mice in fall for later winter consumption.

FLAMMULATED OWL, *Psiloscops flammeolus*

Description: 6.5". Small, **dark-eyed** forest owl with variably **red-tinted facial disk**; short, depressable ear tufts; red-edged line of buff spots delineates shoulder. **Similar Species:** Larger Western Screech-Owl and Whiskered Screech-Owls (p. 219) have yellow eyes; lack any reddish tints. **Voice:** Low, soft, widely-spaced *boop* notes difficult to pin down; seems ventriloquial and may call from inside a nest cavity; becomes quiet in July. **Status:** Fairly common in summer (mid Mar-Sep). **Habitat:** Mountain coniferous forests, especially mixed with Gambel's oaks, and tall canyon groves within Sierra Madrean pine-oak woodland. **Elevations:** Summer 5,000'-9,600'. **Behavior:** Feeds almost exclusively on insects, especially moths. Most active just after dark and just before dawn. Usually perches next to tree trunks. **Noteworthy:** Flammulated Owl is considered the most abundant forest-dwelling owl in Arizona.

Western Screech-Owl
Adult

Juvenile

Whiskered Screech-Owl
Adult

Nest

WESTERN SCREECH-OWL, *Megascops kennicottii*

Description: Description: 8.5". Small "eared" owl of the lowlands and foothills with yellow eyes and **black bill**; relatively **large feet**. Best identified by voice. **Similar Species:** Smaller Flammulated Owl (p. 217) has dark eyes. Whiskered Screech-Owl (below) has green bill. **Voice:** "Bouncing ball" series of short, accelerating whistles. Calls infrequently after July. **Status:** Fairly common resident. **Habitat:** Saguaro desert, river cottonwoods, open canyon groves, and open oak woodlands. **Elevations:** Resident 100'-7,100'.
Behavior: Ambushes prey from perches on lower limbs. Primarily eats small rodents, as well as some birds and large insects. **Noteworthy:** Western is replaced by Whiskered Screech-Owl at higher elevations in SE Arizona, where stream cottonwood groves and open oak woodlands transition into denser sycamore groves and pine-oak woodlands.

WHISKERED SCREECH-OWL, *Megascops trichopsis*

Description: 7.25". Small "eared" owl of the mountains with yellow eyes and **greenish bill**; relatively **small feet**. Best identified by voice. **Similar Species:** Smaller Flammulated Owl (p. 217) has dark eyes. Western Screech-Owl (above) has black bill. **Voice:** Syncopated "Morse Code" series of short and long toots. Calls infrequently after July. **Status:** Fairly common resident. **Habitat:** Reaches its greatest density in mid-elevation mountain canyon sycamore groves and Sierra Madrean pine-oak woodland; sparingly occurs in high elevation Ponderosa pine forest. Most nests are in sycamore trees. **Elevations:** Resident 3,800'-9,400'. **Behavior:** Ambushes prey from perches on lower limbs. Primarily consumes large insects, as well as some small rodents and birds. **Noteworthy:** At their northern limits in SE Arizona, these owls inhabit the Sierra Madre chain south to Nicaragua.

Great Horned Owl
Adult

Juvenile

"Mexican" Spotted Owl
Adult

Juveniles

GREAT HORNED OWL, *Bubo virginianus*

Description: 22", wingspan 44". **Big, boxy, ear-tufted owl** with **yellow eyes**. Females are generally larger, darker, and have higher pitched voices than males. **Similar Species:** Smaller, lankier Long-eared Owl (p. 227) has longer, more closely-spaced ear tufts. **Voice:** Territorial hoot is a rolling *huh h'oooh hoo hoo*. **Status:** Common resident. **Habitat:** Saguaro desert, urban areas, valley and foothill groves, and open woodlands. Sparse in dense forest or open desert lacking trees, canyons, or cliffs. **Elevations:** Resident 100'-9,800'. **Behavior:** Ambushes rodents, rabbits, skunks, and snakes from perches overlooking open areas. Nests are often "borrowed" from large hawks, herons, and ravens; also nests in tree hollows, under bridges, and inside old buildings. **Noteworthy:** Great Horned is Arizona's largest and most widespread owl.

"MEXICAN" SPOTTED OWL, *Strix occidentalis lucida*

Description: 18", wingspan 40". Bulky, **big-headed forest owl** with **dark eyes** and **no ear tufts**. **Similar Species:** Larger Great Horned Owl (above) has yellow eyes and obvious ear tufts. **Voice:** Hooted *hoo hoo wa-hoooh*. **Status:** Uncommon resident; casual in adjacent lowlands in winter. **Habitat:** Mountain canyon groves, tall pine-oak woodland, and shady stands of mixed coniferous forest. Slot canyons with widely scattered trees are preferred in NW Arizona and the Grand Canyon area. **Elevations:** Resident 3,700'-9,800'. **Behavior:** Ambushes mice, woodrats, bats, small birds, and insects from open perches. Day roosts in large trees are usually on lower limb, well away from tree trunk, or in a small tree. Most nests are in potholes in cliffs; occasionally uses old Red-tailed Hawk tree nests. **Noteworthy:** "Mexican" race Spotted Owls are somewhat paler and more spotted on upperparts than Pacific Northwest race; ranges do not overlap. Competition and an inability to dissipate body heat probably lead Spotted Owls to prefer cooler habitats than Great Horned Owls.

Northern
Pygmy-Owl

"Cactus"
Ferruginous
Pygmy-Owl

Rear eye spots

NORTHERN PYGMY-OWL, *Glaucidium gnoma*

Description: 6.75". Mountain gnome with **spotted crown; long, white-barred tail.** Large "eye-spots" on hindcrown. **Similar Species:** Northern Saw-whet Owl (p. 217) has big head with streaked crown and shorter tail, and larger Whiskered Screech-Owl (p. 219) has ear tufts. Lower elevation, desert-dwelling Ferruginous Pygmy-Owl (below) has streaked crown and rusty-barred tail. **Voice:** Repeated, slow, single toots—once per 2 seconds (Rocky Mountain form), or fast double toots—once per second ("Mountain" form south of the Gila River); if very excited both subspecies emit low, rapid *popopopopopo too too too* notes reminiscent of a Screech-Owl. **Status:** Uncommon resident. Rocky Mountain form of Northern Arizona is rarely reported in winter. **Habitat:** Mountain canyon groves, pine-oak woodland, and open coniferous forest. **Elevations:** Resident 3,600'-10,500'. **Behavior:** Chases down birds, rodents, and lizards at dawn and dusk. Aggressively defends territories. **Noteworthy:** Northern Pygmy-Owls sometimes kill birds and mammals larger than themselves.

'CACTUS" FERRUGINOUS PYGMY-OWL, *Glaucidium brasilianum cactorum*

Description: 6.75". Desert gnome with **streaked crown; long, rusty-barred tail.** Large "eye-spots" on hindcrown. **Similar Species:** Larger Western Screech-Owl (p. 219) has ear tufts. Mountain-dwelling Northern Pygmy-Owl (above) has spotted crown and white-barred tail. **Voice:** Long, monotonous series of toots. **Status:** Rare resident. **Habitat:** Saguaro cactus desert and foothill thorn forest canyon groves. **Elevations:** Resident 1,300'-4,200'. **Behavior:** Chases down birds, rodents, lizards, and scorpions at dawn and dusk. Nests almost exclusively in saguaro cavities. **Noteworthy:** Loss of contiguous saguaro stands and eradication of valley cottonwood groves threatens Arizona's Ferruginous Pygmy-Owls. In 2006 researchers documented only 26 individuals in the state. Wild at Heart, a non-profit group, began a reintroduction program in 2016.

223

Elf Owl

Burrowing Owl

Juveniles

ELF OWL, *Micrathene whitneyi*

Description: 5.75". **Tiny**, round-headed, **short-tailed owl**. **Similar Species:** Both Ferruginous and Northern Pygmy-Owls are much larger and have long tails. **Voice:** Wild, giggling chirps and winnies *he-ha-ha-he-he*. Descending, whistled *feeoh*. Usually silent after mid July. **Status:** Common summer resident (early Mar-Aug)); casual in fall (Sep-early Nov). **Habitat:** Saguaro cactus desert, and valley, foothill, and lower mountain canyon groves. **Elevations:** Summer 450'-5,800'. **Behavior:** Forages for moths, scorpions, and other arthropods. Also takes very small vertebrate prey. Most nest in old woodpecker holes in saguaros, cottonwoods, sycamores, and utility poles. **Noteworthy:** Weighing only slightly more than an ounce, Elf Owl is the smallest member of its family in the world.

BURROWING OWL, *Athene cunicularia*

Description: 9.5". **Long-legged**, round-headed, diurnal **ground owl** of open terrain. JUVENILE: Unmarked buffy underparts. **Similar Species:** Much larger Short-eared Owl (p. 227) has boldly-streaked underparts. **Voice:** Hollow, laughter-like *huh-huh* or *hoh-hoh*; rapid, raspy *kwik-kwik-kwik*. **Status:** Uncommon in summer (mid Mar-Oct) and rare in winter (Nov-mid Mar). **Habitat:** Open deserts, barren fields and pastures, golf courses, cemeteries, and valley grasslands. **Elevations:** Summer 100'-6,600'; Winter 100'-4,900'. **Behavior:** Forages for insects and rodents, primarily at dawn and dusk. Often perches most of the day on rocks, mounds, cemetery monuments, or low, dead stumps. Nests in abandoned rodent burrows or–where available–in old drainage pipes and under cement slabs. **Noteworthy:** Elimination of Black-tailed Prairie Dogs in the late 1930s--and the subsequent loss of their burrows for nests--severely reduced Burrowing Owl populations in SE Arizona.

Adult

Long-eared Owl

Short-eared Owl

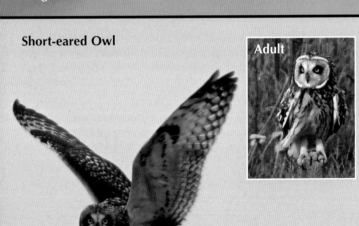

Adult

LONG-EARED OWL, *Asio otus*

Description: 15", wingspan 36". **Long, slim owl** with **long, close-set "ears;"** orange face. FLIGHT: Broad wings buff below with orange crescents on upperwing. **Similar Species:** Larger, boxier Great Horned Owl (p. 221) has widely spaced ear tufts; belly is barred--not cross-hatched. Short-eared Owl (below) has white--not orange--facial disk, miniscule ear tufts, and striped underparts. In flight shorter-tailed Short-eared Owl has more coarsely barred flight feathers; primaries above show a broader patch of paler cinnamon. **Voice:** Regularly spaced *boo boo boo* hoots at three-second intervals. **Status:** Rare and irregular, primarily in winter (Oct-Mar). **Habitat:** Desert mesquite, valley willows, foothill oak thickets, and plateau pinyon-juniper stands, often in riparian stands, or in dry washes, ravines, or canyons, especially adjacent to open areas. **Elevations:** Nomadic 100'-9,600'. **Behavior:** Quarters across open, usually flat terrain at night, flying low as it searches for small rodents; often perches near ground in dense thickets. In winter, may join communal roosts from a few to up to 30 birds. **Noteworthy:** Possible anywhere in Arizona, these nomadic owls materialize when plagues of small rodents develop—and disappear almost as suddenly.

SHORT-EARED OWL, *Asio flammeus*

Description: 15", wingspan 38". **Pale, open country owl** with tiny "ears;" streaked underparts. FLIGHT: Buoyant, moth-like; very long wings with large **buffy patches on upper side. Similar Species:** Long-eared Owl (above). Female Northern Harrier (p. 193) has smaller head, white rump, and longer tail. **Voice:** Silent in our area. **Status:** Rare in winter (early Oct-Mar). **Habitat:** Valley grasslands, farmlands, and seasonal marshes, often near ponds or lakes. **Elevations:** Winter 350'-7,100'. **Behavior:** Flies near ground hunting rodents at dawn and dusk. Frequently perches on ground. **Noteworthy:** In Arizona, may occur singly, or sometimes in small, loosely associated groups of five or more birds.

Elegant Trogon
Male

Juvenile

Female

ELEGANT TROGON, *Trogon elegans*

Description: 12". Medium-large tropical bird of the border range canyons with **yellow bill, orange eyering, white breast band**, and **long tail barred black-and-white** on the underside. MALE: Emerald green above, scarlet red below; uppertail coppery-green and underside finely barred with wavy black lines. FEMALE: White "teardrop" behind eye; neutral grayish-brown upperparts; brownish vest; pink abdomen; uppertail bronze and undertail heavily barred black. FIRST SPRING MALE: Iridescent green on back and largely crimson below, but thick bars on undertail. Some retain shadowy "teardrop" behind eye, and may have "vest coat" with incomplete red underparts. JUVENILE: Like female but with rows of large white spots on the wing coverts. Fledges with only half-grown tail, but in the first month the tail attains full length.

Similar Species: Larger Eared Quetzal (p. 231) has relatively smaller head, black bill, lacks orange eyering, lacks white breast band, and has uppertail blue and undertail mostly white.

Voice: Advertises its territory with loud *koink* or croaking *koa* notes, usually delivered in a series of 4-6 calls; soft *kuh* notes indicate intensity; alarm is a sharp *w-kkkk*. Becomes mostly silent after July.

Status: Fairly common but local in summer (mid Apr-Oct); rare and local in winter (Nov-mid Apr).

Habitat: Summer: Major mountain canyons, usually with sycamore groves; Winter: Foothill and lower mountain canyon groves.

Elevations: Summer 3,700'-7,100'; Winter 2,750'-6,200'.

Behavior: Although males may advertise for mates and announce territorial boundaries from treetops, trogons usually hover-pluck berries and insects from boughs below the canopy. Most nests are in sycamore cavities that have been excavated by Acorn Woodpeckers and Northern Flickers--even those appearing natural.

Noteworthy: Recent surveys sponsored by Tucson Audubon Society have usually recorded approximately 150-170 Elegant Trogons in SE Arizona.

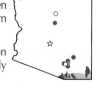

Eared Quetzal
Male

Female

Male

"Ear tufts"

EARED QUETZAL, *Euptilotis neoxenus*

Description: 14″. Large-bodied, **small-headed** trogon of the border ranges with small **black bill**, iridescent blue-green back, **green wing coverts**, flame-red belly, and broad **tail rich blue above** and white below. Wispy, elongated ear feathers are usually not visible. MALE: Blackish head and foreneck; emerald green hindneck and breast. FEMALE: Grayish-brown head, neck, and breast. IMMATURE MALE: Blotchy gray marks on an iridescent green chest. JUVENILE: Like female but with rows of large white spots on the wing coverts.

Similar Species: Smaller Elegant Trogon (p. 229) has relatively larger head, yellow bill, bold orange eyering, white breast band, and the proportionately longer tail is barred below. Its iridescent tail may appear either coppery or greenish above.

Voice: Loud, usually repeated squeal-chuck *wEEE-k* contact call; flight call a cackled *kac-ka-k-kac*; song is an ascending bisyllabic, whistled tremolo.

Status: Rare and irregular year-round, but most often observed in fall and early winter (Oct-Dec).

Habitat: Mountain canyon groves with adjacent pine-oak woodland or—infrequently—in Ponderosa pine forest.

Elevations: 5,000′-8,500′.

Behavior: Eared Quetzals court in spring and early summer, but delay nesting until after the summer rains begin when berries and insects are most abundant. In Mexico, young fledge in late summer and early fall.

Noteworthy: The first record of Eared Quetzal in the U.S. was in the Chiricahua Mountains in Oct., 1977. A nesting attempt in 1991 in Ramsey Canyon of the Huachuca Mountains was unsuccessful.

Belted Kingfisher
Male

Female

Ringed Kingfisher
Male

Green Kingfisher
Male

Female

BELTED KINGFISHER, *Megaceryle alcyon*

Description: 13". Stocky, big-billed, bull-headed **blue-gray** kingfisher with **blue-gray chest band** and white belly. MALE: Single blue-gray chest band. FEMALE: Two chest bands, bottom band rusty. FLIGHT: White upperwing patch. **Similar Species:** Larger Ringed Kingfisher (below) has solid red belly. **Voice:** Long and loud staccato rattle. **Status:** Uncommon in Central and casual in SE in summer (mid May-mid Aug); fairly common migrant and winter visitor (mid Aug-mid May). **Habitat:** Streams, rivers, ponds, lakes, and marshes; requires clear waters to detect prey. **Elevations:** Summer 2,000'-9,400'; Winter 100'-8,400'. **Behavior:** Often takes open perches overlooking water. Hovers before plunging for fish or other prey. Nests in tunnels up to 9-feet-long. **Noteworthy:** Migration peaks in Arizona occur in Apr and again from mid Aug-mid Oct.

RINGED KINGFISHER, *Megaceryle torquata*

Description: 16". Very large, **huge-billed**, blue-gray kingfisher with a **rufous belly.** MALE: Entirely rusty underparts. FEMALE: Blue band on upper chest. FLIGHT: Male has white underwing linings; female has rusty underwing linings. **Similar Species:** Smaller Belted Kingfisher (above) has white belly. **Elevations:** 3,000'-3,100'. **Noteworthy:** One Arizona record near Safford from Oct 2018-early Mar 2019.

GREEN KINGFISHER, *Chloroceryle americana*

Description: 8.75". Small, plunge-diving bird with very long, heron-like bill and white collar. **Oily green above** with **white wing spots**. MALE: Broad rufous chest band. FEMALE: Two splotchy green chest bands. FLIGHT: White outer tail feathers. **Similar Species:** Much larger Belted Kingfisher (above) is blue-gray overall. **Voice:** Insect-like *ch-dit ch-dit*; harsh *chrrrt* notes. **Status:** Rare and irregular year-round, with large population fluctuations. Has nested. **Habitat:** Woodland ponds, rivers, and streams with sluggish, fairly clear waters. **Elevations:** 1,900'-5,400'. **Behavior:** Perches low over water; dives without hovering.

Lewis's Woodpecker

Acorn Woodpecker Male

Juvenile

Female

LEWIS'S WOODPECKER, *Melanerpes lewis*

Description: 10.75". Large, dark, **glossy green woodpecker**. ADULT: Raspberry-red face inside black bonnet and gray macintosh; **pink belly**. JUVENILE: Lacks red face and gray mac'. FLIGHT: Broad wings; slow, crow-like flapping. **Similar Species:** Distinctive. **Voice:** Churring *rippp-rippp-ripp*; also a high-pitched *peek!* **Status:** Fairly common but local resident; uncommon and irregular away from breeding areas in migration and in winter (mid Oct-mid May; casual in Sep). **Habitat:** Summer: Open Ponderosa pine forest and high elevation cottonwood groves. Winter: Some descend to pecan orchards and urban parks; also use desert, valley, foothill, and lower mountain canyon groves. **Elevations:** Summer 5,500'-9,400'; Winter 400'-8,500'. **Behavior:** Harvests pecans, acorns and berries and stores them in crevices; sorties for insects from high, exposed perches. **Noteworthy:** Historically formed large wintering aggregations. Ten or fewer Lewis's Woodpeckers is more typical of recent flock size in Arizona.

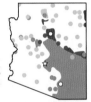

ACORN WOODPECKER, *Melanerpes formicivorus*

Description: 9". Black and white woodpecker with **white iris** and **"clown" face**. MALE: Red cap borders white forehead. FEMALE: Black bar separates red cap from white forehead. JUVENILE: Dark eye. FLIGHT: White rump and wing patches. **Similar Species:** Larger Lewis's Woodpecker (above) lacks any white. **Voice:** Aggravated, nasal *drat-it, drat-it, drat-it!* **Status:** Common resident, rare above upper limits of oaks to 9,500', primarily in summer (mid May-mid Sep); rare and irregular year-round down to 1,000' in lowlands. **Habitat:** Foothill and mountain canyon groves, exceptionally Ponderosa pine forest and old burns with nearby oaks, and to urban oases, especially in winter. **Elevations:** Resident 3,500'-8,700'. **Behavior:** Families harvest acorns and store them until winter in "granary trees"—dead snags peppered with small holes. **Noteworthy:** Acorn Woodpeckers in Arizona ordinarily never leave their group's territory.

Red-breasted
Sapsucker
daggetti race

Red-breasted
Sapsucker
ruber race

Red-headed
Woodpecker

RED-HEADED WOODPECKER, *Melanerpes erythrocephalus*

Description: 9.25". Half-black and **half-white woodpecker** with **entirely red head** and neck. JUVENILE: Brown head. FLIGHT: White rump fuses with white inner-wing patches. **Similar Species:** Smaller Red-breasted Sapsucker (below) has white moustache stripes and lacks white inner wings and rump. **Voice:** Squeaky *squee squee* calls and repeated sneezy *squew* and *whirrr* notes. **Status:** Casual visitor (mid Oct-early Aug). **Habitat:** Pecan groves in valleys, and open woodlands in canyons and highlands. **Elevations:** Year-round 1,500'-7,000'. **Behavior:** Uses conspicuous perches in tall trees to sortie out for flying insects. **Noteworthy:** Once found, a Red-headed Woodpecker occasionally stays within a small area well into summer. Only singles have been found in Arizona.

RED-BREASTED SAPSUCKER, *Sphyrapicus ruber*

Description: 8.5". **Red head and breast;** white moustache. SOUTHERN FORM: Long white moustache extends beyond eye to neck. NORTHERN FORM: Short white moustache ends under front of eye. **Similar Species:** Red-naped Sapsucker (p. 245) has bold head stripes and—except for fall molt—show black breast band. **Status:** Rare in winter (Oct-mid Mar); casual until mid April. **Habitat:** Desert oases, wooded urban areas, and lower mountain canyon groves. **Elevations:** Winter 200'-6,900'. **Behavior:** Drills small holes—sap wells—primarily on tree trunks and major limbs, and consumes both the sap and the insects that frequent them. **Noteworthy:** Both forms, southern *daggetti*, and northern *ruber*, have occurred. In Arizona, hybrids with Red-naped Sapsuckers (photo on p. 244) may outnumber pure Red-breasted Sapsuckers. These show a suffusion of red over Red-naped Sapsucker head pattern and breast band.

MALE

FEMALE

Ladder-backed
Woodpecker

Gila Woodpecker

Gilded Flicker

LADDER-BACKED WOODPECKER, *Dryobates scalaris*

Description: 7.25″. Small, bar-backed woodpecker with **black facial bridle**. MALE: Red cap. **Similar Species:** Larger Gila Woodpecker (below) has unmarked face and underparts. **Voice:** Well-spaced *peach* notes; whinny call is a series of run-on *quick-quicks*. **Status:** Common resident. **Habitat:** Saguaro desert, valley and foothill canyon groves, and hillside agave stands. **Elevations:** Resident 100′-6,800′. **Behavior:** Pecks for insects. Preferred nest tree is paloverde. **Noteworthy:** Most nest cavities are on the underside of branches or "lean" side of agave stalks.

GILA WOODPECKER, *Melanerpes uropygialis*

Description: 9.25″. Bar-backed woodpecker with **unmarked tan underparts**. MALE: Red cap. **Similar Species:** Larger Gilded (below) and Northern Flickers (p. 247) have black chest bands. **Voice:** Squealed *wheek* and *slurrr* calls. **Status:** Common resident in Sonoran Desert; uncommon in SE corner. **Habitat:** Saguaro desert, valley cottonwoods, and towns. **Elevations:** Resident 100′-5,400′. **Behavior:** Probes for fruits and insects. Most nests are in saguaros and cottonwoods. **Noteworthy:** Its "cactus boot" nest cavities in saguaros are subsequently used by many other birds.

GILDED FLICKER, *Colaptes chrysoides*

Description: 11.5″. Large, brown, bar-backed woodpecker with **black chest band**; yellow wing and tail shafts. MALE: Red moustache. FLIGHT: **Yellow underwings and undertail**; white rump. **Similar Species:** "Red-shafted" Northern Flicker (p. 247) has salmon-pink underwings and undertail. **Voice:** Poignant *clear* calls; *wika-wika-wika* notes in a long series. **Status:** Fairly common resident. **Habitat:** Saguaro desert; rare in cottonwood groves in SE Arizona valleys. **Elevations:** Resident 100′-4,100′. **Behavior:** Mostly eats ants. Nests almost exclusively in saguaros. **Noteworthy:** Gilded Flickers are largely confined to the range of saguaro cactus in Arizona and adjacent California.

HAIRY WOODPECKER

"Rocky Mtn." Male

"SE Arizona" Male

Female

DOWNY WOODPECKER

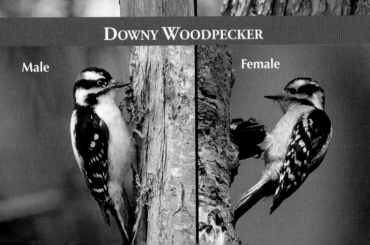

Male

Female

HAIRY WOODPECKER, *Dryobates villosus*

Description: 9". Black-and-white woodpecker of mountain highlands. Long white back stripe; **entirely white outer tail feathers.** MALE: Red bar on the nape; longer bill than female. FEMALE: All black nape. **Similar Species:** Much smaller Downy Woodpecker (below) has very small bill and black barring on white outer tail feathers. **Voice:** Sharp *peek* calls, repeated *teuk* notes; Also a hard rattling *ch'r-ch'r-ch'r-ch'r-ch'r* whinny. **Status:** Fairly common resident. **Habitat:** Upper mountain canyons and coniferous forest, especially in recent burns. **Elevations:** Resident 5,000'-11,000'. **Behavior:** Pecks and scales bark searching for insects and grubs on trunks and large limbs. **Noteworthy:** Post-breeding wandering can take these woodpeckers down to sycamores groves in mountain canyon outlets, well below coniferous forest. SE Arizona form may show a brownish hue on back and wings.

DOWNY WOODPECKER, *Dryobates pubescens*

Description: 6.25". **Short-billed**, quite small black-and-white woodpecker of mountain highlands. Long white back stripe; **black-barred white outer tail feathers.** MALE: Red bar on the nape. FEMALE: All black nape. **Similar Species:** Much larger Hairy Woodpecker (above) has much longer bill and completely white outer tail feathers. **Voice:** Quick *prrk*, burrier than Hairy Woodpecker call. Shrill descending whinny *wi-wi-wi-wi-wi-wilt*. **Status:** Uncommon resident. **Habitat:** Aspen glades and other deciduous groves within coniferous forest; exploits recent burns. Rare wanderer down to 2,000' in riparian woodlands. **Elevations:** Resident 6,200'-10,800'. **Behavior:** Pecks bark and small limbs and gleans twigs, needles, and even weed stalks searching for insects. Streamside deciduous growth like willows and alders are a favorite feeding substrate. **Noteworthy:** Males tend to forage higher up trees and out on thinner twigs than females.

241

MALE

FEMALE

American
Three-toed
Woodpecker

Arizona Woodpecker

AMERICAN THREE-TOED WOODPECKER, *Picoides dorsalis*

Description: 8.75". Black-and-white woodpecker of mountain highlands with **narrow white facial stripes**; a **bar-edged white back** stripe and **barred flanks**. MALE: **Gold forecrown**. FEMALE: Crown is sprinkled with white dots. **Similar Species:** Hairy and Downy Woodpecker have bold white facial stripes, crisp white back stripes, and lack black barring on flanks; males have red nape marks—not gold forecrown. **Voice:** Liquid *whip* notes. Accelerating, petulant whinny *tuoy-tuoy-tuoy-kii-kii-kii-kii*. **Status:** Uncommon resident. **Habitat:** Boreal spuce-fir or mixed coniferous forest, especially in recent burns. **Elevations:** Resident 6,650'-11,300'. **Behavior:** Pecks and scales bark searching for bark beetle grubs on trunks and large limbs. Piles of bark chips may surround the base of a favorite feeding tree. **Noteworthy:** New areas may be colonized or numbers may increase a year or two after timber stand die-offs, especially after forest fires or bark beetle outbreaks.

ARIZONA WOODPECKER, *Dryobates arizonae*

Description: 8". The only woodpecker in the United States with **solid brown upperparts**. MALE: Red hindcrown. FEMALE: Entirely brown crown. **Similar Species:** Flickers and juvenile Sapsuckers have barring on their brown backs. **Voice:** Loud *keek!* Rattle is harsh *whawhawhawha* rolled into rapid series. **Status:** Fairly common resident. **Habitat:** Sierra Madrean pine-oak woodland, especially in major canyons. **Elevations:** Resident 3,800'-7,800'. **Behavior:** Pecks and scales bark, searching for insects and grubs on trunks and large limbs. Adults call infrequently in spring and early summer when nesting, and while their young are still dependent. **Noteworthy:** Except for limited populations in the panhandle mountains of adjacent SW New Mexico, in the United States this woodpecker only occurs in Southeastern Arizona.

YELLOW-BELLIED SAPSUCKER

Male

Juvenile

Female

RED-NAPED SAPSUCKER

Male

Female

Hybrid
with
Red-breasted

YELLOW-BELLIED SAPSUCKER, *Sphyrapicus varius*

Description: 8.5". Red forecrown; **white nape**; long **black whisker fuses with black bib**. MALE: Red throat. FEMALE: White throat. JUVENILE: Muted pattern of adult superimposed over brownish ground color: Retains juvenile plumage until March. **Similar Species:** Red-naped Sapsucker (below) almost always shows a red nape; black whisker does not fuse with black bib. **Voice:** Abrupt but plaintive *Weea* and a rubber stopper squeal. **Status:** Rare in winter (late Sep-mid May). **Habitat:** Desert, valley, and canyon orchards, urban parks, and riparian groves. **Elevations:** Winter 100'-7,700'. **Behavior:** All sapsuckers eat sap and insects. **Noteworthy:** The majority of Yellow-bellied Sapsucker records in Arizona pertain to brownish juveniles before they molt in spring.

RED-NAPED SAPSUCKER, *Sphyrapicus nuchalis*

Description: 8.5". Red forecrown; **red nape**; thin **black whisker does not fuse with black bib.** MALE: Red throat. FEMALE: White chin; red throat. IMMATURE: Lacks solid black breast band. **Similar Species:** Yellow-bellied Sapsucker (above) usually lacks red nape; black whisker fuses with black bib. **Voice:** Explosive *Weea* and squealing *jijijiji-jeel* similar to Yellow-bellied Sapsucker. **Status:** Fairly common but local in summer (May-Aug); common and widespread in migration (Mar-Apr and Sep-Oct); uncommon in winter (Nov-Feb). **Habitat:** Summer: Coniferous forest mixed with aspen, alder, and other broadleaf trees. Winter: Desert oases to open forests, especially orchards. **Elevations:** Summer 6,500'-10,100'; Winter 100'-8,200'. **Behavior:** In Arizona aspen is the tree most commonly used for nests; nest cavities are usually under 15' high. **Noteworthy:** Except for lacking a solid black breast band, by early October young Red-napes look like adults. Hybrids with Red-breasted Sapsucker (page 236) show a suffusion of red over the Red-nape's black nape and chest bands.

MALE

FEMALE

Williamson's
Sapsucker

Northern Flicker
"Red-Shafted"

"Red-Shafted"

"Yellow-Shafted"
Female

WILLIAMSON'S SAPSUCKER, *Sphyrapicus thyroideus*

Description: 9". Large **black-breasted** sapsucker. MALE: White facial stripes; red throat; **solid black back**. FEMALE: Plain brown head; **barred back**; JUVENILE: Like female but lacks black breast. **Similar Species:** Larger Gilded (p. 239) and Northern Flickers (below) resemble female Williamson's, but have boldly spotted underparts. **Voice:** Screechy *ooeek* calls, as if distressed; churring *wrrrrrr*. **Status:** Fairly common in summer (May-Sep); uncommon in winter (Oct-Apr). Prolonged migration with rare summer records from low elevations and south of breeding range. **Habitat:** Summer: Mixed coniferous forest and Ponderosa pines, usually with broadleaf trees. Winter: Desert oases and towns; valley groves; mountain canyon groves, and coniferous forest. **Elevations:** Summer 4,800'-9,700'; Winter 1,000'-9,500'. **Behavior:** Eats sap, insects, and fruit. Most nests are in aspens, usually dead trees. **Noteworthy:** Female Williamson's Sapsucker looks so different from the male that for 20 years—until 1873—the sexes were thought to constitute two different species.

"RED-SHAFTED" NORTHERN FLICKER, *Colaptes auratus collaris*

Description: 12.5". Large, **brown**, bar-backed woodpecker with **black chest crescent**. MALE: Red moustache. FLIGHT: **Salmon-pink underwings and undertail**; white rump. **Similar Species:** Gilded Flicker (p. 239) has yellow underwings and undertail and entirely cinnamon crown. "Yellow-shafted" Northern Flicker, rare in winter (Sep-Apr) in valley and lower canyon groves, has yellow underwings and tail, gray crown with red crescent on hindhead. Male "Yellow-shafted" has black moustache. **Voice:** Poignant *clear*; also a long series of run-on *wika-wika-wika* notes. **Status:** Fairly common in summer (mid Mar-Aug); common and widespread in winter (Sep-mid Mar). **Habitat:** Summer: Woodlands and coniferous forest. Winter: Desert oases to open coniferous forests. **Elevations:** Summer 4,000'-11,000'; Winter 100'-9,500'. **Behavior:** Mostly eats ants. **Noteworthy:** Northern Flicker occurs in more habitats than any other woodpecker in Arizona.

247

Crested Caracara
Adult

Aplomado Falcon
Adult

Juvenile

CRESTED CARACARA *Caracara plancus*

Description: 23", wingspan 50". Large, brownish-black scavenger falcon of the subtropics. **Naked red foreface, long white neck**, and **long naked legs.** JUVENILE: Brown. FLIGHT: "Flying compass" with four points of white on the neck, near the wingtips, and at base of tail. **Similar Species:** Turkey Vulture (p. 191) has entirely naked red head, lacks short crest, and has no true white on body or wings. **Voice:** Sputtering *purrrt purrrt, pur-rrtt.* **Status:** Uncommon in summer (Mar-Oct); fairly common but local in winter (Nov-Feb), when northward wandering from Mexico apparently augments the resident population. **Habitat:** Lower central valleys of the Sonoran Desert, especially within the range of saguaro cactus. Often found in fields, pastures, and garbage dumps. Strays occur from the Lower Colorado River Valley at Yuma east all the way to the New Mexico border near Portal. **Elevations:** Summer 1,500'-3,300'; Winter 100'-4,200'. **Behavior:** With bare facial skin and long legs, Caracaras are well adapted for scavenging. They are even capable of driving vultures off carrion. Flies low, and may take reptiles and small mammals by surprise. Prey remains at some nests show a strong predilection for Horned Lizards. Nests are frequently located in the lower arms of a saguaro cactus, usually below 15 feet. **Noteworthy:** Some winters 50 Crested Caracaras may be observed in a single day of driving through the agricultural fields between Phoenix and Tucson. In Jan., 2014 over 100 were observed there.

APLOMADO FALCON, *Falco femoralis*

Description: 16", wingspan 35". Large, **black-vested, buffy-thighed** falcon with black and white tail. ADULT: Slaty above with white chest. JUVENILE: Dark brown above with streaked, cinnamon chest. FLIGHT: Low and direct with **blackish underwings**. **Similar Species:** Both Peregrine and Prairie Falcons (p. 253) lack black vest and buffy thighs. **Status:** Extirpated former resident. Records from SW New Mexico in 2015 may stem from the population in Chihuahua. **Habitat:** SE valley grasslands. **Elevations:** 3,500'-5,000'. **Noteworthy:** Accidental since 1910, last Arizona records were in Nov, 1939 and Oct, 1940.

249

MALE

FEMALE

American Kestrel

"Taiga" Merlin

"Prairie" Merlin

AMERICAN KESTREL, *Falco sparverius*

Description: 10", wingspan 21". Slim little falcon with **two vertical face stripes; red tail**. MALE: Blue-gray wings. FEMALE: Larger; rusty-barred wings, back, and tail. FLIGHT: Frequently hovers; underwings whitish. **Similar Species:** Merlin (below) shows only one facial stripe and lacks red tail. **Voice:** Rapid *kli kli kli* notes. **Status:** Uncommon in summer (mid Apr-mid Aug); common in winter (mid Aug-mid Apr) when migrants swell populations at elevations below 7,500'. **Habitat:** Open deserts; valley fields, pastures, and grasslands; woodlood savannahs; mountain burns and large meadows. **Elevations:** Resident 100'-9,500'. **Behavior:** Takes open perches; often hovers hunting insects, small birds, and mice. Nests in holes in saguaros and trees, burrows in banks, cracks in cliffs, and under palm fronds. **Noteworthy:** American Kestrel is the most abundant falcon in Arizona and North America.

MERLIN, *Falco columbarius*

Description: 11", wingspan 23". Boxy little falcon with **thin eyebrow** and **one indistinct vertical face stripe** below eye, and narrowly gray-banded dark tail. MALE: Upperparts gray. FEMALE: Upperparts brown. FLIGHT: Powerful, direct, and rapid; pointed underwings dark. **Similar Species:** Juvenile Sharp-shinned Hawk (p. 199) has yellow eye, lacks vertical face stripe, and has dark tail with broad gray bands. **Voice:** Usually silent in winter. **Status:** Uncommon in winter (Nov-Mar) and in migration (Apr-mid May and Sep-Oct). **Habitat:** Valley grasslands and farms, especially near wetlands with concentrations of birds. **Elevations:** Winter 100'-7,100'; Migration 100'-9,500'. **Behavior:** Small bird specialist. Usually hunts from exposed perches. Overtakes prey with speed. Hunts bats at dusk. **Noteworthy:** Two races regularly winter in Arizona: slate-gray male or dark brown female "Taiga," *F. c. columbarius,* and pale blue male or brown female "Prairie," *F. c. richardsonii.* Black Merlin, *F. c. suckleyi*--lacking eyebrows on its black face--is casual.

Peregrine Falcon

Adult

Prairie Falcon
Adult

Juvenile

PEREGRINE FALCON, *Falco peregrinus*

Description: 17", wingspan 41". Husky, **helmet-headed** falcon. ADULT: Slate-gray above; black-barred below. JUVENILE: Sooty brown above; heavily streaked below. FLIGHT: Uniform gray underwings concolor with breast. **Similar Species:** Sandy-brown Prairie Falcon (below) has pale eyebrows, thin moustachial stripes, and black "wingpits" in flight. **Voice:** Strident, harsh *weh weh weh*. **Status:** Uncommon in summer (mid Apr-Aug); more numerous but still uncommon in winter (Sep-mid Apr). **Habitat:** Summer: Mountains, especially in cliff areas near water. Winter: Deserts and valleys, especially near water. **Elevations:** Summer 100'-10,000'; Winter 100'-7,000'. **Behavior:** Aerial hunter, power-diving on birds at speeds exceeding 100 mph. Nests on cliff ledges. **Noteworthy:** Although perhaps half of the approximately 300 pairs nesting in Arizona are found within the Grand Canyon, a large concentration also occurs in SE Arizona, and they have even bred on an office building ledge in downtown Phoenix.

PRAIRIE FALCON, *Falco mexicanus*

Description: 16", wingspan 40". Lanky, long-tailed falcon with **pale eyebrow** and **thin moustache**. ADULT: Sandy-brown above; spotted below. JUVENILE: Dark brown above; streaked below. FLIGHT: **Black "wingpits"** contrast with pale breast. **Similar Species:** Peregrine Falcon (above) has solid black "helmet"; lacks black "wingpits" in flight. **Voice:** Strident *kree kree kree*. **Status:** Rare in summer (May-Jul); uncommon in winter (Aug-Apr). **Habitat:** Summer: Requires cliffs for nest eyries near deserts, valley grasslands and fields, prairies, and large mountain meadows, especially near water. Winter: Open areas, including deserts, agricultural fields and pastures, and large, flat mountain clearings and lakes. **Elevations:** Summer 100'-10,500'; Winter 100'-9,000'. **Behavior:** Hunts for birds and small mammals by overtaking them with speed. Often uses open perches in dead trees and utility poles. **Noteworthy:** Prairies tend to nest on lower cliffs in more arid areas than Peregrine Falcons.

Rosy-faced Lovebird

Monk Parakeet

Stick nest

ROSY-FACED LOVEBIRD, *Agapornis roseicollis*

Description: 6.5". Small, mostly grass-green parrot with a big head and a **pink-red foreface and throat**; blue rump; short tail. **Similar Species:** Escaped <u>Budgerigars</u> (the familiar pet "Parakeet") have long, tapering tails. **Voice:** Screeching *shreep* calls. **Status:** Fairly common resident in Phoenix; rare in Tucson. **Habitat:** Established neighborhoods and city parks with shade trees and water. **Elevations:** Resident 950'-2,400'. **Behavior:** Nests colonially in holes in saguaros, under palm fronds, and under roof eaves. **Noteworthy:** Native to southwestern Africa, Rosy-faced Lovebirds were already established in the greater Phoenix area when they were first officially documented in 1987.

MONK PARAKEET, *Myiopsitta monachus*

Description: 11.5". Big-headed, dove-sized, pale green parrot with a coral bill; bicolored head with **gray forehead** and **gray lower face**; long tail with blunt tip. FLIGHT: Aquamarine flight feathers contrast with much paler wing linings and body color. **Similar Species:** Much smaller Rosy-faced Lovebird (above) has a short tail and blue rump. Much larger <u>Thick-billed Parrot</u>, extirpated in 1938, has massive black bill and green chest. Last Thick-bills from reintroduction attempts in the Chiricahua Mountains in 1986 disappeared in 1989. **Voice:** Screeches of variable length with a slightly trilled quality: *shre-e-e-a*. **Status:** Uncommon resident in greater Phoenix area; casual elsewhere. **Habitat:** Prefers neighborhoods with tall palm trees and open water. **Elevations:** Resident 950'-1,450'; Vagrant: 1,450-4600'. **Behavior:** Multiple pairs create massive communal stick nests, often conspicuously positioned on utility poles or in dead trees. **Noteworthy:** Originally from the pampas in southern South America, Monk Parakeets were first recorded in the U.S. from New York in 1967. They colonized Casa Grande in 2004, but they disappeared from there in 2011, and they are still not considered established in Arizona.

ROSE-THROATED BECARD

Male

Female

GRAY-COLLARED BECARD

Male

Juvenile
Male

ROSE-THROATED BECARD, *Pachyramphus aglaiae*

Description: 7″. Stout, bull-headed, short-winged and short-tailed near-relative of flycatcher clan with **unicolored wings**. MALE: Smoke gray above and pale gray below with **rose-pink throat**. FEMALE: Buff hindcollar and underparts; cinnamon-brown upperparts. **Similar Species:** Smaller Gray-collared Becard (below) has short eyebrow and bold, bright wing edgings. **Voice:** High, squeaky *whee-chee-e*. Also whining, violin-like *fewww* notes, and thin, excited chatter abruptly dying away like a ricocheting "BB". **Status:** Rare and irregular resident. **Habitat:** Valley rivers or foothill canyons with tall sycamores or cottonwoods, some permanent water, and a well-developed understory. **Elevations:** Resident 3,100′-5,300′. **Behavior:** Hunts insects in the canopy, but descends into understory for small fruits or berries. Huge globular nests are ordinarily suspended from the tip of a sycamore or cottonwood branch directly over a streambed. Dimensions usually range from 15-30″ in length by 12-20″ in width; single entrance is located low on the structure. **Noteworthy:** After the first Rose-throated Becard was discovered in the Huachuca Mountains in 1888, none were seen again until 1947, when a small colony appeared near Patagonia. Since 2017, after a decade of sporadic observations, the Santa Cruz River near Tubac has hosted multiple nesting pairs.

GRAY-COLLARED BECARD, *Pachyramphus major*

Description: 6″. Becard with **short eyebrow** and **bright wing-edgings**. MALE: Black cap and black back; white wing edgings. JUVENILE MALE: Cinnamon crown outlined in black; cinnamon back. FEMALE: Black crown; cinnamon back; bronze wing edgings. **Similar Species:** Larger Rose-throated Becard (above) lacks eyebrow or contrast in wings. **Voice:** Piercing *whip-whip-whi-chew*. **Status:** Accidental in summer. **Habitat:** Mountain canyon groves in pine-oak woodland. **Elevations:** Resident 5,200′-5,400′. **Noteworthy:** One record, June, 2009, from South Fork Cave Creek in the Chiricahua Mountains.

Northern Beardless-Tyrannulet

Olive-sided Flycatcher

NORTHERN BEARDLESS-TYRANNULET, *Camptostoma imberbe*

Description: 4.5". **Tiny flycatcher with bushy crest** and stubby, orange-based bill; **short, faint eyebrow**; grayish wingbars. Orange mouth sometimes visible when calling. **Similar Species:** Larger Gray Flycatcher (p. 265) may share same habitat, lacks crest, has eyering and long bill; long tail has obvious white edges. Frequently dips tail down. **Voice:** Descending series of four (usually) clear notes *peer peer peer peer;* call is sharp *pee-uk!* **Status:** Fairly common in summer (Mar-Sep); rare in winter (Oct-Feb), sporadically descending to elevations below 2,000'.

Habitat: Valley and foothill canyon cottonwood groves, mesquite bosques, and hackberry thickets–or any combination of them. **Elevations:** Summer 1,900'-5,400'; Winter 1,200'-4,600'. **Behavior:** Forages actively for insects low in the subcanopy. **Noteworthy:** Northern Beardless-Tyrannulet is the smallest U.S. flycatcher.

OLIVE-SIDED FLYCATCHER, *Contopus cooperi*

Description: 7.5". **Dark, bulky, bull-headed** flycatcher with white "zipper" down center of breast; white ovals may show above wings when perched; short tail. **Similar Species:** Paler gray, crested Greater Pewee (p. 261) has smaller head, lacks white mid-stripe on breast, and has a longer tail. **Voice:** Call is *pip-pip-pip;* song is loud *pip-WEE-deer* ("Quick, three beers!"). Usually silent in migration. **Status:** Fairly common in summer (Jun-mid Aug) and migration (late Apr-May and mid Aug-mid Oct).

Habitat: Summer: Tall, dead treetops in mountain coniferous forest, especially with Ponderosa pines. Migration: Lowlands to mountain ridges and peaks. **Elevations:** Summer 6,900'-10,000'; Migration 100'-10,000'. **Behavior:** Sallies from tall, exposed—often dead—treetop perches to capture flying insects, and frequently returns to its original perch. **Noteworthy:** Competition with Greater Pewees seems to push nesting Olive-sided Flycatchers into forests north of SE Arizona.

GREATER PEWEE

WESTERN WOOD-PEWEE

GREATER PEWEE, *Contopus pertinax*

Description: 8". Slim, peak-headed flycatcher with **short crest**; long bill with **orange lower mandible**. **Similar Species:** Smaller, more compact Western Wood-Pewee (below) lacks obvious crest and has shorter, black-tipped bill; wingbars show greater contrast than Greater Pewee's. **Voice:** Pleasant, whistled *José Maria* song; call consists of *pip* notes. **Status:** Uncommon in summer (Apr-Sep); rare in winter (Oct-Mar). **Habitat:** Summer: Upper mountain canyons, pine-oak woodland, and Ponderosa pine forest. Winter: Desert oases; valley, foothill, and lower mountain canyon groves. **Elevations:** Summer 5,500'-10,700'; Winter 400'-6,200'. **Behavior:** Usually sallies from perches at mid-height up to treetops to capture flying insects, and often returns to same perch. **Noteworthy:** This Sierra Madre highland species reaches the northern limits of its range in central Arizona.

WESTERN WOOD-PEWEE, *Contopus sordidulus*

Description: 6.25". Compact, peak-headed flycatcher with short, orange-based bill; faint eyering; **long wings** with gray wingbars. **Similar Species:** Willow Flycatcher (p. 265) has entirely orange lower mandible, shorter wings, and flicks its tail up. Eastern Wood-Pewee (accidental Jun-mid Oct in SE Arizona), essentially identical, only safely identified by its slow *pee-a-wee* song. **Voice:** Burry descending *bee-zee*; clear *p-pe-pee* and *p'weet* notes. **Status:** Common in summer (mid Apr-Sep); common lowland migrant (mid Apr-late May and mid Aug-mid Oct), casual outside of expected dates. **Habitat:** Summer: Valley, foothill and mountain canyon groves, pine-oak woodland, and open Ponderosa pine forest. Migration: Also riparian woodlands, pecan groves, and urban areas; avoids treeless landscapes. **Elevations:** Summer 3,400'-10,000'; Migration 100'-5,000'. **Behavior:** Perches from low to high and sallies out to capture flying insects, often returning to original perch. **Noteworthy:** Wintering in South America, Western Wood-Pewees perform one of the longest migrations of any Arizona passerine.

Tufted Flycatcher

Buff-breasted Flycatcher

Immature

TUFTED FLYCATCHER, *Mitrephanes phaeocercus*

Description: 5". **Small, cinnamon-colored** flycatcher with **conspicuous crest**. **Similar Species:** Buff-breasted Flycatcher (below) has rounded crown–not crested head–and obvious wingbars. **Voice:** Clear *pweep* similar to Hammond's Flycatcher (p 267); slightly burry *treee-tweee*. **Status:** Rare in summer (early Mar-mid Oct); accidental in Feb. **Habitat:** Canyon riparian in pine-oak woodland; casual migrant in lowland valley river and stream woods. **Elevations:** Summer 4,900'-7,400'; Winter 600'-700'. **Behavior:** Sallies from exposed perches, and often returns to its original perch. In winter in northern Mexico some Tufted Flycatchers are altitudinal migrants to lowland river groves. **Noteworthy:** Arizona's first record of Tufted Flycatcher came from Lower Colorado River at Lake Mohave in Feb, 2005.

BUFF-BREASTED FLYCATCHER, *Empidonax fulvifrons*

Description: 4.7". Small flycatcher with **cinnamon-buff underparts**; oval eyering; small bill with entirely orange lower mandible; wingbars tinged buff. IMMATURE: Black-tipped bill; buffier plumage overall. **Similar Species:** Similarly-colored and sized Tufted Flycatcher (above) has tall crest. **Voice:** High, sharp *pit!* Also *chidew chdip* song. **Status:** Fairly common but local in summer (late Mar-mid Sep); casual in early Mar and mid Sep-mid Oct. **Habitat:** Open Chihuahua and Apache pine stands, primarily in canyons, usually with an understory of seeding pines and grasses. Inter-montane valley migrant. **Elevations:** Summer 5,000'-8,800'. **Behavior:** Often sorties below canopy. Most nests are on lower limbs of pines. Buff-breasted Flycatchers usually nest in loose colonies of two or more pairs. **Noteworthy:** Periodic wildfires may help maintain its specialized habitat. Estimated Arizona population in 1996 was about 120.

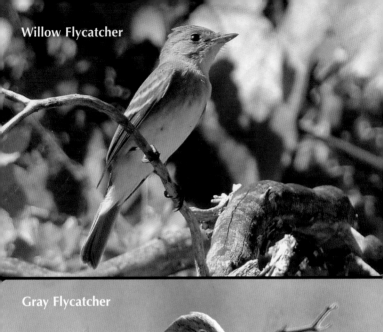
Willow Flycatcher

Gray Flycatcher

WILLOW FLYCATCHER, *Empidonax traillii*

Description: 5.75". **Large brownish *Empidonax* flycatcher without obvious eyering**; long, broad **bill with lower mandible entirely orange**; flips tail up. IMMATURE: Olivaceous above and tinged yellowish below. **Similar Species:** Mostly gray Gray Flycatcher (below) shows white eyering, has narrow lower mandible tipped black, and drops white-edged tail down. **Voice:** Sharp *whit*; burry *witz-beeer* or *fitz-bew* song. **Status:** Uncommon summer resident (May-mid Oct); fairly common migrant (May-early Jun and late Jul-mid Oct). **Habitat:** Summer: Meandering river valleys with extensive subcanopy thickets. Migration: Prefers riparian growth, but uses all low profile, dense vegetation from desert to mountain tops. **Elevations:** Summer 100'-8,500'; Migration 100'-9,100'. **Behavior:** Forages for insects in understory thickets. Flicks tail up. **Noteworthy:** Most nests are now in introduced tamarisk trees. Fewer than 600 "Southwestern" Willow Flycatchers breed in Arizona, and this race is classified as endangered by the U.S. Fish and Wildlife Service.

GRAY FLYCATCHER, *Empidonax wrightii*

Description: 6". **Large grayish *Empidonax* flycatcher with narrow eyering**; long, narrow orange **bill with ink-black tip**; dips long, **white-edged tail down**. **Similar Species:** Willow Flycatcher (above) is mostly brown, lacks eyering, has lower mandible wholly orange, and flips its tail up. **Voice:** Sharp, dry *wit*; sibilant *chi-lip* song. **Status:** Fairly common summer resident (mid Apr-Sep); uncommon in winter (mid Aug-early May). **Habitat:** Summer: Plateau and foothill pinyon-juniper woodlands, especially with an admixture of sagebrush, chaparral, or shrubby oaks. Winter: Valley and foothill mesquite thickets and adjacent riparian groves. **Elevations:** Summer 4,300'-7,600'; Winter 100'-4,500'. **Behavior:** Forages for insects in understory thickets. Drops tail down. **Noteworthy:** Below 4,500', Gray is the most common wintering *Empidonax* flycatcher in Arizona.

Hammond's Flycatcher

Dusky Flycatcher

HAMMOND'S FLYCATCHER, *Empidonax hammondii*

Description: 5.5". Small, **bull-headed *Empidonax*** flycatcher, with an oval eyering; very **short, dark bill**; long primary extension; **tail looks short**. **Similar Species:** Slimmer Dusky Flycatcher (below) has longer bill, shorter wings, and longer tail. Dusky's molt timing—dullest in early fall—is the opposite of Hammond's Flycatcher. Distinctive calls clinch identifications. **Voice:** High, moist *puip* call; breathy, scratchy, trisyllabic song has pause *hdik-prrrh* (pause) *prhh*. **Status:** Irregular and local in summer (mid May-July); common migrant (Apr-mid May and mid Aug-Sep); uncommon in winter (Oct-Mar). **Habitat:** Summer: Montane pine-fir-spruce forest. Migration: Lowland river groves to mountain coniferous forest. Winter: Valley and foothill canyon groves. **Elevations:** Summer 7,500'-9,500'; Winter 100'-5,500'. **Behavior:** Usually forages for insects in canopy. Flicks tail up and often simultaneously flicks wings. **Noteworthy:** Hammond's Flycatcher is dullest in spring and brightest during fall migration.

DUSKY FLYCATCHER, *Empidonax oberholseri*

Description: 5.75". Slender, **small-headed *Empidonax*** flycatcher with subtly oval **eyering connected to pale lore**; short, **orange-based bill**; short wing extension; **tail looks long**. **Similar Species:** See Hammond's Flycatcher (above). <u>Least Flycatcher</u>, casual in migration (May and Sep-Dec) has a shorter, wider, more orange bill, whiter throat, and bold white wingbars. **Voice:** Husky *whit* call, similar to Gray Flycatcher's; burry, three-part song *dwit-dirrrt-deee*. **Status:** Fairly common in summer and in migration (Apr-mid Oct); uncommon in winter (mid Oct-Mar). **Habitat:** Summer: Mountain thickets of short Gambel's oak, aspen, or streamside shrubbery. Winter: Understory in lowland and foothill riparian groves. **Elevations:** Summer 6,000'-9,500'; Winter 100'-4,800'. **Behavior:** Usually sallies from low perches to catch insects. Flicks its tail up. **Noteworthy:** Fall Dusky Flycatchers have dull plumage and spring migrants are bright.

Pine
Flycatcher

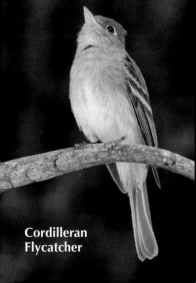

Cordilleran
Flycatcher

Pacific-slope
Flycatcher

PINE FLYCATCHER, *Empidonax affinis*

Description: 5.5". **Pale lemon-throated *Empidonax* flycatcher with eyering wider on rear half; long, narrow bill with entirely orange lower mandible; grayish-olive above and pale yellowish below, brightest on belly. Best identified by voice. **Similar Species:** Cordilleran Flycatcher (below) in same habitat has shorter wings and tail and is usually much brighter yellow on throat and underparts; triangular bill is much broader at base. **Voice:** Mellow *pwip* notes. **Status:** One record of nesting female from late May-early July, 2016. The nest failed. **Elevations:** Summer 5,800'-5,900'.

CORDILLERAN FLYCATCHER, *Empidonax occidentalis*

Description: 5.6". **Yellow-throated *Empidonax* flycatcher with teardrop-shaped eyering; spade-shaped bill with orange lower mandible; olive above and yellowish below. Best identified by voice. **Similar Species:** Pacific-slope Flycatcher (below) should be distinguished by voice, but habitat is a valuable clue. In Arizona Pacific-slope is a valley and foothill grove species. **Voice:** High *seep* and *pdip* calls; male uses *wh-seeet*, accented on second syllable. **Status:** Fairly common in summer (late Apr-late Sep). **Habitat:** Wet mountain canyon groves and coniferous forest. **Elevations:** Summer 5,200'-10,500'. **Behavior:** Nests in niches in boulders in major canyons, and at higher elevations uses stump grottos, tree cavities, and cabin porch eaves. **Noteworthy:** Based on DNA, "Western Flycatcher" was split into Pacific-slope and Cordilleran Flycatcher in 1989.

PACIFIC-SLOPE FLYCATCHER, *Empidonax difficilis*

Description: 5.5". **Yellow-throated *Empidonax* in appearance identical to Cordilleran Flycatcher. Best identified by voice. **Voice:** Tiny, bell-like *tink* and *pdip* calls; male uses up-slurred *s-weeet*. **Status:** Fairly common migrant (mid Mar-May and Aug-mid Oct); rare in winter (mid Oct-mid Mar). **Habitat:** Valley and foothill groves. **Elevations:** Migration 100'-7,100'; Winter 200'-4,000'. **Noteworthy:** In Arizona, all winter "Western Flycatcher" records seem to pertain to Pacific-slope Flycatchers.

Black Phoebe

Say's Phoebe

Eastern Phoebe

BLACK PHOEBE, *Sayornis nigricans*

Description: 6.75". **Black and white** wetlands flycatcher. **Similar Species:** Rare Eastern Phoebe (below), in same riparian habitats in winter, is brown above with whitish throat. **Voice:** Whistled *pdeee*; dying *cheer* call. **Status:** Common resident below about 5,500'; most withdraw from highlands in winter (mid Oct-mid Feb). **Habitat:** Desert oases, valley rivers, ponds, and lakes, and foothill and mountain canyon streams. **Elevations:** Summer 100'-9,400'; Winter 100'-5,500'. **Behavior:** Forages low over water or adjacent grasses, shrubs, or boulders. All three U.S. phoebes often dip and spread tails and all frequently nest on man-made structures. **Noteworthy:** Most diurnal birds and animals are darker above and paler below, but none exemplifies the biological precept of "counter-shading" better than Black Phoebe.

EASTERN PHOEBE, *Sayornis phoebe*

Description: 6.75". **Brown and white** wetlands flycatcher with dusky chest and yellow-tinged belly. **Similar Species:** Black Phoebe (above) has black throat, chest, and flanks. **Voice:** Husky, whistled *fee-bee*; also *chep* calls. **Status:** Rare in winter (Oct-mid May) and migration (Apr-mid May and mid Aug-Sep); casual in summer. **Habitat:** Desert oases to mountain canyon streams. **Elevations:** Winter 150'-7,000'.

SAY'S PHOEBE, *Sayornis saya*

Description: 7.75". **Gray**, open-country flycatcher with **apricot belly** and black tail. **Similar Species:** Larger kingbirds have yellow—not apricot—bellies. Larger American Robin (p. 357) has black-streaked white throat and orange chest. **Voice:** Down-slurred whistled *pdeeew*; also rising *pidireep*. **Status:** Common resident below 5,500'; most withdraw from highlands in winter (mid Oct-mid Mar). **Habitat:** Open landscapes including deserts, valleys, plateaus, mountain clearings, and urban areas. **Elevations:** Summer 100'-9,400'; Winter 100'-5,500'. **Behavior:** Forages low. Nests on horizontal substructures such as ledges or porch beams.

271

Male

Juvenile

Female

Description: 6". Compact, **boxy-headed flycatcher** with long wings and short tail. MALE: **Flaming red crown** with short, erectable crest and **fiery red underparts**; dark brown back, wings, and tail. FEMALE: Big head with peaked nape and diffuse white eyebrow; neutral brown upperparts; streaked breast; "monokini" of **watermelon pink on lower belly**. JUVENILE: Streaked white underparts, becoming red in first winter male and yellow in first winter female.

Similar Species: Adult male is distinctive. Larger Say's Phoebe (p. 271) lacks female Vermilion's whitish eyebrow and streaked breast.

Voice: Rapid-fire series of sweet *ti-ti-ti-ti-tit-hee* notes.

Status: Common—although local—in summer (Mar-mid Sep); fairly common but local in winter, usually withdrawing from areas above 4,200' (mid Sep-mid Feb).

Habitat: Valley and broad foothill canyon pastures and fields adjacent to mesquite, willow, and cottonwood groves with nearby permanent water. Also uses grassy urban area parks, golf courses, and athletic fields.

Elevations: Summer 100'-7,000'; Winter 100'-4,200'.

Behavior: Sallies out from low, conspicuous perches, usually staying low and occasionally snatching insects from ground. When perched dips tail like a phoebe. Male performs spectacular "butterfly dance" display flight, singing as it flutters high in the sky with chest puffed out.

Noteworthy: In Arizona, it is estimated that Brown-headed Cowbird parasitism impacts about 20 percent of Vermilion Flycatcher nests. Red pigment of males begins to fade by mid-summer, and they do not become radiant again until their pre-nuptial molt in spring (Feb-Mar).

Dusky-capped Flycatcher

Undertail

Brown-crested Flycatcher

Undertail

DUSKY-CAPPED FLYCATCHER, *Myiarchus tuberculifer*

Description: 7.25". Medium-sized flycatcher with **dusky-brown, bushy crest**; long, thin-based bill; **pewter gray chest** and yellow belly; **gray undertail**. JUVENILE: Coppery tail edges. **Similar Species:** Larger Brown-crested Flycatcher (below) has big, thick-based bill, medium-brown crest, and extensive rufous in undertail. **Voice:** Mournfully-whistled *Pierre* or *wee-earrr*. **Status:** Common in summer (late Mar-mid Oct); casual in winter (mid Oct-late Mar). **Habitat:** Summer: Valley cottonwood gallery forest, foothill groves within oak woodland, and mountain canyons and adjacent slopes within Sierra Madrean pine-oak woodland. Winter: River valley and large foothill canyon groves. **Elevations:** Summer 3,300'-7,000'; Winter 400'-3,900'. **Behavior:** Hunts insects within canopy. Nests in woodpecker holes or natural cavities. **Noteworthy:** One of Arizona's earliest fall migrants, most Dusky-caps are gone by late August. Occurring south to Argentina, Arizona is their northernmost outpost.

BROWN-CRESTED FLYCATCHER, *Myiarchus tyrannulus*

Description: 8.75". Medium-large flycatcher with **medium-brown, bushy crest**; long, thick-based bill; pale gray chest and yellow belly; **rufous undertail** with parallel gray outer edges. **Similar Species:** Smaller, overall paler Ash-throated Flycatcher (p. 277) has medium-long bill, light-brown crest, whitish chest, and undertail has large dark corners. **Voice:** Sharp *hwhit* and a rolling *brit-r-bewww*. **Status:** Common in summer (mid Apr-Aug); rare earlier or later (late Mar-mid Apr and Sep-Oct). **Habitat:** Sonoran Desert saguaro stands, foothill cottonwood groves, and mountain canyon sycamore groves. Rare above upper limits of sycamores. **Elevations:** Summer 100'-6,500'. **Behavior:** Hunts large insects within canopy. Quite rarely catches hummingbirds near feeding stations. Nests in woodpecker holes. **Noteworthy:** Saguaros and big trees like cottonwoods and sycamores with cavities large enough for nesting Brown-cresteds apparently limit this flycatcher's distribution within Arizona.

275

Ash-throated Flycatcher

Nutting's Flycatcher

Undertail

Description: 8". Medium-sized flycatcher with **light-brown, bushy crest;** medium-long, medium-thick bill; pink interior mouth; grayish ears; **off-white chest; yellow-tinged belly;** rufous **undertail with dusky corners that usually merge to form bar across tip. Similar Species:** Larger Brown-crested Flycatcher (p. 275) has bigger, thicker-based bill, medium-brown crest, and tail with parallel dark outer edges. **Voice:** Sharp *pit;* also *ka-beerrr* and *ka-brick.* **Status:** Common in summer (mid Mar-mid Sep); rare in mid winter (mid Sep-mid Mar), primarily west of Sonoita Creek. **Habitat:** Deserts, grasslands, woodlands, mountain canyon groves, and arid pinyon-juniper slopes.
Elevations: Summer 100'-6,800'; Winter 100'-4,200'. **Behavior:** Hunts insects from a watch-post. Also eats cactus fruits and berries. Low nests—average about 7' high—are in almost any available hole, including pipes and hollow fence posts. **Noteworthy:** Ash-throated is the most common and widespread *Myiarchus* flycatcher in Arizona.

Description: 7.3". Medium-sized flycatcher with medium-brown, **rounded crest;** relatively short, thin-based bill; **orange interior mouth;** brownish ears; yellow belly; rufous **undertail with dusky outer edge widening slightly at tip.** Voice useful for identification. **Similar Species:** Larger Ash-throated Flycatcher (above) has bushier crest, whitish breast, paler belly, and undertail has large dark corners that often form a bar across tip. **Voice:** Sharp *wheep!* Whining *ka-wheek whe-eek whe-eek* calls. **Status:** Rare but erratic year-round. **Habitat:** Foothill canyon riparian woodland with thickets of tamarisk, mesquite, and hackberry trees. **Elevations:** Summer 500'-600'; Winter 500'-4,100'. **Noteworthy:** After the first record of Nutting's Flycatcher in Arizona near Roosevelt Lake in Jan., 1952, the next report was not until Dec., 1997. In 2013 nested on the Bill Williams River.

Sulphur-bellied Flycatcher

Great Kiskadee

Couch's Kingbird

SULPHUR-BELLIED FLYCATCHER, *Myiodynastes luteiventris*

Description: 8.5". Medium-sized flycatcher with **dingy facial stripes; streaked back** and streaked underparts; coppery rump and tail. **Similar Species:** Larger Great Kiskadee (below; accidental) has bolder, cleaner black and white facial stripes, reddish wings, unstreaked back, and unstreaked underparts. **Voice:** Squealing *queee-u* notes; series of emphatic *p'dee* calls; squeaky *pee-d'ree* dawn song. **Status:** Fairly common but local in summer (early May-mid Sep); casual earlier or later (late Apr and early Oct). **Habitat:** Canyon sycamores within pine-oak woodland. Migrants are rare in valley groves. **Elevations:** 3,600'-6,600'. **Behavior:** Sallies for insects from canopy perches; eats some fruit. **Noteworthy:** Limited nest cavities may lead to prolonged battles with earlier-arriving Elegant Trogons--which the trogons typically win.

GREAT KISKADEE, *Pitangus sulphuratus*

Description: 9.75". Large, heavy-set flycatcher with **black and white facial stripes; reddish wings** and tail; egg-yolk yellow belly. **Similar Species:** Smaller Sulphur-bellied Flycatcher (above) has dingy facial stripes, streaked back and underparts. **Voice:** Squealing *greee* and *greea*; explosive *kis-ker-wah* similar to its name. **Status:** Accidental in winter and spring (late Dec-mid May). **Habitat:** Valley and foothill groves near water. **Elevations:** 2,800'-4,000'. **Noteworthy:** Several records since 1978, including Sonoita Creek in March, 2000.

COUCH'S KINGBIRD, *Tyrannus couchii*

Description: 9.25" Large, gray-headed kingbird with a long, **broad-based bill**; greenish back; **yellowish breast; notched brown tail**. **Similar Species:** Almost identical Tropical Kingbird (p. 281), accidental in winter, has slightly slimmer bill and is best separated by voice. **Voice:** Harsh *beerrr*; abrupt, often repeated *pt* notes. **Status:** Casual in winter (early Nov-late Feb). **Habitat:** Desert and foothills with gentle relief. **Elevations:** 450'-5,000'. **Noteworthy:** First discovered in Arizona in 2007.

Tropical Kingbird

Thick-billed Kingbird

TROPICAL KINGBIRD, *Tyrannus melancholicus*

Description: 9.25". Large, gray-headed kingbird with **long bill**; greenish back; **yellowish breast; notched brown tail**. **Similar Species:** Western Kingbird (p. 283) has short bill, pale gray breast, square-ended, jet-black tail usually showing white outer edges. Almost identical Couch's Kingbird (p. 279), casual in Winter (early Nov-late Feb) has broader-based bill, but is best identified by its *beerrr* or *kip* call notes. **Voice:** Accelerating *pt pt prrt prrrrrrrrrt* ending in a high, thin, musical trill. **Status:** Fairly common but local in summer (May-Sep); otherwise casual. **Habitat:** Valley cottonwood and pecan groves bordering open pastures, fields, or golf courses, usually near permanent water. **Elevations:** Summer 150'-4,200'. **Behavior:** Hunts insects from open, often high perches. **Noteworthy:** Although its distribution is spotty, since first recorded in Arizona near Tucson in 1905, Tropical Kingbird has expanded its range from New Mexico to California.

THICK-BILLED KINGBIRD, *Tyrannus crassirostris*

Description: 9.5". Large, heavy-set kingbird with **bicolored head**, blackish above and whitish below; **big, thick bill**; dark back; whitish breast, variably yellow belly; dark tail. **Similar Species:** Smaller Eastern Kingbird (p. 285) has small bill, white belly, and white-tipped black tail. **Voice:** Loud and abrupt *purrppt* and a questioning *pureerr?* Alarm call is explosive, loud "rattlesnake" rattle. **Status:** Fairly common but local in summer (late Apr-mid Sep); casual in winter (mid Sep-late Apr). **Habitat:** Foothill sycamore and cottonwood groves, usually near permanent water; rarely in valley gallery forest with nearby bluffs. Has wintered in cottonwoods and tamarisk on Lower Colorado River. Casual north of central Arizona. **Elevations:** Summer 2,000'-5,400'; Winter 100'-400'. **Behavior:** Hunts insects from open, high perches. **Noteworthy:** Thick-billed Kingbird was first discovered in extreme SE Arizona in Guadalupe Canyon in 1958. In shared sites Thick-bills are usually subordinate to Cassin's Kingbirds.

281

Cassin's Kingbird

Western Kingbird

CASSIN'S KINGBIRD, *Tyrannus vociferans*

Description: 9". Stocky kingbird with **blue-gray head**; medium-sized bill; **white chin**; gray back tinged olive; lead-gray breast; dark **tail with translucent tip**. **Similar Species:** Pale gray Western Kingbird (below) has much paler gray breast that does not contrast with its chin, and a jet-black tail usually showing white outer edges. **Voice:** Rough, imperative *c'mere!* call; rapidly repeated *ch'keer ch'keer ch'keer*. **Status:** Common in summer (mid Mar-Nov); rare in winter (Dec-mid Mar). **Habitat:** Open areas adjacent to woodlands: urban parks, farms, and valley cottonwoods, usually above elevations of 2,000'; foothill woodlands, open mountain canyon groves, open pinyon-juniper stands, and open Ponderosa pine forest. Exploits burns at high elevations. **Elevations:** Summer 350'-9,200'; Winter 750'-4,600'. **Behavior:** Hunts insects from exposed, often high perches. **Noteworthy:** Cassin's is the only kingbird expected to over-winter in Arizona.

WESTERN KINGBIRD, *Tyrannus verticalis*

Description: 8.75". Pale gray kingbird with **short bill**; gray back tinged with olive; pale gray breast; **jet-black tail with white outer edges**. **Similar Species:** Darker Cassin's Kingbird (above) has white chin contrasting with lead-gray breast, dark tail lacking white outer feathers, and usually showing a paler, translucent tip. **Voice:** Querulous, rolling *p'dik p'dik p'dik dik dik dik dik*. **Status:** Common in summer (mid Mar-Oct); more common south of the Mogollon Rim; casual in winter (Nov-mid Mar). **Habitat:** Flat and open deserts, valleys, grasslands, and farms, up to the base of the mountains. Casual at high elevations and in mountains. **Elevations:** Summer 100'-9,000'; Winter 100'-4,000'. **Behavior:** Hunts insects from open, often low perches. Nests in the highest available saguaro, tree, utility pole, or tower. Although both species may occupy the same site, usually prefers more open habitats than Cassin's Kingbird. **Noteworthy:** Loose flocks of hundreds may stage in S. Arizona valleys from mid August-early October prior to fall migration.

Eastern Kingbird

Scissor-tailed Flycatcher

EASTERN KINGBIRD, *Tyrannus tyrannus*

Description: 8.5". **Two-toned kingbird** with black head and slaty upperparts; white below; black tail with **white tail tip**. **Similar Species:** Larger Thick-billed Kingbird (p. 281) has much larger bill, yellowish wash on belly, and lacks white terminal band on tail. **Voice:** Tiny, buzzy, insect-like *bzeer*; series of sharp, sputtering *bzeet* notes. **Status:** Rare migrant (May-mid Jun and Aug-early Oct); with a concentration of records in September; casual in summer (mid Jun-Jul). **Habitat:** Open flat areas within deserts, valleys, foothill and lower mountain canyon groves, and plateaus, usually near water. **Elevations:** Migration 700'-7,100'. **Behavior:** Hunts insects from open, often low perches. **Noteworthy:** Although it migrates and winters in flocks in South America, only single Eastern Kingbirds have been recorded in Arizona.

SCISSOR-TAILED FLYCATCHER, *Tyrannus forficatus*

Description: 13". **White-headed kingbird** with salmon-pink belly; extravagant, **long, black-and-white tail**. JUVENILE: Yellowish belly and underwings; shorter tail than adult. FLIGHT: Pink underwings; tail splayed like open scissor blades. **Similar Species:** Adults are unmistakable. Immature resembles Western Kingbird (p. 283) but has white head and underparts, and lacks any yellow on belly. **Voice:** Deliberate *pek pek pek pur-ree* rising in pitch and speeding up at end; loud *pip* calls. **Status:** Rare in summer (mid Apr-mid Oct), especially from early June to mid July; casual in winter (mid Oct-mid Apr). **Habitat:** Open areas in deserts, valleys, and–exceptionally–in lower mountain canyons. **Elevations:** Summer 500'-5,800'. **Behavior:** Hunts insects from open, often low perches. **Noteworthy:** Pairs have been found on several occasions, and it nested once at Dudleyville on the San Pedro River.

Loggerhead Shrike

Northern Shrike
Adult

Juvenile

Description: 9". Compact shrike with hooked, thick black bill; bold **black mask envelopes eyes, joins above bill**. JUVENILE: Finely barred above and below. FLIGHT: Conspicuous white patches on black wings; Arizona birds have a white rump that contrasts with the black tail. Flight is low and rapid, ending with upsweeping glide to perch. **Similar Species:** See Northern Shrike (below). Longer and slimmer Northern Mockingbird (p. 341) lacks black mask and has a small, thin bill; does not show white rump in flight. **Voice:** Thin and squeaky *squeent*; repeated gurgles; electric buzzer *bzzz*. **Status:** Uncommon in summer (Apr-Sep) and fairly common in winter (Oct-Mar) when migrants from north augment resident population. Most common south of the Mogollon Rim. **Habitat:** Open, flat or gently rolling deserts, valley grasslands, farm fields and pastures, and open juniper woodlands. Post-breeding wandering may take them into large mountain meadows up to 9,200'. **Elevations:** Resident 100'-7,400'. **Behavior:** Takes watch-posts on fence lines, utility wires, and tops of shrubs; primarily consumes large insects, but also pursues lizards and small birds, overtaking them with bursts of speed. **Noteworthy:** Impaling prey on thorns or barbed wire to store for later use earned it the colloquial name of "Butcher Bird."

Description: 10". **Long-tailed** shrike with comparatively narrow black stripes through eyes; **white forehead line**; hooked, long black bill; faintly barred underparts. JUVENILE: Dusky facial stripes; brownish barring below. **Similar Species:** Smaller Loggerhead Shrike (above) has thick black mask, black line on forehead above shorter bill, and lacks faint barring on underparts. **Status:** Casual but almost annual in winter (Nov-late Mar). **Habitat:** Open, flat to gently rolling Great Basin Desert scrub, juniper grasslands, pasturelands, open lake shores. Most records are from north of the Mogollon Rim. **Elevations:** Winter 3,900'-7,100'.

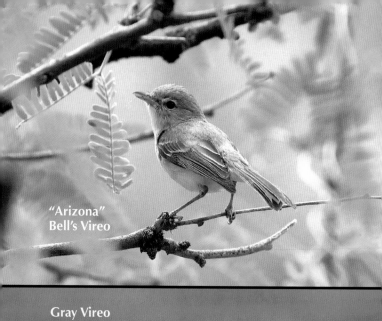

"Arizona"
Bell's Vireo

Gray Vireo

"ARIZONA" BELL'S VIREO, *Vireo bellii arizonae*

Description: 4.75". **Small, desert-dwelling vireo** with **both a pale eyebrow and a broken eyering**, neither sharply defined; forward wingbar weaker than rear wingbar; long tail expressively waved. **Similar Species:** Larger Gray Vireo (below) has unbroken white eyering and lacks eyebrow. **Voice:** Song usually consists of a question, often repeated, and an answer *cheedle-cheedle-cheedle-dee? cheedle-cheedle-cheedle-der;* also nasal *cherr cherr cherr* calls. **Status:** Common in summer (early Mar-Sep); rare in winter (Oct-early Mar). **Habitat:** Dense thickets in desert, valley, and foothill washes up to lower mountain canyons. **Elevations:** Summer 100'-6,800'; Winter 100'-4,400'. **Behavior:** Hunts insects actively in dense thickets and vine tangles. Sings throughout the summer. **Noteworthy:** "Arizona" race birds are intermediate between green and yellow forms of the eastern U. S. and monochromatic "Least" Bell's Vireos of California.

GRAY VIREO, *Vireo vicinior*

Description: 5.5". **Gray and white, juniper-dwelling vireo** with a narrow **white eyering**; usually shows only **one wingbar**; flicks long tail. **Similar Species:** Plumbeous Vireo (p. 293) has bold white "spectacles," two conspicuous white wingbars, shorter tail never flicked. **Voice:** Musical series of deliberate *cheup cheuu* notes delivered faster than Plumbeous Vireo song; also nasal *cheh* calls. **Status:** Fairly common but often local in summer (mid Mar-Sep); rare in winter (Oct-mid Mar). **Habitat:** Summer: Arid pinyon-juniper woodlands, and chaparral with pinyon pines and junipers scattered through the brush. Winter: Sonoran desert scrub and lower scrubby oak chaparral. **Elevations:** Summer 3,500'-6,800'; Winter 1,000'-4,500'. **Behavior:** Hunts insects actively at low levels in brush and short trees. Sings often during the breeding season. **Noteworthy:** A short-distance, although rarely-encountered migrant, most Gray Vireos winter in lowlands of NW Mexico.

White-eyed Vireo

Yellow-throated Vireo

WHITE-EYED VIREO, *Vireo griseus*

Description: 5". **Small vireo** with **yellow spectacles**; two white wingbars; yellow flanks. ADULT: Green cap; **white iris**. JUVENILE: Gray cap; brown iris. **Similar Species:** None similar. **Voice:** Song rendered *chick-for-free, you!*; also nasal *breh breh breh breh* scold. **Status:** Casual in summer (Apr-Aug). **Habitat:** Dense thickets in desert, valley, and foothill washes up to lower mountain canyons. **Elevations:** Summer 200'-6,700'. **Behavior:** Hunts insects actively in dense thickets and vine tangles. Sings throughout the year. **Noteworthy:** Approximately one-third of a White-eyed Vireo's diet consists of moths, butterflies, and their larvae.

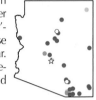

YELLOW-THROATED VIREO, *Vireo flavifrons*

Description: 5.5". **Yellow-headed vireo** with **bright yellow spectacles**; two bold white wingbars; short tail. **Similar Species:** Cassin's Vireo (p. 293) has grayish or greenish—not yellow—head, and has bold white—not yellow—spectacles. **Voice:** Loud series of *chu-wee che-uu cher-ruu* notes similar to Plumbeous Vireo song; also harsh, nasal *cheh cheh cheh* scold. **Status:** Rare in summer (May-Sep); accidental in spring (Apr) and fall (Oct.). **Habitat:** Valley, foothill, and mountain canyon groves, especially cottonwoods, usually with permanent water. **Elevations:** Summer 100'-6,500'. **Behavior:** Moves deliberately through the canopy as it hunts for insects. Visitants sing throughout the breeding season. **Noteworthy:** In Arizona, foothill and mountain canyon records usually come in May and June. Valley cottonwood grove records of Yellow-throated Vireos span May-September; some valley birds stay for weeks or months.

Plumbeous Vireo

Cassin's Vireo

PLUMBEOUS VIREO, *Vireo plumbeus*

Description: 5.5". **Lead-gray vireo** with bold white spectacles; **white wing edgings**; whitish underparts. **Spring:** Gray flanks. **Fall:** Flanks on adults tinged yellow after Jul-Aug molt. **Similar Species:** Cassin's Vireo (below) has greenish back, greenish wing edgings, and yellow flanks. See Gray Vireo (p. 289) **Voice:** Slow, conversational *wheeu wheeu wheeu wheeyou*; loud, harsh *jhhh jhhh jhhh* scold. **Status:** Common in summer (Apr-Sep); rare in winter (Oct-Mar). **Habitat:** Summer: Mountain canyon groves, pine-oak woodland, and Ponderosa pine forest. Winter: Sonoran Desert oases, and valley, foothill, and mountain canyon riparian groves. Uses winter habitats in migration periods (Apr and Sep). **Elevations:** Summer 3,400'-9,100'; Winter 100'-5,700'. **Behavior:** Forages for insects methodically along branches and in leaves. Persistent singer, often heard throughout the day during summer. **Noteworthy:** Plumbeous is usually the easiest summering Arizona vireo species to observe.

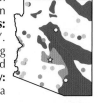

CASSIN'S VIREO, *Vireo cassinii*

Description: 5.25". **Greenish-backed, greenish-naped vireo** with bold white spectacles; **greenish wing edgings**; yellow flanks. **Similar Species:** Plumbeous Vireo (above) has gray back, white wing edgings, and--from Oct-Jun--grayish flanks. Eastern <u>Blue-headed Vireo</u> with crisp contrast between blue-gray head and white throat, blue-gray nape and green back, is casual in fall (late Sep-mid Dec) in valley riparian below 4,000'. **Voice:** Similar to Plumbeous, but slightly higher and faster. **Status:** Uncommon spring (mid Mar-May) and fairly common fall (mid Aug-Oct) migrant; casual (Jun-Jul); rare in winter (Nov-mid Mar). **Habitat:** Migration: Wooded areas from desert oases to mountain Ponderosa pine forest. Winter: Desert oases and valley groves. **Elevations:** Migration 100'-9,100'; Winter 500'-5,100'. **Behavior:** Forages methodically for insects along branches and in leaves. **Noteworthy:** In central and S. Arizona lowlands, wintering Cassin's is as expected as Plumbeous Vireo.

Hutton's Vireo

"Western" Warbling Vireo

HUTTON'S VIREO, *Vireo huttoni*

Description: 5". **Chubby, oak-dwelling vireo** with pale lores and a **white eyering broken at top**; greenish wing edgings. **Similar Species:** Smaller, more energetic Ruby-crowned Kinglet (p. 323) has thin bill and black bar behind rear wingbar. **Voice:** Whiny, oft-repeated *zu-whee*; buzzy *whe-eah* scold notes, as if the bird is struggling for air. **Status:** Fairly common in summer (late Mar-mid Oct); uncommon in winter (mid Oct-late Mar). **Habitat:** Summer: Foothill groves, mountain canyon groves, pine-oak woodland, and Ponderosa pine forest mixed with Gambel's oak. Winter: Desert oases and valley, foothill, and lower mountain canyon groves. **Elevations:** Summer 3,800'-9,100'; Winter 150'-5,500'. **Behavior:** Actively hops and hovers through mid-levels of trees in search of insects. Sings monotonously throughout the summer. **Noteworthy:** Summer range of Hutton's Vireo largely mirrors the distribution of oaks in Arizona.

"WESTERN" WARBLING VIREO, *Vireo gilvus swainsonii*

Description: 5.2". **Slim vireo** with small head and **white eyebrow**; lacks wingbars. **Similar Species:** Larger, darker Red-eyed Vireo (casual; p. 297) has much sharper facial stripes, contrasty gray cap, and much longer bill. **Voice:** Song is a pleasant jumbled warble, slightly slurred; harsh *whe-cheh-cheh* scold. **Status:** Fairly common in summer (Jun-Jul) and common migrant (mid Mar-early Jun and mid Jul-Oct); casual in winter (mid Oct-mid Mar). **Habitat:** Summer: Upper mountain canyon groves, especially near water, and coniferous forests mixed with Gambel's oak and aspen. Migration: From desert oases and towns to mountain forest. **Elevations:** Summer 6,000'-11,300'; Migration 100'-10,700'. **Behavior:** Forages for insects in leafy trees and shrubs. Avoids conifers. **Noteworthy:** In Arizona, Warbling is the only expected vireo that lacks wingbars. Slightly larger "Eastern" form with paler gray cap has been documented once in late Jun 2014 at Las Cienegas NCA.

Red-eyed Vireo

Yellow-green Vireo

RED-EYED VIREO, *Vireo olivaceus*

Description: 6". Large vireo with **long dark bill** and **obvious eyebrow**; blue-gray crown bordered with **distinct black line**; dark loral stripe passes through coral-red eye; **drab green upperparts;** mostly white below with yellowish undertail coverts. JUVENILE: Brown eye. **Similar Species:** Yellow-green Vireo (below) has larger pale bill, gray lores, lacks crisp black lines above its off-white eyebrows. Amount and intensity of yellow on its sides is highly variable. **Voice:** Rich series of whistled and deliberate robin-like *chewee cherup cherah* phrases; nasal, often descending *meyaah* scold. **Status:** Rare visitant (late Apr-early Nov), with records peaking in fall (early Sep-Oct). **Habitat:** Desert oases and valley, foothill, and mountain canyon groves; mountain gambel's oak and maple stands. **Elevations:** Summer 200'-8,500'. **Behavior:** Searches deliberately through canopy for insects. Sings throughout the day in breeding season. **Noteworthy:** Red eye color is often not visible. Winters in the Amazon Basin.

YELLOW-GREEN VIREO, *Vireo flavoviridis*

Description: 6". Large vireo with **very long pale bill** and **off-white eyebrow**; gray crown blends into olive nape; **gray loral stripe** passes through red eye; olive green upperparts; amount and intensity of yellow on sides is highly variable. **Similar Species:** Red-eyed Vireo (above) has shorter dark bill, blackish lores, crisp black lines above conspicuous eyebrows, and usually mostly white underparts, yellowish often confined to undertail coverts. **Voice:** Similar to Red-eyed Vireo but faster phrasing and higher pitched. **Status:** Casual in summer (mid Jun-late Sep), with records peaking in July. **Habitat:** Valley and foothill groves, usually with cottonwood trees and permanent water. **Elevations:** Summer 500'-4,800'. **Behavior:** Same as Red-eyed Vireo. **Noteworthy:** Almost all records for Yellow-green Vireo in Arizona have occurred at elevations above 2,300'. Eye color may be difficult to discern.

Woodhouse's Scrub-Jay

Mexican Jay

Juvenile

WOODHOUSE'S SCRUB-JAY, *Aphelocoma woodhouseii*

Description: 11.25". Blue and gray jay with **thin white eyebrow; streaky white throat**. ADULT: brownish back. JUVENILE: Gray head and back; lacks eyeline and throat streaks are inconspicuous. **Similar Species:** Huskier Mexican Jay (below) lacks white eyebrows and streaked white throat. Arizona's first --and still only--record of <u>California Scrub-Jay</u> with thick, blue "lapels" framing the streaky white throat was present in Yuma Aug, 2016-May, 2017. **Voice:** Squeaky upslurred *shriee* and a series of *sheelp sheelp* notes. **Status:** Fairly common resident. Irruption winters (mid Oct-Apr) bring small numbers of Woodhouse's Scrub-Jays from northern populations down to Tucson, Phoenix, and the lower Colorado River. **Habitat:** Pinyon-juniper woodland, interior chaparral, scrub oak, and mesquite-hackberry thickets in foothill canyons. Recent forest fires have extended the upper elevational limits for wanderers. **Elevations:** Summer 3,600'-8,400'; Winter 100'-8,400'. **Behavior:** Omnivorous. Usually in pairs, except when with new fledglings. **Noteworthy:** Unlike closely related species in California and Florida, Woodhouse's Scrub-Jay is usually shy and prefers dense cover.

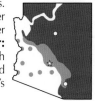

MEXICAN JAY, *Aphelocoma wollweberi*

Description: 12". A plain-faced jay, pale blue above and pale gray below, **lacking distinctive field marks**. ADULT: Black bill. JUVENILE: Mottled pink bill, unlike any other Arizona jay. **Similar Species:** Slender Woodhouse's Scrub-Jay (above) has white eyebrow and white throat. Grayish juvenile has all black bill. **Voice:** Primary call is *wink wink wink*. **Status:** Common resident. **Habitat:** Mountain pine-oak woodland and mountain canyon groves. Dispersing birds are casual in lowlands below 3,000' and in mountains above 9,000'. **Elevations:** Resident 3,500'-8,400'. **Behavior:** Omnivorous, but primary food is acorns. Usually a sentinel bird watches while family feeds. **Noteworthy:** The preceding generation of young help adult pairs feed new offspring, and stay with their siblings for six months or longer, acquiring parenting skills. Flock size averages 10 birds.

Steller's Jay

Pinyon Jay

STELLER'S JAY, *Cyanocitta stelleri*

Description: 11.5". Deep-blue jay with white-streaked, **crested blackish head**. **Similar Species:** <u>Blue Jay</u>, accidental in fall (late Oct-mid Dec) in NE and SE Arizona, has short blue crest and black necklace on pale underparts. **Voice:** Harsh *shreeh shreeh* and higher *whek* notes. Imitates other birds, notably Red-tailed Hawk. **Status:** Common in summer (Apr-Oct); usually less common in winter (Nov-Mar). **Habitat:** Resident: Mountain coniferous forest and upper canyon groves. Winter: May descend to lower canyon groves. Irruptions: Sonoran Desert groves and urban areas. **Elevations:** Summer 5,300'-11,600'; Winter 4,800'-10,000'. **Behavior:** Omnivorous. Food includes seeds, nuts, eggs, and nestlings. In summer usually in pairs, except with fledglings. Winter groups may number 5-10 or more. **Noteworthy:** Summer wanderers can occur down to canyon outlets below an elevation of 5,000', well below breeding areas. Irruption winters at 10-25 years intervals bring Steller's Jays into Tucson, Phoenix, and even to Yuma.

PINYON JAY, *Gymnorhinus cyanocephalus*

Description: 10.5". **Entirely dull-blue jay** with **long, awl-like bill; short tail. Similar Species:** Larger Mexican Jay (p. 299) is gray below with proportionately longer tail. **Voice:** Human-sounding *hah-ha-ha*; mewing *spii spii spii*. **Status:** Fairly common resident. Uncommon irruptive in some winters (Sep-late May), occurrences may be separated by 5 or more years. **Habitat:** Summer: Pinyon-juniper woodlands and pinyon-Ponderosa pine stands. Winter: Arid lower mountain oaks, junipers, and chaparral. Irruptions: Possible to desert foothills. **Elevations:** Summer 4,600'-8,600'; Winter 200'-7,000'. **Behavior:** Roams widely for food. Although omnivorous, primary food is pinyon pine nuts, which it caches in fall for winter consumption. Flocks nest colonially and remain together throughout the year. **Noteworthy:** In central Arizona flocks usually average from 100-200 birds; in fall flocks may coalesce into a super-flock of up to 1,000 birds.

Canada Jay

Juvenile

Clark's Nutcracker

CANADA JAY, *Perisoreus canadensis*

Description: 11.5". Ash gray jay with short bill; dusky nape band; fuzzy, soft-looking feathers on belly; white-tipped tail. JUVENILE: Darker, charcoal gray overall. FLIGHT: Low through trees with frequent glides.
Similar Species: Slightly larger Clark's Nutcracker (below) lacks dark nape band; has black-and-white wings and a black tail with white edges. **Voice:** Harsh *chek* calls and high whistles. **Status:** Uncommon resident. **Habitat:** Spruce forest borders. **Elevations:** Resident 8,750'-11,000'. **Behavior:** Pairs and family groups defend a large, irregularly-shaped territory averaging a quarter-mile square. **Noteworthy:** They are campground regulars in the highest areas of the White Mountains.

CLARK'S NUTCRACKER, *Nucifraga columbiana*

Description: 12". Large, **gray-bodied jay** with **black and white wings and tail**. FLIGHT: White bars on inner wings and white outer tail feathers.
Similar Species: Canada Jay (above) lacks black and white patterns in wings and tail. **Voice:** Long, harsh and penetrating *kraaaah* notes; calls are clicks and rattles. **Status:** Uncommon resident. Casual irruptive to southern Arizona in some winters (Sep-mid Jun, accidentally through entire summer). Occurrences may be separated by 5 or more years. **Habitat:** Summer: Mountain coniferous forest, especially in pines. Winter: Usually in pines, but in irruption years possible to desert foothills. **Elevations:** Summer 6,200'-11,600'; Winter 2,400'-11,600'. **Behavior:** Mainly feeds on pine seeds, which it caches in late summer for winter use. Flocks may number up to 12, rarely more in Arizona. **Noteworthy:** Although Clark's Nutcrackers have exhibited courtship behavior in the Chiricahua and Santa Catalina Mountains, nests have never been documented south of central Arizona.

Black-billed Magpie

American Crow

BLACK-BILLED MAGPIE, *Pica hudsonia*

Description: 19". Large, slim, black-and-white **corvid with a long tail**; in favorable lighting wings and tail show blue, violet, and oily green gloss. FLIGHT: White flight feathers contrast with black inner wings. **Similar Species:** Distinctive. **Voice:** Series of conversational, variable *whek whek* calls. **Status**: Uncommon resident. **Habitat:** Cottonwood riparian, often in conjunction with introduced tamarisk and Russian olive trees along arroyos, and village and ranch groves within sparsely vegetated Great Basin Desert. **Elevations:** Resident 4,700'-5,800'. **Behavior:** Opportunistically feeds on seeds, nuts, fruits, insects, small animals, and carrion. Caches food when abundant. Builds huge stick nests with two entrances. **Noteworthy:** Once fairly common, Arizona population was almost extirpated in the first half of the twentieth century. Since about 1970 it has been slowly recovering.

AMERICAN CROW, *Corvus brachyrhynchos*

Description: 17.5". Big, all-black corvid with stout bill; **short, square-tipped tail**. FLIGHT: Fan-shaped tail. **Similar Species:** Larger Chihuahuan Raven (p. 307) has longer bill, mostly feathered upper mandible, white neck visible in wind; wedge-shaped tail shows in flight. **Voice:** Usually rendered *caw caw*. **Status:** Common resident. Rare in winter (late Oct-Mar) along Colorado River and in lowland agricultural areas. **Habitat:** Open ponderosa pine forests; forest meadowlands; open woodland edges. Winter: Farms, irrigated pastures, and pecan groves. **Elevations:** Summer 5,000'-9,500'; Winter 150'-9,500'. **Behavior:** Usually forages on ground and eats almost anything. In Arizona may form flocks of well over 100 crows. **Noteworthy:** Among the most intelligent of all birds, American Crows are capable of counting up to 16 and using simple tools like twigs to jab food out of crevices.

Chihuahuan Raven

Common Raven

CHIHUAHUAN RAVEN, *Corvus cryptoleucus*

Description: 19.5". Large, all-black corvid; long bill with **mostly-feathered upper mandible**; shaggy throat; wind ruffled **neck shows white**. FLIGHT: Somewhat rounded, often only slightly wedge-shaped tail. **Similar Species:** Larger Common Raven (below) has upper mandible only feathered half of its length; thick, all-black neck ruff. In flight its tail is usually strongly wedge-shaped. **Voice:** Reverberant *wantt wantt* croaks. **Status:** Common resident. **Habitat:** Chihuahuan Desert flats and valley grasslands; farms fields and pecan groves. **Elevations:** Resident 1,500'-5,300'. **Behavior:** Frequently scavenges road kills, but feeds opportunistically on fruits, eggs, lizards, etc. Nests usually have sweeping views and are located in isolated trees or on utility poles. **Noteworthy:** Forms large winter flocks that may number in the hundreds. Chihuahuan Ravens are extremely rare visitors inside mountain perimeters, the purview of larger Common Ravens.

COMMON RAVEN, *Corvus corax*

Description: 24". Very large, all-black corvid with violet gloss in good light; long bill with **upper mandible only half-feathered**; shaggy throat. FLIGHT: Wedge-shaped tail. **Similar Species:** Smaller Chihuahuan Raven (above) shows white on neck in wind, and is confined to largely treeless habitats on flat or gently sloping terrain. In flight shows a shallow wedge-shaped, slightly rounded tail. **Voice:** Resonant *wahh wahh* croaks, deeper than Chihuahuan Raven. **Status:** Common resident. **Habitat:** Desert, woodlands, and forest. Usually infrequent in open Chihuahuan Desert and valley grasslands, but uses river groves, orchards, and enters towns and cities. **Elevations:** Resident 100'-12,600'. **Behavior:** Unlike crows, ravens routinely soar high above ground like Red-tailed Hawks. **Noteworthy:** Bold and resourceful, Common Ravens are widely considered the most intelligent of all North American birds.

Horned Lark
Male

Juvenile

Purple Martin
Male

Female

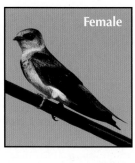

Female

HORNED LARK, *Eremophila alpestris*

Description: 7". Slim pinkish-tan bird with **black horns, mask, and collar**; tiny bill; white underparts. MALE: Yellow throat. FEMALE: Duller overall with thinner horns. JUVENILE: Blackish crown and back heavily spotted with white. FLIGHT: **Black tail** with narrow white edges. **Similar Species:** Wintering "big-eyed" Sprague's Pipit (p. 365) arrives after juvenile Horned Larks molt. **Voice:** Tinkling flight calls include *tseep*, *tew*, and *zip* notes. Song starts with very high, thin *terp* notes, followed by a rising, tinkling flourish, often given in sustained flight. **Status:** Fairly common in summer (Apr-Oct); common in winter (Nov-Mar). **Habitat:** Open flat deserts, valley grasslands, pastures, freshly tilled fields, golf courses, and barren pond edges. Casual in summer above timberline. **Elevations:** Summer 100'-11,400'; Winter 100'-9,200'. **Behavior:** Terrestrial; may perch on fence lines. Forms large winter flocks. **Noteworthy:** Unlike most birds, Horned Larks thrive on heavily grazed pastures.

PURPLE MARTIN, *Progne subis*

Description: 7.5". Large swallow with large bill. MALE: Glossy **purple-black**. FEMALE: Blue-black above with frosty forehead; whitish half-collar; whitish underparts. FLIGHT: **Very broad-based wings**. **Similar Species:** Much smaller Tree Swallow (p. 311) is sharply bicolored. In flight Tree Swallow's clean white underparts contrast with blackish wings. Brown-chested Martin (accidental at Patagonia Lake, Feb 2006) from South America is brown above with a distinct, soft brown chest band. **Voice:** Rich, liquid, gurgling *w'chu cheup churrr cheup* notes. Begins to sing well before dawn. **Status:** Fairly common in summer (May-Sep); common fall migrant (Aug-early Sep) in S. central Arizona when flocks form of up to 1000 birds. **Habitat:** Requires permanent water within a mile of nest. S. Arizona: saguaros. N.Arizona: pine forest. **Elevations:** Summer 1,800'-9,100'; Migration 100'-9,100'. **Noteworthy:** S. Arizona race, *P. s. hesperia*, averages about 7% smaller.

MALE

FEMALE

Male

Tree Swallow

Violet-green
Swallow

Male

Description: 5.5". Bicolored swallow; **dark cap extends below eyes**; wings reach tail tip. MALE: Glossy **deep blue** above. FEMALE: Dark brown above. JUVENILE: Brown above with diffuse gray breast-band. **Similar Species:** Smaller Violet-green Swallow (below) has white above the eyes and white patches on the sides of rump. Juvenile Tree is whiter below than Northern Rough-winged Swallow (p. 313). **Voice:** Pleasant, liquid *sidilip* or *chirrip*. **Status:** Uncommon and local as a breeding bird in summer (May-Jul). Common migrant (mid Jan-mid May and Jul-Nov), with summer stragglers. Fairly common in Western Arizona in winter (Dec-mid Jan), decreasing eastwards. **Habitat:** Summer: Mountain forests of pine, mixed conifers, and aspens near water. Migration and Winter: Valley rivers, marshes, ponds, and lakes. **Elevations:** Summer 5,100'-9,500'; Winter 100'-8,300'. **Behavior:** Usually forages over water. **Noteworthy:** Tree Swallows are among the first birds to arrive in spring. In prime locations single day migrants may exceed 100,000 birds. The first known nest in Arizona was on the Kaibab Plateau in 1973.

Description: 5". **Green-backed** swallow; **white on cheeks curls over eyes; white-sided rump**; wings extend well beyond tail tip. MALE: Green cap; emerald-green back; violet rump. FEMALE: Tan cap; indistinct facial pattern; dull overall. **Similar Species:** Tree Swallow (above) lacks white above eye and on sides of rump; male has a deep blue back. **Voice:** Burry *chidip* calls; also paper-crackle *chip* notes. **Status:** Common in summer (Jun-Jul) and migration (Feb-May and Aug-Nov); rare in winter (Dec-Jan). **Habitat:** Summer: Mountain forests, canyons, and cliffs. Rare--but recently confirmed nesting--in saguaro cactus. Migration and Winter: Valley rivers, ponds, and lakes. **Elevations:** Summer 500'-11,300'; Winter 100'-6,800'. **Behavior:** Nests colonially in woodpecker holes and crevices on cliff faces. **Noteworthy:** Common in spring along the Colorado River, but rare in fall.

311

Northern Rough-winged Swallow

Bank Swallow

NORTHERN ROUGH-WINGED SWALLOW, *Stelgidopteryx serripennis*

Description: 5.25". Brown-backed swallow with drab **buffy throat** and **dingy underparts**, darkest on breast. **Similar Species:** Smaller Bank Swallow (below) is white below with crisp brown breast band. **Voice:** Buzzy *jippt jippt*. **Status:** Fairly common in summer (Feb-Oct); rare in winter (Nov-Jan). **Habitat:** Valley and foothill streams, rivers, ponds, and lakes and adjacent farm fields and pastures, usually forages outside of mountain perimeters. **Elevations:** Summer 100'-9,000'; Winter 100'-4,100'. **Behavior:** Nests are burrows in stream and river banks, less often in dry arroyo banks, or holes in irrigation canals and in unused pipes. Forages for insects over water or nearby fields. **Noteworthy:** Northern Rough-wings are the only bank nesting swallow in Arizona.

BANK SWALLOW, *Riparia riparia*

Description: 5". **Small** brown-backed swallow with **white of throat** curling up behind ears; **crisp brown breast band**; clean white belly. **Similar Species:** Northern Rough-winged Swallow (above) has faintly buff throat and breast, lacks distinct breast band. Larger juvenile Tree Swallow (p. 311) has diffuse gray breast band. **Voice:** Dirty buzzing *zippur* or *chrrt*, often repeated rapidly; its notes are slightly deeper and slightly slower than Northern Rough-winged Swallow calls. **Status:** Uncommon spring (Apr-May) and fall (mid Jul-mid Oct) migrant, with summer stragglers. Rare in lowlands in winter (mid Oct-Mar). **Habitat:** Valley rivers, ponds, and lakes. **Elevations:** Migration 100'-7,100'. **Behavior:** Like most other swallows in migration, forages primarily over water for flying insects, often in mixed flocks with other swallow species. **Noteworthy:** Bank Swallow is the smallest member of the martin and swallow family in the world. It occurs on every continent but Antarctica.

CLIFF SWALLOW

BARN SWALLOW

CLIFF SWALLOW, *Petrochelidon pyrrhonota*

Description: 5.5". **Black-capped swallow** with variably chestnut or whitish forehead, depending on subspecies; chestnut throat; white-striped black back; **cinnamon rump**; square tail. **Similar Species:** Juvenile Barn Swallow (below) has solid blue back and long forked tail. <u>Cave Swallow</u>, accidental in fall and winter in lowlands (Aug-Jan), has clear, pale orange throat. **Voice:** Creaks like a swinging rusty gate *veeehh*. **Status:** Common migrant and summer resident (early Feb-mid Oct), casual in winter. **Habitat:** Open areas in deserts and valleys near rivers, ponds, and lakes, or buildings, especially with nearby irrigated lawns or fields. **Elevations:** Summer 100'-9,400'. **Behavior:** Usually forages in flocks and nests colonially. Adobe nests are attached to cliff faces, dams, bridges, and buildings. About 25% of females lay their eggs in another female's nest. **Noteworthy:** The "Mexican" Cliff Swallow, *P. p. melanogaster*, breeding in SE Arizona has a chestnut forehead. Northern races of Cliff Swallow have white or pale cinnamon foreheads.

BARN SWALLOW, *Hirundo rustica*

Description: 6.75". Large, slender, blue-backed swallow with a **long, deeply-forked tail**. **Similar Species:** Cliff Swallow (above) has cinnamon rump and shorter, square-tipped tail. **Voice:** Jumbled, squeaky *whee* or *whitt-wheal* notes alternating with low buzzes. **Status:** Common migrant and summer resident (Mar-Oct); rare in winter (Nov-Feb). **Habitat:** Summer: Desert oases, fields, pastures, golf courses, ponds, and lakes from lowlands to highlands. Winter: Confined to lowlands, primarily wetlands. **Elevations:** Summer 100'-9,500'; Winter 100'-4,200'. **Behavior:** Flies low over fields or water. Mud-based nests are on man-made structures such as bridges, barns, and verandas. **Noteworthy:** Availability of mud for nests probably determines the breeding distribution of Barn Swallow in Arizona.

Mountain Chickadee

Mexican Chickadee

MOUNTAIN CHICKADEE, *Poecile gambeli*

Description: 5.25". Small forest acrobat with black crown and bib; **white eyebrow**; white cheek patches; pale gray flanks. **Similar Species:** <u>Black-capped Chickadee</u>, casual year-round, primarily in winter (Oct-mid Feb), usually in small towns within 15 miles of Utah, lacks a white eyebrow and has a white panel on its upper wing. **Voice:** Harsh *shika-dee-dee*; whistled *fee dee dee*. **Status:** Common resident; casual winter (Dec-Jan) visitant to lowlands (250'-4,000') in ones and twos, once or twice per decade. **Habitat:** Mountain coniferous forests up to timberline, pinyon-juniper woodland, and upper mountain canyon groves. **Elevations:** Resident 5,500'-11,600'. **Behavior:** Gleans insects from leaves and needles; forages for small seeds. Nests in tree cavities, usually created by woodpeckers, but occasionally excavated by themselves. After breeding, they often form the nucleus of traveling mixed species flocks. **Noteworthy:** Arizona's southernmost resident population of Mountain Chickadees are in the Santa Catalina and Rincon Mountains outside of Tucson, but they have bred in the Santa Rita Mountains and wintered in the Chiricahua Mountains.

MEXICAN CHICKADEE, *Poecile sclateri*

Description: 5". Small forest acrobat with black crown and white cheek patches; **large black bib** extending onto upper breast; smoke gray flanks. **Similar Species:** Mountain Chickadee (above, accidental in the Chiricahua Mountains) has white eyebrow, less extensive black bib, and pale gray flanks. **Voice:** Querulous *zhika dee*; nasal *b-zzz b-zzz*. **Status:** Fairly common resident. **Habitat:** Mountain canyon groves, upper pine-oak woodland, and coniferous forests in the Chiricahua Mountains. **Elevations:** Resident 5,300'-9,800'. **Behavior:** Considered a mixed flock leader in its highland habitat. Nests in tree cavities. **Noteworthy:** In the U.S., Mexican Chickadee occurs on public lands only in the Chiricahua Mountains of SE Arizona.

Bridled Titmouse

Juniper Titmouse

BRIDLED TITMOUSE, *Baeolophus wollweberi*

Description: 5.25". Titmouse with **white cheek outlined in black**. **Similar Species:** Juniper Titmouse (below) lacks any pattern on gray face. **Voice:** Wren-like *che-che-che-che*; trilled *tra-la-la-la-la* notes; sputtering scold. **Status:** Common resident. **Habitat:** Two disjunct populations in two different habitats. A lowland population exploits river valley cottonwood groves, and a larger montane population uses canyon riparian, oak woodland, and pine-oak up to Ponderosa pine. **Elevations:** Resident 2,000'-8,400'. **Behavior:** Gleans insects from the surfaces of leaves and eats seeds. Nests in natural tree cavities. In winter some small flocks may join the small population that breeds in river valley groves. **Noteworthy:** A third adult Bridled Titmouse regularly joins the nucleus pair in feeding their nestlings and defending their nest.

JUNIPER TITMOUSE, *Baeolophus ridgwayi*

Description: 5.25". Entirely gray titmouse lacking field marks. Blank face with black eyes often gives it a vaguely puzzled expression. **Similar Species:** Bridled Titmouse (above) has boldly-patterned black and white face. Bushtit (p. 321) lacks crest. **Voice:** Speedy *che-che-che-che-che-eap*; trilled *gid-dy-up gid-dy-up gid-dy-up*. **Status:** Fairly common resident. **Habitat:** Arid mountain areas with juniper as a major component, including chaparral, oak-juniper woodland, pinyon-juniper woodland, and mountain canyon groves. **Elevations:** Resident 3,400'-7,800'. **Behavior:** Gleans insects from the surfaces of leaves and eats seeds. Nests in both natural tree cavities and woodpecker holes. **Noteworthy:** SE Arizona represents the southernmost range limits of Juniper Titmouse in the U.S., although an isolated population exists just below the border in the Sierra San Luis in Mexico.

Verdin

Juvenile

Bushtit
Male

Female

VERDIN, *Auriparus flaviceps*

Description: 4.5″. Tiny gray songbird with sharp bill, dark eyes, and medium-length tail. ADULT: **Yellow head**; oft-concealed rufous shoulder patch. JUVENILE: Entirely gray with pale-based bill. **Similar Species:** Bushtit (below) has fawn-brown ears and noticeably long tail. Juniper Titmouse (p. 319) has crest; Lucy's Warbler (p. 431) has eyering and chestnut rump. **Voice:** High clear *chee* notes; also plaintive, sweet *tea-for-you, tea-for-you-too*. **Status:** Common resident. **Habitat:** Desert scrub and lowland urban areas up to foothill thorn scrub and open oak woodland. **Elevations:** Resident 100′-5,400′. **Behavior:** Verdins are primarily insectivores, but will exploit nectar and eat fruit. Construct large, oval twiggy nests for both roosting and nesting. After young birds become independent they build their own roost nests. **Noteworthy:** The distribution of Verdins in Arizona is almost identical to the range of mesquite. Accidental once in fall (Nov) in pine forest at 8800′.

BUSHTIT, *Psaltriparus minimus*

Description: 4.5″. Tiny, usually social, gray song bird with **long tail. Ears fawn brown**. MALE: Eyes dark. FEMALE: Eyes creamy white. **Similar Species:** See juvenile Verdin (above). **Voice:** Tiny, twittering *pit pit pit* notes that sound like jingling dimes in someone's pants pocket. **Status:** Fairly common resident. **Habitat:** Primarily mid-elevation woodlands, chaparral, and mountain canyons, but some also nest locally in river valley and foothill groves. Post-breeding flocks (after August) disperse from desert mesquites to high mountain coniferous forest. **Elevations:** Summer 3,000′-9,000′; Winter 500′-7,100′. **Behavior:** After fledging, flocks usually number 10-50 birds. Bushtit stocking nest is flexible enough to accommodate 7-14 birds at once. **Noteworthy:** Bushtit nests may be attended by several unmated adults, as well as the nucleus pair.

Golden-crowned Kinglet
Male Displaying Crest

Female

Ruby-crowned Kinglet
Male

Female

GOLDEN-CROWNED KINGLET, *Regulus satrapa*

Description: 4". **Tiny** songbird of boreal forest with **incandescent crown** trimmed in black; broad **white eyebrow**; white wingbars; dark flight feathers with golden edgings. MALE: Orange crown. FEMALE: Golden-yellow crown. **Similar Species:** Ruby-crowned Kinglet (below) lacks black and white facial stripes and whitish underparts. **Voice:** Hypersonic *tseee* trill; song of almost inaudibly high, thin notes accelerating into bubbly finale. **Status:** Uncommon resident; rare and irregular at lower elevations in winter (Nov-mid Apr). **Habitat:** Summer: Mountain spruce and fir forests. Winter: Valley, foothill and mountain groves, as well as coniferous forests. **Elevations:** Summer 6,800'-10,900'; Winter 400'-10,000'. **Behavior:** Energetically forages in conifer twig tips. **Noteworthy:** Arizona's breeding Golden-crowned Kinglet populations are the southernmost in the United States.

RUBY-CROWNED KINGLET, *Corthylio calendula*

Description: 4.25". **Tiny** olive-colored songbird with **split white eyering** broken above and below; **rear wingbar edged with black bar.** MALE: Flaming red crest often concealed. FEMALE: Lacks red crown. **Similar Species:** Stripe-headed Golden-crowned Kinglet (above) is whitish below. Hutton's Vireo (p. 295) has pale lores, eyering is only broken at top, and it lacks black border behind rear wingbar. **Voice:** Dry, scolding *tsit* notes; song is high, thin *tsee* notes that build into full-throated warble. **Status:** Common in summer (early May-late Sep); common and widespread in winter (late Sep-early May), especially south of Mogollon Rim. **Habitat:** Summer: Mountain coniferous forest, sometimes mixed with Gambel's oak or aspen. Winter: Desert oases and thickets to upper limits of Ponderosa pine. **Elevations:** Summer 6,800'-11,100'; Winter 100'-8,000'. **Behavior:** Energetically hovers and gleans from shrub-level to treetops. **Noteworthy:** Arizona's Pinaleno Mountains near Safford host the southernmost breeding population of Ruby-crowned Kinglets in the United States.

Red-breasted Nuthatch

White-breasted Nuthatch

RED-BREASTED NUTHATCH, *Sitta canadensis*

Description: 4.5". Medium-sized nuthatch with a **white eyebrow** and **apricot underparts**. **Similar Species:** Both larger White-breasted Nuthatch (below) and smaller Pygmy Nuthatch (p. 327) lack white eyebrow and have mostly white underparts. **Voice:** Deliberate, clarion *yenk yenk yenk* notes, like a child's noisemaker. **Status:** Fairly common resident. Small numbers are irruptive to lowlands below 5,000' during winter (Sep-May) usually once or twice per decade. **Habitat:** Mountain coniferous forest and upper canyon groves with standing dead trees. **Elevations:** Summer 6,400'-10,700'; Winter 100'-9,500'. **Behavior:** Climbs head-first down tree trunks probing for insects. Stores food for later use under bark, in holes, and in the ground. Smears pine pitch around its nest entrance. **Noteworthy:** Food shortages in states farther north probably accounts for "lost" Red-breasted Nuthatches using the Arizona lowlands during irruption winters.

WHITE-BREASTED NUTHATCH, *Sitta carolinensis*

Description: 5.75". Large nuthatch with **white face**; white underparts; rusty vent patch. **Similar Species:** Red-breasted Nuthatch (above) has white eyebrow and reddish underparts. Smaller Pygmy Nuthatch (p. 327) has black eyestripe. **Voice:** Nasal *ank-ank-ank* notes in a series. **Status:** Common resident; most withdraw from highest elevations in winter (mid Oct-Mar). **Habitat:** Summer: Valley, foothill, and mountain canyon groves, pine-oak woodland, and coniferous forest. Winter: Desert oases and urban parks to mountain Ponderosa pine forest. **Elevations:** Summer 3,400'-11,300'; Winter 1,000'-9,100'. **Behavior:** Climbs head-first down tree trunks probing for insects. Hammers at bark and seeds with wedge-tipped bill. Often seen in pairs or family groups. Nests in cavities. **Noteworthy:** White-breasted Nuthatches "wipe" ants and beetles around their nest entrances, apparently as a chemical defense against mammalian predators.

Pygmy Nuthatch

"Rocky Mountain"
Brown Creeper

"Mexican"

PYGMY NUTHATCH, *Sitta pygmaea*

Description: 4.25". Excitable little nuthatch with **grayish-brown crown** bordered by **dark eye-line**; white lower face and throat. **Similar Species:** Larger White-breasted Nuthatch (p. 325) has white face encircling eye. Slightly bigger Red-breasted Nuthatch (p. 325) has a bold white eyebrow and reddish underparts. **Voice:** High pleasant *peep peep* notes, and rapid twittering *pip-pip-pip* calls, often given in chorus by a flock. **Status:** Common resident. **Habitat:** Mountain Ponderosa pine forests. **Elevations:** Resident 5,100'-10,700'.

Behavior: Acrobatically forages for insects or pine seeds high in Ponderosa branches and needle clusters. Usually gregarious and often joins mixed species flocks with other birds. Roosts and nests in tree cavities. Caches seeds for winter consumption. **Noteworthy:** Nesting pairs often have 1-3 helpers, usually males, that assist in feeding the young.

BROWN CREEPER, *Certhia americana*

Description: 5.25". Thin, cryptic, **trunk-creeping bird** with a long, thin, **downcurved bill**. **Similar Species:** Nuthatches lack mottled-brown upperparts and downcurved bill. **Voice:** Very high, tremulous *tseeee* notes; rhythmic *wee-dee-seedly-see* song. **Status:** Fairly common resident. Rare and irregular in lowland groves in winter (Nov-Mar). **Habitat:** Summer: Mountain canyon groves and coniferous forest. Winter: Desert oases and urban parks to mountain Ponderosa pine forest. **Elevations:** Summer 5,100'-11,800'; Winter 100'-9,500'. **Behavior:** Hunts insects by flying to the base of a tree and spiraling upward around the trunk until it reaches the top, or by inching along major limbs. Builds nest under loose sections of tree bark. **Noteworthy:** Border range "Mexican" Brown Creeper, *C. a. albescens*, usually exhibit dark upper parts, white throat contrasting with a gray breast and belly.

Black-tailed Gnatcatcher
Breeding Male

Nonbreeding Male

Blue-gray Gnatcatcher
Male

Female

Black-capped Gnatcatcher
Male

Female

BLACK-TAILED GNATCATCHER, *Polioptila melanura*

Description: 4.1". Gnatcatcher with **short bill**; narrow white **eyering broken on rear edge; mostly black undertail feathers** with oval white tips. BREEDING MALE (Feb-Jul): Black cap crosses eye, accenting white upper half of thin eyering. WINTER (Aug-Jan): Short black eyebrow. FEMALE: Lacks black on head. **Similar Species:** Blue-grays (below) always show mostly white undertail. **Voice:** Coarse *shesh-shesh-shesh* calls; childish *whee-e* note, often repeated. **Status**: Common resident in Sonoran Desert; fairly common in Chihuahuan Desert. **Habitat:** Desertscrub and foothill thornscrub, especially thickets in arroyos. **Elevations:** Resident 100'-5,000'. **Behavior:** Typically nests in mistletoe clumps.

BLUE-GRAY GNATCATCHER, *Polioptila caerulea*

Description: 4.3". Gnatcatcher with medium-length bill; **obvious white eyering**; white undertail. BREEDING MALE (Mar-Jul): Narrow black forehead crescent. **Similar Species:** Winter Black-capped Gnatcatcher (below) has longer bill, thinner eyering, and—with a good view—distinctly tiered pairs of undertail feathers. **Voice:** Plaintive, nasal *speew*; conversational *H'do you, you, H'do you do do?* **Status:** Fairly common in summer (mid Mar-mid Sep); withdrawing from higher elevations in winter (mid Sep-mid Mar). **Habitat:** Summer: Foothill and mountain chaparral and woodlands. Winter: Lowland and foothill scrub. **Elevations:** Summer 3,000'-9,000; Winter 100'-5,000'. **Noteworthy:** Only migratory gnatcatcher.

BLACK-CAPPED GNATCATCHER, *Polioptila nigricepstt*

Description: 4.2". Gnatcatcher with **long bill**; three widely separated tiers of white undertail feathers. BREEDING MALE (Feb-Aug): Black cap surrounds eye and accentuates white lower half of eyering. WINTER (Sep-Jan): Thin black eyebrow. **Voice:** Mewing *beeww*, fading at end; imperative, hoarse *burrr*. **Status:** Rare resident. **Habitat:** Foothill thornscrub and adjacent canyon groves. **Elevations:** Resident 3,400'-5,000'. **Noteworthy:** First U.S. record was near Patagonia in May, 1971.

Cactus Wren

Sinola Wren

Carolina Wren

CACTUS WREN, *Campylorhynchus brunneicapillus*

Description: 8.5". **Very large wren** with **scaly black throat and breast**; long white eyebrow; **red eye**; striped white above; streaked black below. FLIGHT: Tail is spread and white-tipped. **Similar Species:** All other wrens are much smaller. **Voice:** Chugging song, a series of *krr krr krr* notes, suggests someone cranking the balky motor on an old car. Loud and often heard, for many the song of the Cactus Wren evokes the Arizona desert. **Status:** Common resident. **Habitat:** Sonoran, Mohave, or Chihuahuan Desert scrub, urban areas, valley mesquite grasslands, and foothill thornscrub. **Elevations:** 100'-6,600'. **Behavior:** Forages primarily on the ground for insects and cactus fruits. Obtains all the water it needs from food. Large, straw-colored, oven-shaped nests are woven from fine materials and usually placed in a thorny plant—especially cholla cactus—or in a spiny tree. Males may build up to five extra "dummy" nests, which can be used as roosts, nests for second broods, or to discourage would-be predators. **Noteworthy:** Largest member of its family in the U.S., Cactus Wren is the Arizona State Bird.

SINALOA WREN, *Thryophilus sinaloa*

Description: 5.5". Brown, heavyset wren with white eyebrow; **sides of neck striped** black and white; reddish rump and tail; underparts gray without flank barring. **Similar Species:** Slimmer, longer-tailed Bewick's Wren (p. 335) lacks rusty rump and tail. **Status:** Rare year-round. **Habitat:** Understory of valley and mountain canyon groves. **Elevations:** 3,200'-5,600'.

CAROLINA WREN, *Thryothorus ludovicianus*

Description: 5.5". Warm-brown, heavyset wren with black-bordered white eyebrow; "wingbars" are series of white dots; **underparts cinnamon** with faint flank barring. **Similar Species:** Sinaloa Wren (above) has striped sides of neck, only rump and tail are rusty, and underparts are gray. **Status:** Casual year-round. **Habitat:** Valley and mountain canyon thickets. **Elevations:** 2,150'-6,600'. **Noteworthy:** May stay at a site up to 8 months.

Rock Wren

Canyon Wren

ROCK WREN, *Salpinctes obsoletus*

Description: 6". **Large, pale wren** with faint breast streaks; buff belly; thin eyebrow. FLIGHT: Dull rusty rump; cinnamon tail corners. **Similar Species:** Canyon Wren (below) is rich rusty overall with white throat and breast. **Voice:** High, trilled, bisyllabic *j'deee j'deee* and *t'rreee*. **Status:** Fairly common resident. **Habitat:** Summer (mid Apr-mid Sep): Open, rocky foothills and mountain slopes; talus slides above timberline in the San Francisco Peaks. Winter (mid Sep-mid Apr): Open deserts, valleys, agricultural areas, and rocky foothills. **Elevations:** Summer 150'-12,200'; Winter 100'-7,700'. **Behavior:** Bobs when perched. Forages on ground and under rocks. Paves entrance to crevice nests with pebbles. **Noteworthy:** With a summer range from 150' along the Colorado River to above 12,000' on the San Francisco Peaks, Rock Wrens match the widest elevational extremes of any bird in Arizona.

CANYON WREN, *Catherpes mexicanus*

Description: 5.75". **Large, rusty-red wren** with snow-white throat and breast. FLIGHT: Bright red rump and tail. **Similar Species:** Rock Wren (above) much paler overall with thin eyebrow; lacks immaculate white throat and breast. **Voice:** Downward spiraling series of pure clear whistles, often ending with sneezy *beeep* notes; hard, harsh *jeeet!* calls. **Status:** Common resident. **Habitat:** Summer (Apr-Sep): Foothill and mountain cliffs, rocky ridgelines, and rock-walled canyons. Winter (Oct-Mar): Desert oases, valley, foothill, and mountain canyon groves, especially with nearby rocky walls, cliffs, or rock formations. **Elevations:** Summer 100'-9,400'; Winter 400'-8,000'. **Behavior:** Bobs when perched and its white throat signals location to other Canyon Wrens. Forages under rocks and inside crevices; in winter some follow streambeds and probe flood debris. **Noteworthy:** Canyon Wrens sing their descending carols throughout the year, apparently to defend their large territories.

Bewick's Wren

House Wren
"Northern"

House Wren
"Brown-throated"

BEWICK'S WREN, *Thryomanes bewickii*

Description: 5.25". Lanky, gray woodland wren with bold **white eyebrow**; largely unmarked upperparts, and **long gray tail**, often expressively waved. **Similar Species:** Smaller, shorter-tailed House Wren (below) lacks a bright white eyebrow. **Voice:** Two-note *eek-Pierre* song begins with a burry inhale and ends in an exhaled trill; many calls, including *clenk clenk* notes. **Status:** Common in summer (Mar-mid Oct), withdrawing from highest elevations in winter (mid Oct-Feb). **Habitat:** Desert mesquite bosque and hackberry thickets; valley, foothill, and mountain canyon groves and oak woods; open stands of Ponderosa pine. **Elevations:** Summer 500'-9,400'; Winter 100'-7,000'. **Behavior:** Actively gleans understory for insects. Nests in cavities. **Noteworthy:** Grayish-brown Arizona Bewick's Wrens lack reddish tones of other U.S. races and sing the least complex song.

HOUSE WREN, *Troglodytes aedon*

Description: 4.75". Small wren with **pale bill**; jaunty, **medium-long tail**. "NORTHERN": Neutral gray-brown with indistinct eyebrow; gray throat and breast. "BROWN-THROATED": Cocao overall with a buff eyebrow and a grayish-buff throat and breast. **Similar Species:** Smaller Pacific and Winter Wrens (p. 337) have stubby tails. **Voice:** Musical trills and tinkles, richer and slower than Pacific or Winter Wrens; *beeerr beeerr beeerr* calls. **Status:** Fairly common in summer (Apr-Aug); common migrant (late Mar-mid May and mid Aug-Oct); fairly common in winter (Nov-late Mar). **Habitat:** Summer: Undergrowth and brush piles in mountain canyons and coniferous forests. Migration: Throughout. Winter: Desert thickets and valley, foothill, and lower mountain canyon undergrowth. **Elevations:** Summer 4,300'-11,300'; Winter 100'-7,000' **Behavior:** Strongly territorial, and will destroy the eggs of other wrens or songbirds. Often sings defiantly from conspicuous perches. **Noteworthy:** The "Brown-throated" race of House Wren, *T. a. brunneicollis*, is confined to the mountains of SE Arizona.

Winter Wren

Pacific Wren

WINTER WREN, *Troglodytes hiemalis*

Description: 4". **Medium brown**, mouse-like wren with black bill, thin, but distinct buffy eyebrow; **obvious, white-dotted wing coverts**; pale, **grayish-brown breast**; short tail usually cocked upward. **Similar Species:** Larger House Wren (p. 335) has pale bill, indistinct eyebrow, and longer tail. **Voice:** Song Sparrow-like *chimp* notes; song is a long and complex series of high, thin, tinkling trills delivered about half as fast as that of Pacific Wren. **Status:** Rare in winter (late Oct-early Apr). **Habitat:** Dense undergrowth in valley, foothill, and mountain canyon groves. **Elevations:** Winter 100'-7,100'. **Behavior:** Searches for insects in dark tangles and flood debris, usually near running water. **Noteworthy:** Call notes and—in spring—song are important for separating Winter Wren from Pacific Wren.

PACIFIC WREN, *Troglodytes pacificus*

Description: 4". **Dark brown**, mouse-like wren with black bill, thin, but distinct buffy eyebrow; **faintly-dotted wing coverts; cinnamon breast;** short tail usually cocked upward. **Similar Species:** Winter Wren (above) has paler upperparts with more pronounced constellation of white dots on wing coverts; its pallid breast is much more coffee latte than cinnamon. **Voice:** Dry, Wilson's Warbler-like *tic-tic* notes; long, high song phrases are executed about twice as fast as those of Winter Wren. **Status:** Rare and local in summer (mid Apr-mid Oct); rare and more widespread in winter (mid Oct-mid Apr). **Habitat:** Summer: Deadfall and tangles in wet canyons below the Mogollon Rim. Winter: Dense undergrowth in valley, foothill, and mountain canyon groves. **Elevations:** Summer 5,400'-7,000'; Winter 500'-7,600'. **Behavior:** Searches for insects in dark tangles and flood debris, usually near running water. **Noteworthy:** First confirmed nesting in Arizona in 1999, Pacific Wren was split from Winter Wren in 2010.

Marsh Wren

American Dipper

MARSH WREN, *Cistothorus palustris*

Description: 5". Small **marsh denizen** with distinct, pale eyebrow; **black and white striped back**; oft-cocked short tail. **Similar Species:** Smaller Sedge Wren, one record from late Nov 2010-early Apr 2011 at Pena Blanca Lake near Nogales, has finely streaked crown, boldly barred wings, and lacks the rust in wings, rump, and tail of Marsh Wren. **Voice:** Dry *kek kek* followed by an explosive, accusatory rattle. **Status:** Fairly common along lower Colorado River in summer (May-Aug), but rare in other locations. Common and widespread in winter (Sep-Apr) when migrants augment resident population. **Habitat:** Emergent vegetation around valley marshes, ponds, lakes, and slow-moving rivers. **Elevations:** Resident 100'-7,400'. **Behavior:** Gleans for insects and often calls from under cover. Males may build ten or more nests, although only one is used. **Noteworthy:** Lack of deep water marshes in Arizona means the areas where Marsh Wrens breed is much smaller than the areas where they may appear in summer.

AMERICAN DIPPER, *Cinclus mexicanus*

Description: 7.5". **Chunky**, brown-headed streamside bird with a **slate-gray body**; short tail. When blinking the nictitating membranes over the eyes flash white. **Similar Species:** Wren-like shape but—unlike any wren—swims and dives. **Voice:** High, buzzy *dzeet*; song is series of high whistled or trilled phrases. **Status:** Uncommon in summer (mid May-Oct). Withdraws from higher elevations in winter (Nov-mid May) when uncommon but more widespread. **Habitat:** Clear mountain streams, usually with waterfalls. **Elevations:** Summer 1,850'-9,500'; Winter 2,500'-7,400'. **Behavior:** Bobs when perched. Forages underwater for aquatic insects and fry-sized fish. Builds domed moss nest under waterfalls and bridges. **Noteworthy:** There is a disjunct, desert-dwelling population inside the Grand Canyon. American Dipper is the only passerine that swims and walks underwater. Unique second eyelids enable Dippers to forage while submerged.

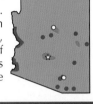

Gray Catbird

Northern Mockingbird

GRAY CATBIRD, *Dumetella carolinensis*

Description: 8.5". **Slate-gray** mimic-thrush with short bill, **black cap,** and rufous undertail. **Similar Species:** Larger Crissal Thrasher (p. 343) is paler gray with much longer, curved bill. **Voice:** Hoarse *mew* scolds. Song is disjointed, squeaky, scratchy, random notes. **Status:** Rare and local in summer (May-Sep); uncommon and more widespread in migration and winter (Oct-Apr). **Habitat:** Summer: Mountain streamside willow and alder thickets. Migration/Winter: Desert oases and urban plantings; foothill and lower mountain canyon thickets. **Elevations:** Summer 5,000'-8,500'; Migration and Winter 200'-7,000'. **Behavior:** Forages on ground or in dense cover for insects, seeds, and small fruits. Flight is typically low. Avoids crossing large openings. **Noteworthy:** Possible statewide at any season in Arizona.

NORTHERN MOCKINGBIRD, *Mimus polyglottos*

Description: 10". **Pale gray** mimic-thrush with short bill and dull yellow eyes. FLIGHT: **Large white wing patches** and **white outer tail feathers**. **Similar Species:** Smaller Townsend's Solitaire (p. 353) has stubbier bill, white eyering, and buffy wing patch. **Voice:** Repeats sounds, often other bird vocalizations, an average of three times each, then begins new series with another bird call, dog bark, or mechanical noise, etc.; calls include loud *shack* notes. **Status:** Common resident, most withdrawing from higher elevations in winter (Sep-mid Mar). **Habitat:** Deserts, especially near water or irrigation, urban areas, and open areas in valleys, foothills, plateaus, and mountains. Avoids extremely arid areas, treeless savanna, and heavy timber. **Elevations:** Resident 100'-7,800'. **Behavior:** Both sexes sing throughout the day, and unmated males sing at night. Average repertoire may include 150 different calls. **Noteworthy:** Usually scarce away from towns and water in SW Arizona, in wet years mockingbirds may also breed in desolate desert valleys.

LeConte's Thrasher

Crissal Thrasher

LeConte's Thrasher, *Toxostoma lecontei*

Description: 11". **Pale gray**, plain-breasted mimic-thrush with long, scythe-like bill; conspicuous **dark eye** on plain gray face; **buffy undertail coverts; dark tail** contrasts with pale body. **Similar Species:** Brownish-gray Crissal Thrasher (below) is overall much darker, has pale eyes, bold, black whiskers, and russet undertail coverts. **Voice:** Call is a questioning, deep-throated whistle *qu-eat?*; song is a happy, whistled series of clear and scratchy notes. **Status:** Rare resident. **Habitat:** Sparsely vegetated Sonoran Desert saltbush and creosote flats from Phoenix west. **Elevations:** Resident 450'-3,100'. **Behavior:** Usually shy, but sings from shrub tops from December through February. Ordinarily runs and does not fly from danger. **Noteworthy:** Breeding Bird Atlasers found nests of Arizona LeConte's Thrashers average just less than 4 feet above the ground.

Crissal Thrasher, *Toxostoma crissale*

Description: 11.5". **Large**, plain-breasted mimic-thrush with very long, **scythe-like bill**; black whisker; dull yellow eye; **russet undertail coverts**; long tail. **Similar Species:** Cobweb-gray LeConte's Thrasher (above) has dark eye and lacks russet undertail coverts. Curve-bill Thrasher has straighter bill, orange eye, and spotted chest. **Voice:** Loud *cheer-ry cheer-ry* call; song is long series of musical phrases, sometimes doubled. **Status:** Fairly common resident. **Habitat:** Desert thickets and valley mesquite grasslands, especially in dry washes, foothill thornscrub, arid oak-juniper, and mountain chaparral below Ponderosa pines. **Elevations:** Resident 100'-6,700'. **Behavior:** Usually shy, but sings from January through March, usually from within the tallest tree or shrub in its territory. **Noteworthy:** Near New Mexico, Crissals usually outnumber Curve-billed Thrashers in Chihuahuan Desert scrub on the Portal Christmas Bird Count.

Bendire's Thrasher

Curve-billed Thrasher
oberholseri

Curve-billed Thrasher
palmeri

Description: 9.75". **Medium-sized** mimic-thrush of the flatlands with straight, medium-length bill, **pale at the base**; yellow eye; **sharp, arrowhead-shaped spots below**. **Similar Species:** Larger adult Curve-billed Thrasher (below) has longer, more curved bill, lacks pale-based lower mandible, and has blurry spots below. Beware of juvenile Curve-billed Thrasher with its short bill, yellow eye, and sharp breast spots, only lacking Bendire's pale-based bill. Look for parent bird. **Voice:** Loud *chup*. Song is squeaky, unbroken, double-noted. **Status:** Uncommon statewide in summer (Apr-Aug), most common in S. Arizona; withdrawing from N. Arizona in winter (Sep-Mar). **Habitat:** Desert flats with fringing brush or cholla cactus, grasslands with mesquite strands or scrubby juniper, and agricultural areas with hedgerows. **Elevations:** Summer 300'-6,100'; Winter 700'-4,100'. **Behavior:** Singing begins in mid-January—later in N. Arizona—a month after most Curve-billed Thrashers. **Noteworthy:** Found in all four North American deserts, Arizona is the center of Bendire's Thrasher range within the U.S.

Description: 11". **Large** mimic-thrush with long, slightly-curved bill; **bright orange eye; blurry gray spots below**. **Similar Species:** See Bendire's Thrasher (above). **Voice:** Loud *whit-wheet!* Song is rich, puppy-like mixture of barks and whines. **Status:** Common resident. **Habitat:** Desert and foothill habitats, including urban areas, especially with cholla cactus. **Elevations:** Resident 150'-5,300'. **Behavior:** Begins singing from a conspicuous perch in December. Usually nests in cholla cactus. After dry winters nests later and lays fewer eggs. **Noteworthy:** Curve-bills east of the Chiricahua Mountains, *T. c. oberholseri*, show dotted white wingbars, more pronounced breast spots, and large white under tail spots. *T. c. palmeri*, occupying all of Arizona west of the Chiricahuas, is ordinarily the most easily seen member of the thrasher tribe.

Sage Thrasher

Blue Mockingbird

SAGE THRASHER, *Oreoscoptes montanus*

Description: 8.5". **Small** mimic-thrush with **short bill** and yellow eye; two narrow white wingbars; **crisp, dark streaking below**. **Similar Species:** Larger Bendire's Thrasher (p. 345) has longer bill, lacks white wingbars, and has finer, lower-contrast streaking on underparts. **Voice:** Low *chup* call; song is long, clear series of warbled phrases. **Status:** Fairly common in summer (Apr-mid Sep); uncommon and irregular in winter (mid Sep-Mar). **Habitat:** Summer: Swales, valleys, and mesas with sagebrush or other low, sparse, desert cover. Winter: Sparsely vegetated desert and juniper stands in valleys, foothills, and lower mountains. **Elevations:** Summer 4,800'-7,200'; Winter 100'-7,100'. **Behavior:** Forages on the ground. Nests in Arizona are under three feet, usually less than half that high. **Noteworthy:** Winter abundance in Arizona is correlated to food availability.

BLUE MOCKINGBIRD, *Melanotis caerulescens*

Description: 10". **Deep blue mimic-thrush** with straight bill; black mask; red eyes; silvery streaking on throat and breast. **Similar Species:** Paler blue Woodhouse's Scrub-Jay (p. 299) has much stouter bill, thin white eyebrows, and mostly gray underparts. **Voice:** Loud, often explosive, *tchook, shiek, wheeal* and *whup* calls; variable song has five or six quick, rich, and very different phrases, followed by a brief break, before resuming. **Status:** Accidental in winter and early spring (late Dec-mid May). **Habitat:** Foothill canyon thickets, especially with thornscrub on adjacent slopes. **Elevations:** Winter 3,700'-4,900'. **Behavior:** Forages primarily on the ground, turning over leaves for fallen hackberry fruits and insects. Once detected, Arizona birds have not been particularly wary. **Noteworthy:** The first Arizona Blue Mockingbird was found in December 1991 on Sonoita Creek near Patagonia.

Brown Thrasher

Wood Thrush

BROWN THRASHER, *Toxostoma rufum*

Description: 11". **Reddish-brown** mimic-thrush with **bright yellow eye**; relatively short, straight bill with pink-based lower mandible; obvious white wingbars; **crisp, reddish-brown spots in rows on underparts.** **Similar Species:** No other Arizona thrasher has reddish-brown upperparts. **Voice:** Loud *chttt* like striking a flint. Song is rich assortment of phrases repeated several times, a pause, then a new set of repeated phrases. **Status:** Rare in winter (Oct-May); casual in summer (Jun-Sep). **Habitat:** Desert oases; valley, foothill, and lower mountain canyon groves. **Elevations:** Summer 2,300'-8,000'; Winter 300'-7,000'. **Behavior:** Forages on the ground for insects and berries, usually remains low in thickets. **Noteworthy:** Brown Thrashers may sing over 1,000 song types, more than Northern Mockingbirds or any other species of mimic-thrush.

WOOD THRUSH, *Hylocichla mustelina*

Description: 7.75". Plump, spot-breasted thrush with **reddish crown and nape**, gradually becoming warm brown towards rump; white eyering; large black spots below; **short tail**. **Similar Species:** Other Arizona spot-breasted thrushes are smaller and lack bright red crown and nape. See larger Brown Thrasher (above). **Voice:** Call is breathy, chortled *whuh-whuh-whuh-whuh*. Evocative gurgling song begins with several swirling phrases, following by trill in a minor key. **Status:** Casual in migration (late Apr-early Jun and Oct-Nov); accidental in summer and winter. **Habitat:** Desert oases; valley, foothill, and lower mountain canyon groves with available surface water. **Elevations:** Migration 400'-6,000'. **Behavior:** Forages on the ground for insects and berries, usually remains low in understory. **Noteworthy:** The majority of Wood Thrush records in Arizona have occurred in October.

EASTERN BLUEBIRD

Male

Female

Juvenile

WESTERN BLUEBIRD

Male

Female

EASTERN BLUEBIRD, *Sialia sialis*

Description: 6.75". Plump blue thrush with **ears bordered orange;** orange breast; **white belly.** MALE: Blue upperparts; **orange throat** and breast. FEMALE: White throat. FLIGHT: Underwings uniform gray. **Similar Species:** Western Bluebird (below) has gray belly. Male has blue throat and breast; rusty sides of back. Female lacks orange bordered ear patches and throat is gray. Male Lazuli Bunting (p. 477) has white wingbars. **Voice:** Rich, gurgled *few-for-you* or *too-few* notes. **Status:** Uncommon in summer (mid Mar-mid Sep); uncommon but more widespread in winter (mid Sep-mid Mar). **Habitat:** Summer: Open foothill groves and oak savannah; montane grassy pine-oak woodland, burns and clearings. Winter: Open valleys, farms, golf courses, city parks, and open foothill and mountain areas. **Elevations:** Summer 3,500'-9,000'; Winter 1,750'-8,200'. **Behavior:** Hunts ground insects from low perches. **Noteworthy:** In SE Arizona's resident race of "Azure Bluebird", males are paler blue than the violet-blue birds from the eastern U.S. The eastern race is irregular in Arizona, primarily in winter.

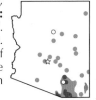

WESTERN BLUEBIRD, *Sialia mexicana*

Description: 6.75". Plump blue thrush with orange breast; **gray belly.** MALE: Blue upperparts with variably **rusty back; blue throat and breast.** FEMALE: **Gray throat.** FLIGHT: Dark underwing linings. **Similar Species:** See Eastern Bluebird (above). **Voice:** Breathy *phew* and *fee-phew* notes; abrupt *chut* calls. **Status:** Fairly common in summer (mid Mar-mid Oct); common in winter (mid Oct-mid Mar). **Habitat:** Summer: Open mountain pine forest and burns; uncommon below the pine belt in open oak woodland. Winter: Open desert oases to mountain pines, especially with mistletoe or juniper berries. **Elevations:** Summer 3,800'-11,300'; Winter 100'-9,100'. **Behavior:** Hunts ground insects from low perches. Winter flocks may number from a few to several hundred. **Noteworthy:** In Arizona, Western Bluebirds compete for cavity nests with Violet-green Swallows.

351

Mountain Bluebird
Male

Female

Townsend's Solitaire

MOUNTAIN BLUEBIRD, *Sialia currucoides*

Description: 7". **Slim** blue thrush with thin bill, long wings, and **long tail.** MALE: **Sky blue.** FEMALE: Gray body; pale blue flight feathers and tail. **Similar Species:** Other bluebirds are plump and have short tails. **Voice:** Pleasant, tremulous *breww* notes and *chuk* calls. **Status:** Common in summer (mid Mar-mid Oct); common but irregular in winter (mid Oct-mid Mar, can linger until early May) when it usually occurs in flocks. **Habitat:** Summer: Flat or gently-sloping terrain with open sagebrush, pinyon-juniper woodland, or large meadows bordering mixed coniferous forest. Winter: Open desert flats, valley fields and pastures, savannas, sagebrush, and open pinyon-juniper woodlands. **Elevations:** Summer 5,200'-11,400'; Winter 100'-7,400'. **Behavior:** Sallies after insects like a flycatcher, often hovers, and frequently uses ground perches. Irruptive to S. Arizona where some years flocks may number in the hundreds. **Noteworthy:** A pair of Mountain Bluebirds nested in grasslands in SE Arizona near Sonoita in 1981.

TOWNSEND'S SOLITAIRE, *Myadestes townsendi*

Description: 8.25". Slender, **gray thrush** that perches upright; white eyering; long tail. FLIGHT: **Buffy wingstripe** and white-sided tail. **Similar Species:** Brown-backed Solitaire (p. 355; accidental) has warm brown back and wings. **Voice:** Bell-timbred *eeh*; warbling, jumbled, continuous, thrasher-like song. **Status:** Fairly common in summer (Apr-mid Sep); uncommon to irregularly fairly common in winter (mid Sep-Apr; rare until late May). **Habitat:** Summer: Montane open coniferous forest, often with aspen edges. Winter: Foothill and mountain juniper woodlands and canyon groves, casual below 3,000' to lower Colorado River. **Elevations:** Summer 6,500'-11,300'; Winter 3,000'-7,800'. **Behavior:** Insectivorous in summer; primarily consumes juniper and mistletoe berries in winter. **Noteworthy:** Unique among Arizona thrushes, Townsend's Solitaire defends a winter territory.

Brown-backed Solitaire

White-throated Thrush

Clay-colored Thrush

BROWN-BACKED SOLITAIRE, *Myadestes occidentalis*

Description: 8.25". Slender, **brown-backed thrush** that perches upright; **broken white eyering**; thin, black whisker; long tail. FLIGHT: White outer tail feathers. **Similar Species:** Townsend's Solitaire has gray back. **Voice:** Poignant *wheep*; evocative song is accelerating tinkling series building to explosive jangling. **Status:** Accidental in summer (mid Jul-early Oct). **Habitat:** Canyons in pine-oak woodland. **Elevations:** 4,500'-6,500'. **Noteworthy:** First Arizona record was from Madera Canyon in the Santa Rita Mountains in Oct, 1996, and second from Miller and Ramsey Canyons in the Huachuca Mountains from Jul-Aug, 2009.

WHITE-THROATED THRUSH, *Turdus assimilis lygrus*

Description: 9.5". Large thrush with neutral, **olive-gray upperparts; slaty upper bill; white crescent** below streaked throat; **café-con-leche breast**. **Similar Species:** American Robin (p. 357) has yellow bill and red breast. **Voice:** Abrupt *zeept*. Rich, thrasher-like, whistled song with notes frequently doubled. **Status:** Accidental in winter (Jan-Feb) and spring (late May). **Habitat:** Desert oases and lower mountain canyon groves, especially with netleaf hackberry and pyracantha. **Elevations:** Winter 4,500'-4,900'; Migrant 2,200'-2,300'. **Behavior:** Skulks in understory. **Noteworthy:** Recorded from early Jan-late Feb, 2019 in lower Madera Canyon, Santa Rita Mountains, and late May, 2019 in Tucson.

CLAY-COLORED THRUSH, *Turdus grayi*

Description: 9.25". Large thrush with murky, **olive-brown upperparts; red eyes; green bill;** lightly streaked throat; **dull buff breast**. **Similar Species:** Grayish White-throated Thrush (above) has dark eyes and bill, and white collar. **Voice:** An inquisitive *wh-heer-rrp?* Song is slow, clearly enunciated whistles at different pitches. **Status:** Accidental in late spring (mid May-mid Jun). **Habitat:** Desert oases and foothill canyon groves, especially with pools of water. **Elevations:** 3,500'-4,700'. **Noteworthy:** Recorded near Portal in mid June, 2015 and Arivaca in mid May, 2020.

Rufous-backed Robin

American Robin
Male

American Robin
Female

American Robin
Juvenile

RUFOUS-BACKED ROBIN, *Turdus rufopalliatus*

Description: 9.5″. Large, plump thrush with solid gray face; black-and-white striped throat; **orange-red back** and breast. **Similar Species:** Darker-headed American Robin (below) has broken white eye crescents and gray back. **Voice:** Abrupt *chupt*. Whistled sing-song carol, notes richer and longer than American Robin's, is almost unheard in Arizona. **Status:** Rare in summer (May-Sep); uncommon in winter (Oct-Apr). **Habitat:** Summer: Valley, foothill, and lower mountain canyon groves. Winter: Desert oases and urban areas; valley, foothill, and lower mountain canyon groves. Accidental in coniferous forest. **Elevations:** Summer 3,900′-4,800′; Winter 400′-5,600′. **Behavior:** Skulks in understory and thickets searching for fruits and insects. **Noteworthy:** Over-wintering birds may spend up to six months at a single location.

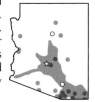

AMERICAN ROBIN, *Turdus migratorius*

Description: 10″. Large, plump thrush with **broken white eye crescents**; brick-red breast. MALE: Head blackish. FEMALE: Head concolor with back. JUVENILE: Heavily spotted. **Similar Species:** Paler-headed Rufous-backed Robin (above) lacks eye crescents, has bright black-and-white striped throat, and rufous back. **Voice:** Typically a four-part, sing-song, reedy carol; also sharp *keup* and squealing *kitty-pup* calls. **Status:** Common in summer (Apr-Sep); common but irregular in winter (Oct-Mar). **Habitat:** Summer: Mountain canyon groves and openings within coniferous forests, also occasionally breeds in city parks and river valley groves. Winter: Desert oases and urban areas; foothill and mountain canyon groves and woodlands; open pine forests, usually below snow line. **Elevations:** Summer 450′-11,300′; Winter 100′-8,400′. **Behavior:** In summer feeds on earthworms and grubs. Winter flocks seek berries and fruit. **Noteworthy:** Migrant and winter flocks may number from a handful to several hundred birds.

SWAINSON'S THRUSH

"Russet-backed"

"Olive-backed"

HERMIT THRUSH

"auduboni"

"guttatus"

SWAINSON'S THRUSH, *Catharus ustulatus*

Description: 7". Plump, spot-breasted thrush with bold, **buffy eyering**; ear patch edged in buff; **buff wash on breast**; flanks vary from olive-brown to tinged with rufous. **Similar Species:** Hermit Thrush (below) has white eyering and contrasting reddish tail. <u>Veery</u>, with gray flanks and smaller, blurrier chest spots, was a very local breeder on Little Colorado River near Eager through 1980. **Voice:** Liquid *whoit* call; musical song is rich paired notes on ascending scale: *wood-whoit, wh-white, whittle-whit* etc. **Status:** Rare and local in summer (early Jun-Aug); uncommon migrant (late Apr-early Jun and Sep-Oct). **Habitat:** Summer: Mountain spruce-fir forest and dense stream-side thickets. Migration: Desert oases; foothill and mountain canyon groves; meadow edges. **Elevations:** Summer 7,800'-9,800'; Migration 100'-9,300'. **Behavior:** Feeds on insects and fruit deep within shady woodland understory. **Noteworthy:** In migration the Pacific coast "Russet-backed" form of Swainson's Thrush, *C. u. ustulatus*, is more common than the Arizona's breeding "Olive-backed" race, *C. u. swainsoni*, from the Rocky Mountains.

HERMIT THRUSH, *Catharus guttatus*

Description: 6.75". Plump, spot-breasted thrush with white eyering; contrasting **reddish rump and tail**; grayish flanks. **Similar Species:** Swainson's Thrush (above) has buffy face pattern and lacks contrasting reddish tail. **Voice:** Call is sharp *chuk-chuk*; also whining *vreee*. Ethereal song begins with clear note, following by several quick, silvery, paired harmonics; successive songs on different pitches. **Status:** Fairly common. **Habitat:** Summer (May-Sep): Undergrowth in mountain canyon groves and coniferous forest. Winter (Oct-Apr): Thickets in desert oases, valley, foothill, and mountain canyon groves. **Elevations:** Summer 5,200'-11,300'; Winter 100'-7,900'. **Behavior:** When water is available, drinks frequently. **Noteworthy:** Summer breeding birds are large, pale gray *C. g. auduboni* of the interior west. Most wintering birds are dark, olive-brown *C. g. guttatus* of the northwest Pacific coast.

Varied Thrush
Male

Female

Aztec Thrush
Male

Female

VARIED THRUSH, *Ixoreus naevius*

Description: 9.5". **Robin-like** thrush with **orange eyebrow, throat,** and **complex orange wing pattern**. MALE: Black mask and breast-band. FEMALE: Dusky mask and breast-band. **Similar Species:** American Robin (p. 357) lacks orange eyebrow, throat, and wing pattern. **Voice:** Deep *tchupp* notes. Song, a long "policeman's whistle" note on one pitch, is followed by a pause of 2-10 seconds, before it's repeated, often on a different pitch. **Status:** Rare in winter (mid Oct-mid May). **Habitat:** Desert oases and urban areas; valley, foothill, and mountain canyon groves. Rare in coniferous forest. **Elevations:** Winter 150'-7,600'. **Behavior:** Forages on ground for insects, also eats seeds and berries. Shy, prefers dense understory. **Noteworthy:** Similarities in wing pattern led legendary Arizona taxonomist Allen Phillips to believe Varied Thrush was closely related to Aztec Thrush.

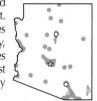

AZTEC THRUSH, *Ridgwayia pinicola*

Description: 9.25". **Blackish, robin-like** thrush with **complex white wing pattern**. MALE: Black hood and back. FEMALE: Dark brown head and back streaked with white. JUVENILE: Brown with heavy white scaling on head and underparts. **Similar Species:** Smaller juvenile Spotted Towhee (p. 409) has shorter, thicker bill and lacks white-streaked crown. **Voice:** High *tseeer* notes; thin, hypersonic *tzeee* calls. **Status:** Accidental in spring (May-early Jun); rare but irregular in late summer (mid Jul-Sep), not seen every year; accidental in winter (Jan-early Feb). **Habitat:** Mountain canyon groves, usually near springs or streams. **Elevations:** Summer 4,900'-7,400'. **Behavior:** Forages primarily for berries in Arizona, especially chokecherries in late summer. Inconspicuous, even when plucking berries. May remain motionless on perches for long periods. **Noteworthy:** The first two records of Aztec Thrush in Arizona were both in May, 1978.

Cedar Waxwing

Phainopepla
Male

Female

CEDAR WAXWING, *Bombycilla cedrorum*

Description: 7". Plump, sleek, cinnamon, and highly sociable berry-eater with black mask and **relaxed crest; yellow-tipped tail**. **Similar Species:** Larger female Northern Cardinal (p. 471) has stout, orange bill, mostly red wings and tail—and is usually alone or with mate. Larger, gray <u>Bohemian Waxwing</u> (acc. in Feb, 1984 at Flagstaff) has cinnamon undertail coverts. **Voice:** Almost inaudible, high-pitched reedy *seee* calls. Large flock in chorus sounds like a steam kettle. **Status:** Fairly common but irregular in winter (mid Sep-mid May); rare statewide in summer (mid May-mid Sep). **Habitat:** Desert oases and urban plantings; valley, foothill, and lower mountain canyon groves. **Elevations:** Winter 100'-7,900'. **Behavior:** Singles occur, but Waxwings typically gather in flocks numbering a few to over 50. Feeds on berries of all varieties. **Noteworthy:** Nomadic; some winters none are found where they were common the preceding year.

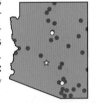

PHAINOPEPLA, *Phainopepla nitens*

Description: 7.5". Slim, silky, **long-tailed** berry-eater with **red eyes** and **spiky crest**. MALE: Black. FEMALE: Gray with white wing edgings. FLIGHT: Male shows white crescents in wings. **Similar Species:** Larger female Pyrrhuloxia (p. 471) has stubby bill, red-tinged wings and tail. **Voice:** Liquid *querp* calls; also quizzical *pretty you?* followed by affirmative *pretty you*. **Status:** Common resident; as mistletoe berries disappear in spring, some move from lower western to higher eastern habitats (May-Aug). **Habitat:** Desert oases and urban plantings; valley and foothill groves. Summer: Also uses lower mountain canyon groves. **Elevations:** Summer 100'-8,500'; Winter 100'-6,600'. **Behavior:** Mistletoe specialist; eats other berries and flycatches. Nests at lower elevations in spring and higher elevations in summer. Forms small flocks after fledging young. **Noteworthy:** Males construct nests alone, but females help incubate, brood, and feed the young.

American Pipit

Sprague's Pipit

AMERICAN PIPIT, *Anthus rubescens*

Description: 6.25". Slender, **dark-faced** pipit with mostly **plain back**; dark legs; long tail with white outer edges. BREEDING: Largely unstreaked underparts. NONBREEDING: Breast and flanks streaked. **Similar Species:** Sprague's Pipit (below) is stockier with pale face, dark-streaked back, obvious white wingbars, pink legs, and short tail. **Voice:** Calls include thin *tseep* and doubled *pi-pit*. **Status:** Common but local in summer (May-Aug); fairly common in winter (late Sep-early May). **Habitat:** Summer: Barren rock and grassy patches above timberline; Winter: Open desert flats; barren pond and river edges; barren fields, golf courses, and turf farms. **Elevations:** Summer 11,000'-12,600'; Winter 100'-7,100'. **Behavior:** Terrestrial, constantly pumping tail as it searches for insects. Forms large winter flocks. **Noteworthy:** Nesting on the San Francisco Peaks north of Flagstaff and possibly in the White Mountains above 11,000', American Pipit is the only Arizona bird that breeds exclusively above timberline.

SPRAGUE'S PIPIT, *Anthus spragueii*

Description: 6". Dumpy, **pale-faced** pipit with **large, dark eye; heavily streaked back**; white wingbars; pink legs; **short tail** with white outer tail feathers. FLIGHT: Flashes white outer tail feathers when flushed. Switchbacks high into sky, then plummets until just above the ground. **Similar Species:** See American Pipit (above). Juvenile Horned Larks (p. 309) molt into adult plumage before Sprague's Pipits arrive in fall. **Voice:** High, thin *squint* note, usually repeated, delivered in flight. **Status:** Rare in winter (early Oct-early Apr). **Habitat:** Native short grass prairie, grassy desert valleys, and lush pasturelands. **Elevations:** Winter 200'-5,500'. **Behavior:** Singles or twosomes, rarely more, lurk in grass and are usually not detected until flushed. **Noteworthy:** With experience, Sprague's distinctive flight style may be sufficient for identification.

European Starling
Breeding

Nonbreeding

House Sparrow
Male

Female

EUROPEAN STARLING, *Sturnus vulgaris*

Description: 8.5". Stocky, **blackish** bird with **straight, sharp bill; short, squared tail**. BREEDING: **Yellow bill**; lustrous purple head and green back. NONBREEDING: Bill black; body spangled white. JUVENILE: Gray-brown. FLIGHT: Broad-based, triangular wing silhouette. **Similar Species:** Female Red-winged Blackbird (p. 417) is striped–not spotted. **Voice:** Buzzy *dzrrrr* call. Varied mechanical song of buzzes, clicks, rattles, and squeals. **Status:** Common resident, rare above 9,000' in summer. **Habitat:** Urban areas, farms, and ranches, and nearby riparian groves. **Elevations:** Resident 100'-8,300'. **Behavior:** Waddles on ground and probes for food. Also consumes fruit, grain, and insects. Will usurp saguaro cavities from native birds. Large post-breeding flocks may number in the thousands. **Noteworthy:** White spotting in winter wears away by February to reveal breeding plumage. Introduced to New York in 1890, European Starlings arrived in Arizona in 1946.

HOUSE SPARROW, *Passer domesticus*

Description: 6.25". **Chunky, sparrow-like bird** from Eurasia with a stout bill; **one white wingbar**. MALE: **Black bib, gray crown**; whitish cheeks; striped brown back. FEMALE: Dull yellowish bill; broad, creamy eyebrow; tan and brown back stripes. **Similar Species:** Male Harris's Sparrow (p. 403) lacks a gray crown. In winter, nonbreeding female Thick-billed Longspur (p. 379) lacks female House Sparrow's solid crown and broad back stripes. **Voice:** Cheerful *chirp* or *cheep* notes; song is monotonous series of call notes. **Status:** Common resident. **Habitat:** Urban areas, towns, farms, and ranches. **Elevations:** Resident 100'-8,300'. **Behavior:** Forages for waste foods on ground. Forms small nesting colonies. **Noteworthy:** In 1851 House Sparrows were introduced in New York City, and they arrived in Tucson in 1903.

Cassin's Finch
Male

Female

"Pacific" Purple Finch
Male

Female

House Finch
Male

Female

CASSIN'S FINCH, *Haemorhous cassinii*

Description: 6.25". Stocky red finch with **long, straight bill** and distinct facial stripes; **pale eyering; crisp, contrasting back streaks**; short tail. MALE: Reddest on erectable cap. FEMALE: Underparts white with crisp, dark streaks. **Similar Species:** Purple Finch (below) lacks eyering and crisp, contrasting back streaking. Male Purples have darker red spread more evenly across head. Female Purples have blurry, low-contrast streaking below. **Voice:** Rich *chid-r-rew* calls. Song is rich, slightly reedy caroling, like virtuoso House Finch. **Status:** Uncommon in summer (mid Apr-Oct); irregular and uncommon in winter (Nov-mid Apr). **Habitat:** Summer: Mountain pines and meadow edges. Winter: Desert oases to mountain pines. **Elevations:** Summer 6,750'-9,500'; Winter 200'-9,100'.

"PACIFIC" PURPLE FINCH, *Haemorhous purpureus californicus*

Description: 6". Stocky red finch with **slightly curved bill** and distinct facial stripes; **low-contrast back streaks**; undertail coverts typically lack streaks; short tail. MALE: Uniform red on cap and throat. FEMALE: Underparts off-white with blurry streaks. **Status:** Rare in migration and winter (mid Oct-Apr). **Habitat:** Desert oases; valley, foothill, and mountain canyon groves. **Elevations:** Winter 150'-7,200'. **Noteworthy:** Usually numbers 1-5 birds, often with House or Cassin's Finches.

HOUSE FINCH, *Haemorhous mexicanus*

Description: 5.75". **Slim** red finch with **stubby, curved bill** and indistinct eyebrow; **long tail**. MALE: Red with heavily streaked flanks. FEMALE: Unpatterned face; underparts off-white with blurry streaks. **Similar Species:** Cassin's and Purple Finches (above) have larger bills, bigger heads, striped facial patterns, and short, notched tails. **Voice:** Call is upslurred query *beerr? beerr?* Song is cheerful warble that includes burry notes. **Status:** Common resident, most withdraw from high elevations in winter. **Habitat:** Urban areas; widespread from desert scrub to open pine forest. **Elevations:** Summer 100'-9,500'; Winter 100'-7,500'.

369

PINE GROSBEAK

Male

Female

RED CROSSBILL

Male

Female

PINE GROSBEAK, *Pinicola enucleator*

Description: 9". Dapper finch with **small black bill** and **gray crescent below eyes**; dove gray belly; long notched tail. MALE: Red head and reddish mottled chest. FEMALE: Mustard yellow head. JUVENILE: Lacks white wingbars. **Similar Species**: Stocky female Evening Grosbeak (p. 373) has massive, apple green bill. **Voice:** Chiming call notes, as if from a tiny bell; loud, rich, warbling *whe-wheedle-wee* song. **Status**: Uncommon resident; casual irruptive in winter (Nov-Mar). **Habitat:** Summer: Spruce-fir forest, especially adjacent to moist alpine meadows. Winter: Coniferous forest edges. **Elevations:** Summer 9,250'-10,500'; Winter 6,800'-9,500'. **Behavior:** Staple foods include spruce seeds and buds, but also forages on grass seeds in clearings. Forms winter flocks of up to 25 birds. **Noteworthy:** The small population breeding in the White Mountains represents the southernmost U.S. outpost of this circumpolar, boreal species.

RED CROSSBILL, *Loxia curvirostra*

Description: 6.25". Stocky, big-headed finch with **crossed mandible tips**; long, dark wings; short, notched tail. MALE: Red or orange. FEMALE: Grayish-olive; yellow highlights on crown, breast, and rump. JUVENILE: Streaked brown; short mandibles. **Similar Species:** Female Cassin's Finch (p. 369) lacks crossed mandibles. White-winged Crossbill (accidental at Grand Canyon Nov, 2007 and in Lukachukai Mountains Dec, 2017) has two white wingbars. **Voice:** Smacking *kip kip kip* calls. **Status:** Irregularly fairly common resident; irruptions below 3,000' (Nov-Mar), usually 5-10 years apart. **Habitat:** Pines from urban areas to mountain tops. **Elevations:** Summer 5,500'-11,000'; Winter 400'-9,500'. **Behavior:** Uses strong, crossed bill to extract seeds from cones. Nests in early winter. **Noteworthy:** Accidental as a breeder in Aleppo pines in Phoenix and Tucson. In Arizona most breeding birds are Type 2 or "Ponderosa Pine Crossbills"; in SE Arizona many are Type 6 "Sierra Madre Crossbills," the largest-billed of all 7 types.

Black Rosy-Finch

Gray-crowned Rosy-Finch

Evening Grosbeak Male

Evening Grosbeak Female

BLACK ROSY-FINCH, *Leucosticte atrata*

Description: 6.25". **Blackish finch** with broad gray hind-crown; rosy belly. BREEDING: Black bill; rosy-pink wing patch. NONBREEDING: Yellow bill; scaly black back and underparts. **Similar Species:** Gray-crowned Rosy-finch (below) has warm brown back. **Voice:** Noisy--like a House Sparrow chorus. **Status:** Irregularly uncommon in irruption years in winter (late Nov-mid Mar). **Habitat:** Sparsely vegetated Great Basin desert. **Elevations:** Winter 5,000'-7,500'. **Behavior:** Occurs in flocks of up to 80. **Noteworthy:** Most years no Rosy-Finches are reported from Arizona.

GRAY-CROWNED ROSY-FINCH, *Leucosticte tephrocotis*

Description: 6.25". **Warm brown finch** with broad gray hind-crown; limited pink on shoulders. BREEDING: Black bill; deep pink flanks. NONBREEDING: Yellow bill; rows of blackish-tipped brown back feathers and ill-defined brown scaling on underparts. **Status:** May occur in winter (early Dec-mid Mar) as singles or pairs in large flocks of Black Rosy-Finches (above). **Elevations:** Winter 5,000'-7,500'.

EVENING GROSBEAK, *Coccothraustes vespertinus*

Description: 7". Chunky finch with **massive pale bill; black wings with white patches**; short tail. MALE: Brownish-black head and neck with yellow crescent on forehead. FEMALE: Gray head and yellow nape. **Similar Species:** Larger Yellow Grosbeak (p. 475) has dark bill and yellow head. **Voice:** Pleasant--but sharp--whistle: *pew-w!* **Status:** Uncommon in summer (mid Mar-mid Nov); irregular and usually rare in winter (mid Nov-mid Mar). **Habitat:** Summer: Mountain mixed coniferous forest. Winter: Mountain canyons and lower coniferous forest; casual in desert oases and foothill groves. **Elevations:** Summer 6,200'-9,500'; Winter 400'-7,900'. **Behavior:** Primarily searches for seeds in canopy. **Noteworthy:** In winter irruptions—usually every 5-10 years—flocks away from breeding areas may number from 2 to several hundred.

Pine Siskin

Lawrence's Goldfinch
Male

Female

PINE SISKIN, *Spinus pinus*

Description: 4.75". Small, **streaky finch** with **sharp, straight bill**; yellow wing edges. FLIGHT: **Yellow stripes on underwings**; yellow patches at base of tail. **Similar Species:** Larger female House Finch (p. 369) has bigger, blunt bill and lacks yellow in the wing or tail. **Voice:** Burry questioning *bzzzeee?* rising at end. Song is stuttering *What d'ya what d'ya see see.* **Status:** Fairly common but erratic in summer (Jun-Jul), some withdraw from elevations above 7,500' in winter; common but erratic in winter (Aug-May). **Habitat:** Summer: Mountain coniferous forest. Winter: Desert oases; valley, foothill, and mountain canyon groves; mountain coniferous forest. **Elevations:** Summer 5,500'-11,300'; Winter 100'-8,500'. **Behavior:** Nomadic; flocks—sometimes over 100 birds—follow seed crops after breeding. **Noteworthy:** Pine Siskins are possible throughout the year anywhere in Arizona. Numbers at feeders peak from mid March-mid May. The name "Siskin" is meant to mimic its common call.

LAWRENCE'S GOLDFINCH, *Spinus lawrencei*

Description: 4.5". Small **gray finch** with **stubby gray bill; yellow accents in wings**; yellow blush on chest. MALE: Black foreface. FEMALE: Gray head. **Similar Species:** Nonbreeding female American Goldfinch (p. 377) has lemon yellow surrounding its eyes and a brownish back. **Voice:** Violin-string *tooeee.* Jumbled tinkling imitations of other bird calls, each repeated several times. **Status:** Irregularly rare to fairly common in winter (late Sep-Apr); very rare in summer (May-late Sep), but has nested in SW lowlands. **Habitat:** Weed patches in desert oases, and valley, foothill, and lower mountain canyons, usually near water. **Elevations:** Winter 100'-6,900'. **Behavior:** Forages for seeds in weeds and shrubs. **Noteworthy:** Small to large numbers are present in Arizona every winter, especially during migration peaks in Oct and Mar, but every 3-10 years a major irruption sweeps Lawrence's Goldfinches east to the New Mexico state line.

375

Lesser Goldfinch
Male

Female

American Goldfinch
Nonbreeding Male

Breeding Male

LESSER GOLDFINCH, *Spinus psaltria*

Description: 4.5". Small, yellow finch with **sharp, dark bill;** white flash marks in wings. MALE: Black cap. **Similar Species:** Larger nonbreeding American Goldfinch (below) has thicker bill, limited yellow on face and throat, brownish back, and white undertail coverts. **Voice:** Plaintive *tleeee?* or *wheer?* rising at end. Song is complex, rapid repetitions of local bird calls delivered in minor key. **Status:** Common resident. **Habitat:** Usually near water. Summer (May-Oct): Desert oases and urban areas to mountain coniferous forest. Winter (Nov-Apr): Desert oases to lower mountain canyon groves. **Elevations:** Summer 100'-11,300'; Winter 100'-8,300'. **Behavior:** Forages for seeds in weeds, shrubs, and trees. Found in pairs and flocks throughout the year. Recorded nesting every month but December. **Noteworthy:** Almost all male Lesser Goldfinches in Arizona are "Green-backed" color morph; "Black-backed" color morph is quite rare.

AMERICAN GOLDFINCH, *Spinus tristis*

Description: 5". Small yellow finch with **thick bill; solid dark wings with one broad white wingbar;** white undertail coverts. BREEDING: Pink bill; yellow underparts. NONBREEDING: Black bill; yellow on face and throat; brownish back. **Similar Species:** Smaller Lawrence's Goldfinch (p. 375) has gray back and lacks mostly black wings. **Voice:** Violin-string *toe'o'weee*. Song consists of high, sweet, run-on phrases, oft-repeated. **Status:** Rare wanderer in summer (early May-mid Sep), casual nester at mid-elevations in NE. Irregularly rare to uncommon in winter (mid Sep-early May). **Habitat:** Desert oases; valley, foothill, and lower mountain canyon groves, usually near water. **Elevations:** Summer 1,200'-9,500'; Winter 100'-8,200'. **Behavior:** Forages for seeds in weeds, shrubs, and trees. **Noteworthy:** Most Arizona birds are in nonbreeding plumage. Exhibits alternate plumage April through September.

BREEDING

NONBREEDING

Thick-billed
Longspur

Chestnut-collared
Longspur

Lapland
Longspur

THICK-BILLED LONGSPUR, *Rhynchophanes mccownii*

Description: 6". Stout longspur with **large pinkish bill**; dull ear-patch lacking dark rear border; sometimes-concealed chestnut "shoulder bar" on upper wing. BREEDING MALE: Black cap; black breast-band. NONBREEDING: Unstreaked dusky breast. FLIGHT: **Inverted black "T" on white tail**. **Similar Species:** Nonbreeding Chestnut-collared Longspur (below) has small dark bill, dark but broken rear margin of ear-patch, mottled black underparts, and—in flight—black triangle on white tail. **Status:** Uncommon in winter (mid Oct-Apr). **Habitat:** Valley short grass savanna with bare patches; barren pastures; plowed fields; sod farms. **Elevations:** Winter 300'-5,500'. **Noteworthy:** Usually found mixed in flocks of Horned Larks. Male does not develop black bill while in Arizona.

CHESTNUT-COLLARED LONGSPUR, *Calcarius ornatus*

Description: 5.75". Small longspur with **small bill**; **white eyering**; dark but broken rear margin of ear-patch; short tail. BREEDING MALE: Yellow bill; yellow foreface; chestnut hind-collar. NONBREEDING: Dusky coral bill; mottled black underparts. FLIGHT: **Black triangle on white tail**. **Similar Species:** Larger nonbreeding Lapland Longspur (below) lacks eyering and blotches on breast; in flight shows white outer tail feathers. **Voice:** Repeated rattling *chiddle* calls. **Status:** Common in winter (Oct-mid Apr), forming large flocks. **Habitat:** Short valley grasslands; sod farms; barren stock tank margins. **Elevations:** Winter 200'-7,000'.

LAPLAND LONGSPUR, *Calcarius lapponicus*

Description: 6.25". Slender longspur with **sharp bill**; heavy rear ear-patch outline; long wings and tail. BREEDING MALE: Yellow bill; black foreface and chestnut hind-collar. NONBREEDING: Dusky coral bill; **rusty panel on mid-wing**. FLIGHT: **White outer tail feathers**. **Status:** Rare in winter (mid Oct-Apr). **Habitat:** Valley savanna with bare patches and barren pastures; plowed fields; sod farms. Usually a single or twosome with other longspur species. **Elevations:** Winter 300'-5,100'.

379

Cassin's Sparrow

Botteri's Sparrow

CASSIN'S SPARROW, *Peucaea cassinii*

Description: 6″. Flat-headed sparrow with **black-spotted back**; gray underparts with sparse, **narrow flank streaks**; long, round-tipped tail. FLIGHT: Narrow **white tail corners**. **Similar Species:** Botteri's Sparrow (below) has short, black back-streaks and unmarked, pale buff underparts. Botteri's is subtly warmer brown overall than Cassin's. Both species are best identified by their distinctive songs. **Voice:** Slow, poignant song begins with short chips segueing into trills *pi-ti-d-deeeee-deee-dee*. **Status:** Resident uncommonly reported in spring (mid Mar-May) and fairly commonly reported in summer (Jul-Sep); rarely detected when silent in early summer (Jun) and in winter (Oct-mid Mar). **Habitat:** Valley mesquite grasslands, especially in lightly grazed areas; accidental below 1,000′. **Elevations:** Summer 600′-5,900′; Winter 2,500′-4,300′. **Behavior:** Males "skylark," rising 10-20 feet, then gradually descend with head cocked and tail spread, singing all the while. **Noteworthy:** Displays, singing, and breeding are strongly correlated to summer rains. Cassin's Sparrows also sing in springs following wet winters.

BOTTERI'S SPARROW, *Peucaea botterii*

Description: 6″. Flat-headed sparrow with short **black streaks on back**; unmarked pale buff underparts; long, round-tipped tail. FLIGHT: Narrow gray tail corners. **Similar Species:** See Cassin's Sparrow (above). Best identified by song. **Voice:** Several hesitant notes on different pitches accelerating into one or more trills. **Status:** Resident uncommonly reported in spring (May-late Jun) and fairly commonly reported in summer (late Jun-Sep); rarely detected when silent in winter (Oct-Apr). **Habitat:** Mesquite grasslands in valleys and in gently rolling terrain, especially sacaton grass, within 80 miles of Mexico. **Elevations:** Resident 2,200′-5,600′. **Behavior:** Does not skylark like Cassin's Sparrow. Males may sing from inside mesquite trees, as well as low exposed perches. **Noteworthy:** Breeding coincides with the summer monsoon rains.

Rufous-winged Sparrow

Rufous-crowned Sparrow

RUFOUS-WINGED SPARROW, *Peucaea carpalis*

Description: 5.75". Flat-headed sparrow with **double black whiskers**; divided rufous crown; **rufous shoulder patch** helpful if visible; long, round-tipped tail. **Similar Species:** Smaller Chipping Sparrow (p. 389) lacks double black whisker stripes and has notched tail. **Voice:** One or two introductory notes followed by hard, extended trill *pit-pit-deeeeeee*. **Status:** Fairly common resident. **Habitat:** Primarily level or gently sloping grassy desertscrub and valley mesquite grassland; foothill mesquite and hackberry thickets. **Elevations:** Resident 1,400'-5,600'. **Behavior:** Feeds on seeds and insects on the ground in pairs or in family groups; breeding is timed to take advantage of additional food available during the summer rainy season. **Noteworthy:** One of the last North American birds described to science when discovered near Tucson in 1872, the entire U.S. range of Rufous-winged Sparrow is limited to southern Arizona and the extreme SW corner of New Mexico.

RUFOUS-CROWNED SPARROW, *Aimophila ruficeps*

Description: 6". Flat-headed sparrow with obvious **short white eyebrow and eyering** on dark face; single **heavy black whisker**; rufous crown; long, round-tipped tail. **Similar Species:** Smaller Chipping Sparrow (p. 389) lacks heavy black whisker stripe framing white throat and has a notched tail. No other solidly "rufous-crowned" sparrow in its habitat. **Voice:** Excited *dear dear* calls, usually doubled or tripled. Song is fast, jumbled chatter notes. **Status:** Fairly common resident. **Habitat:** Foothill and mountain rocky or brushy slopes within desertscrub, thornscrub, chaparral, and woodland vegetation. Strays into flat desert lowlands. **Elevations:** Resident 1,500'-7,800'. **Behavior:** Forages on the ground for seeds and insects, usually in pairs. **Noteworthy:** Nests in spring, as well as during the summer monsoon season.

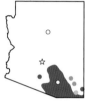

Brown-backed

Five-striped Sparrow

Black-throated Sparrow

Juvenile

FIVE-STRIPED SPARROW, *Amphispizopsis quinquestriata*

Description: 6". Gray-headed sparrow with **five white head stripes**: eyebrows, whiskers, and throat; brown back; gray breast with black spot; white belly. **Similar Species:** Smaller Black-throated Sparrow (below) has four white head stripes and big black bib. **Voice:** Raspy *chept* calls. Squeaky song with deliberate *whee-whee* and *chept* notes and chattered *fa-la-la* figures tunelessly combined. **Status:** Uncommon and local in summer (mid Apr-Sep); rarely detected in winter (Oct-mid Apr). **Habitat:** Hillside foothill thornscrub, usually near permanent water, usually within 30 miles of Mexico. **Elevations:** Resident 3,500'-4,800'. **Behavior:** Although pairs begin to sing in May, frequency of song increases as the summer progresses, and reaches its peak after the onset of the rainy season. **Noteworthy:** Entirely confined to Arizona within the U.S., the first record of a Five-striped Sparrow was in 1957 in the foothills of the western Santa Rita Mountains.

BLACK-THROATED SPARROW, *Amphispiza bilineata*

Description: 5.5". **Black-and-white-headed** sparrow with **big black bib**. JUVENILE: Gray head with bold white eyebrows and white throat; gray-streaked breast. FLIGHT: Black tail with white corners. **Similar Species:** See Five-striped Sparrow (above). Bell's and Sagebrush Sparrows (p. 387) lack long white eyebrow and black bib. **Voice:** Lisping *pizz* and tinkling calls. Song is pleasant, musical *je-je-jeeeeeee* ending with trill. **Status:** Common resident in S. Arizona; common in summer (late Mar-early Sep) and rare in winter (early Sep-late Mar) in N. Arizona. **Habitat:** Desertscrub, valley mesquite grassland, foothill thornscrub, and lower mountain chaparral. Wanders up to lower edge of Ponderosa pines. Avoids inner cities. **Elevations:** Summer 100'-6,900'; Winter 100-5,000'. **Behavior:** Forages on the ground for seeds and insects, usually in pairs and family groups. **Noteworthy:** Black-throated is Arizona's most widespread and numerous breeding sparrow.

Bell's Sparrow

Sagebrush Sparrow

BELL'S SPARROW, *Artemisiospiza belli canescens*

Description: 6". **Lead gray-headed** sparrow with white eyering and white accents on forehead; curving white mustache underlined by **broad, black stripe; finely streaked or unstreaked, brownish-gray back** does not contrast with nape. **Similar Species:** Paler Sagebrush Sparrow (below) has white moustache bordered below by thin gray line; tan, dark-streaked back contrasts with mouse gray nape. **Voice:** Rapid *twee* and *sip* calls. **Status:** Rare in winter (mid Oct-Feb). **Habitat:** Treeless deserts and valleys with somewhat uniform-sized and evenly-spaced shrubs, especially saltbush flats. **Elevations:** Winter 150'-1,800'. **Behavior:** Cocks tail as it forages on ground. Usually runs--instead of flies--from potential danger. **Noteworthy:** Bell's was split from Sagebrush Sparrow (below) in 2013. During winter at low elevations in SW Arizona, both species may occur together.

SAGEBRUSH SPARROW, *Artemisiospiza nevadensis*

Description: 6". **Pale gray-headed** sparrow with white eyering and white accents on forehead; curving white mustache underlined by **thin, gray stripe; dark-streaked, tan back** contrasts with pale gray nape. **Similar Species:** Darker Bell's Sparrow (above) has mustache bordered below by bold black line; unstreaked or finely streaked back does not contrast with nape. **Voice:** Tinkling *tic* calls. Evocative and reedy *twee dweedle-dee dweedle-dee* song. **Status:** Fairly common in summer (mid Mar-Sep); uncommon in winter (Oct-mid Mar). **Habitat:** Summer: Sagebrush flats and valleys. Winter: Level or gently-sloping, treeless deserts and valleys with somewhat uniform-sized and evenly-spaced shrubs, especially in saltbush flats, less commonly in creosote associations. **Elevations:** Summer 5,000'-7,000'; Winter 100'-7,000'. **Behavior:** Cocks tail as it forages on ground. Sings from bush tops. **Noteworthy:** The breeding population in Arizona is noticeably reduced in drought years.

Chipping Sparrow
Breeding

Nonbreeding

Clay-colored Sparrow
Nonbreeding

Nonbreeding

CHIPPING SPARROW, *Spizella passerina*

Description: 5.5". Small-billed, slender sparrow with **dark lores**; gray breast; **gray rump**; long, cleft tail. BREEDING: Chestnut cap; white eyebrow. NONBREEDING: Pink bill; pale gray crown stripe. **Similar Species:** Nonbreeding Clay-colored Sparrow (below) has creamy white crown stripe, pale buff lores, sandy eyebrows, well-defined dark whisker, buffy breast, and buffy rump. <u>American Tree Sparrow</u> (casual mid Nov-Feb) has bicolored bill, yellow below, rufous eyeline, cinnamon flanks, and a spot on its whitish chest. **Voice:** Call is soft *tik* note. Song is long, dry trill. **Status:** Common in summer (Apr-Sep); common and more widespread in migration and winter (mid Aug-mid May). **Habitat:** Summer: Grassy mountain pinyon-juniper and pine-oak woodlands, and Ponderosa pine forest. Winter: Openings within deserts, valleys, foothills, and lower mountain canyon groves. **Elevations:** Summer 4,200'-9,600'; Winter 100'-7,600'. **Behavior:** Often forms large winter flocks. **Noteworthy:** From winter to winter, numbers at a site may vary widely.

CLAY-COLORED SPARROW, *Spizella pallida*

Description: 5.5". Small-billed, slender sparrow with central crown stripe; **pale buff lores**; pale cream to sandy eyebrows; **bold whisker**; buffy breast; **buff rump**; long, cleft tail. NONBREEDING: Pink bill; pale gray crown stripe. **Similar Species:** Nonbreeding Chipping Sparrow (above) has pale gray crown stripe, dark lores, gray eyebrows, gray breast, and gray rump. **Voice:** Call is soft *tik* note. Song is four short, cicada-like buzzes. **Status:** Uncommon in fall migration (Sep); rare in winter and spring (Oct-mid May). **Habitat:** Open areas with grass or weed patches within deserts, valleys, and mountain canyon outlets, often near water. **Elevations:** Winter 950'-6,900'; Migration 100'-7,400'. **Behavior:** Forages on the ground. **Noteworthy:** In Arizona, Clay-colored is often a lone bird or a twosome in a flock of Chipping, Brewer's, or other sparrows. Most are single day migrants, but occasional birds overwinter.

Brewer's Sparrow
Adult

Black-chinned Sparrow
Breeding Male

Female

BREWER'S SPARROW, *Spizella breweri*

Description: 5.25". Small-billed, slender sparrow with **finely-streaked crown** lacking distinct central stripe; **complete white eyering**; dull grayish-brown breast; **gray-brown rump** concolor with back; long, cleft tail. **Similar Species:** Nonbreeding Clay-colored Sparrow (p. 389) has obvious central crown stripe, pale buff lores, sandy eyebrows, well-defined dark whiskers, and pale buff breast. **Voice:** Call is thin *tik* note. Song is varied series of long, dry trills and buzzes. **Status:** Fairly common in summer (early May-late Aug); common in winter (late Aug-early May). **Habitat:** Summer: High desert sagebrush and saltbush plains, valleys, and foothills. Winter: Open, gentle terrain within deserts, valleys, savannas, foothills, and lower mountain canyon outlets. **Elevations:** Summer 4,500'-8,400'; Winter 100'-5,300'. **Behavior:** Forms large flocks in winter. **Noteworthy:** In Arizona, numbers of Brewer's Sparrows and the areas they use for wintering may change from one year to the next.

BLACK-CHINNED SPARROW, *Spizella atrogularis*

Description: 5.75". Small-billed, slender sparrow with pink bill; **dark-streaked rusty back**; plain gray head and underparts; long, cleft tail. MALE BREEDING (mid Mar-Aug): **Black foreface and throat. Similar Species:** "Gray-headed" and "Red-backed" races of Dark-eyed Junco (p. 405) have solid rusty backs and white outer tail feathers. **Voice:** Weak, thin *seet* calls. Song is several short whistles accelerating into trill, like a bouncing ball-bearing coming to rest. **Status:** Fairly common resident. **Habitat:** Summer (May-Sep): Mid-elevation mountain chaparral and pinyon-juniper woodlands. Winter (Oct-Apr): Foothill and lower mountain canyon thickets. Occasionally uses riparian shrubbery and reeds adjacent to brushy slopes. **Elevations:** Summer 3,500'-8,200'; Winter 200'-5,600'. **Behavior:** May join other sparrows in winter flocks. **Noteworthy:** In Central and SE Arizona, some Black-chinned Sparrows are probably only altitudinal migrants, wintering downslope directly below their breeding territories.

Vesper Sparrow

Savannah Sparrow

Grasshopper Sparrow

VESPER SPARROW, *Pooecetes gramineus*

Description: 6.25". Large grassland sparrow with long pink bill, dusky on culmen; **white eyering**; finely-streaked crown; often concealed rufous shoulder patch. FLIGHT: Long tail with **white outer tail feathers**. **Voice:** Chipping *tipt* notes; Sweet song, often delivered at evening "vespers" is *Here here, where?*, and short descending trills. **Status:** Fairly common in summer (mid Apr-mid Sep); common in winter (mid Sep-mid Apr). **Habitat:** Summer: Grasslands and mountain meadows with woody shrubs, small trees, or fence posts for song perches. Winter: Desert and valley savanna, fields, and openings next to ponds and rivers. **Elevations:** Summer 5,600'-9,500'; Winter 100'-5,300'. **Behavior:** Often uses obvious perches. Vesper Sparrows usually winter in small flocks.

SAVANNAH SPARROW, *Passerculus sandwichensis*

Description: 5.5". Small grassland sparrow with **small bill**; well-defined **eyebrow, often yellow between eye and bill**; finely-streaked crown; densely-streaked breast; short, notched tail. **Voice:** Chipping *sipt* notes; Song begins with buzzy introductory chips, a long trill, and a bitten-off chip note. **Status:** Uncommon and local in summer (May-Sep); common in winter (Sep-Apr). **Habitat:** Summer: Wet highland meadows. Winter: Desert and valley grasslands, fields, and openings, often next to ponds, rivers, streams, and marshes. **Elevations:** Summer 8,000'-9,500'; Winter 100'-7,100'. **Behavior:** Not shy; uses conspicuous perches.

GRASSHOPPER SPARROW, *Ammodramus savannarum*

Description: 5". Small grassland sparrow with large flat head; large bill; **yellow-orange between eye and bill; creamy crown stripe**; unstreaked breast; short tail. **Voice:** Insect-like buzz. **Status:** Fairly common in summer (Apr-Sep), but usually inconspicuous before the rains; uncommon in winter (Oct-Mar). **Habitat:** Summer: Tall valley grasslands, especially when ungrazed. Winter: Desert and valley grasslands, primarily in SE Arizona. **Elevations:** Summer 3,400'-5,300'; Winter 350'-7,900'.

Baird's Sparrow

Lark
Sparrow

Lark Bunting
Nonbreeding

Breeding

BAIRD'S SPARROW, *Centronyx bairdii*

Description: 5.5". Small grassland sparrow with large, flat head; large bill; **ochre face; orange crown stripe**; contrasting back streaking; **narrow band of breast streaks**; short tail. **Similar Species:** Savannah Sparrow (p. 393) lacks mostly orange face, orange crown stripe, and narrow, sharply defined band of breast streaks. Smaller Grasshopper Sparrow (p. 393) lacks markings on cheek and has unstreaked breast. **Voice:** High, dry *pit*. **Status:** Uncommon in winter (Sept-Apr). **Habitat:** Tall valley grasslands. **Elevations:** 3,300'-5,300'. **Behavior:** Often solitary and usually shy.

LARK SPARROW, *Chondestes grammacus*

Description: 6.25". **Chestnut-and-white-headed** sparrow with central breast spot. FLIGHT: **Large white tail corners. Similar Species:** Distinctive. **Voice:** Weak *pink* calls. Fast "rock-and-rattle" song like mockingbird on caffeine. **Status:** Fairly common resident; withdraws from N. Arizona in winter (Oct-Mar). **Habitat:** Summer: Valley mesquite grasslands, rolling foothill oak savanna, arid prairies, and open pinyon-juniper woodlands. Winter: Open desert oases, valley groves, pastures, weedy fields, and open woodlands. **Elevations:** Summer 2,200'-9,500'; Winter 100'-4,300'. **Behavior:** During migration (Apr-mid May and Aug-Sep) flocks of 5-100 birds occur from desert oases to mountain meadows.

LARK BUNTING, *Calamospiza melanocorys*

Description: 6.5". **Big sparrow** with **big blue bill; white wing crescents**. BREEDING MALE (May and late Jul-Aug): Black with white wings. FLIGHT: White inner-wing patches; white tail corners. **Voice:** Sweet *heww* calls. **Status:** Irregular but usually common in migration and winter (late Jul-mid May). **Habitat:** Desert and valley openings, grasslands, farm fields, and pastures. **Elevations:** Winter 300'-6,800'; Migration 250'-7,100'. **Behavior:** Usually in flocks as it forages, occasionally numbering more than 100 birds. **Noteworthy:** Migrants have been recorded in every month, but are only casual in June.

395

FOX SPARROW

"Slate-colored"

"Red"

"Sooty"

Description: 7". Large, stocky sparrow with big **yellow-based bill; reddish wings and tail**; white breast with arrowhead-shaped spots. Other markings depend on subspecies.
SLATE-COLORED: Gray head and back; red rump; dark spots on underparts.
RED: Red crown and facial pattern; red back streaks; gray rump; red spots on underparts.
SOOTY: Brownish head and back; brown rump; dark spots densely-packed on breast.

Similar Species: Smaller Song Sparrow (p. 399) is similar to "Red" race of Fox Sparrow, but lacks yellow on bill, has contrasty back streaks, and lacks Red Fox's extensive, arrowhead-shaped spots below.

Voice: Call for Slate-colored and Red races is a smacking *chep* note; Sooty Fox Sparrow has a higher *chip* note. Song, heard after late March, is rich, caroling series of trills.

Status: Uncommon in winter (mid Oct-mid Apr). Casual in early fall (early Sep-mid Oct).

Habitat: Desert oases; valley, foothill, and lower mountain canyon groves; rarely found in deciduous groves within Ponderosa pine stands.

Elevations: Winter 200'-8,000'.

Behavior: Towhee-like, uses both feet simultaneously to scratch the ground for seeds and insects.

Noteworthy: There are four field recognizable subspecies groups of Fox Sparrows, regarded by some taxonomists as separate species. "Slate-colored," *P. i. schistacea*, is the most common race wintering in Arizona. "Red" Fox Sparrows, *P. i. zaboria* and *P. i. altivagans* are rare in our region. "Sooty," *P. i. townsendi*, from the Pacific coast is casual. The aptly-named "Thick-billed" Fox Sparrow, *P. i. stephensi*, from California, is accidental— there are two records from SW Arizona.

Song Sparrow "Mountain"

Song Sparrow "Desert"

Lincoln's Sparrow

Swamp Sparrow

SONG SPARROW, *Melospiza melodia*

Description: 6". Gray-faced sparrow with **rusty eyestripes**; whitish whisker; white throat; **rust or brown-streaked white breast**; central breast spot; reddish wings; long reddish tail. FLIGHT: Low; pumps tail. **Similar Species:** Larger "Red" Fox Sparrow (p. 397, rare in winter) has thicker, yellow-based bill, and extensive, arrowhead-shaped spots on underparts. **Voice:** Husky *chimp* calls. Midway through every song a harsh buzz introduces final notes. **Status:** Common resident, most withdraw from highlands in winter (Sep-Mar). **Habitat:** Prefers still or sluggish waters with wetland plants. **Elevations:** Summer 100'-9,300'; Winter 100'-7,300'. **Noteworthy:** During winter (Sep-Apr) some larger, darker "Mountain" Song Sparrows, *M. m. montana*, of N. Arizona and the Rocky Mountains migrate to S. Arizona and may use brushy areas away from water. "Desert" Song Sparrow, *M. m. fallax*, is resident in S. Arizona.

LINCOLN'S SPARROW, *Melospiza lincolnii*

Description: 5.5". Gray-faced sparrow with small bill; **buffy malar stripe; buffy wash on black-streaked chest**; short tail. **Similar Species:** Larger Song Sparrow (above) has a big bill and a white whisker. **Voice:** Smacking *tchep* and thin *zeet* calls. Song is a mixture of quick notes, ending with a trill. **Status:** Uncommon and local in summer (early May-mid Sep); irregular but usually common in winter (mid Sep-early May). **Habitat:** Summer: Wet mountain meadow willow and alder thickets. Winter: Desert oases; valley, foothill, and lower mountain canyon underbrush. **Elevations:** Summer 7,300'-11,000'; Winter 100'-7,000'.

SWAMP SPARROW, *Melospiza georgiana*

Description: 5.75". Gray-faced sparrow with small bill; contrasty **white throat**; faintly-streaked **gray chest**; wine-red wings and short tail. **Similar Species:** Lincoln's Sparrow (above) has a buff chest with sharp streaks. **Voice:** Snappy *pick* calls. **Status:** Uncommon in winter (Nov-mid Apr). **Habitat:** Marshy wetlands. **Elevations:** Winter 100'-7,100'.

WHITE-THROATED SPARROW

White-striped Adult

Tan-striped

WHITE-CROWNED SPARROW

"Gambel's" Adult

"Mountain" Adult

Immature

WHITE-THROATED SPARROW, *Zonotrichia albicollis*

Description: 6.25". Stocky, stripe-crowned sparrow with **gray bill; yellow lores; white throat**; rich rufous wings; dark gray breast; long tail. WHITE-STRIPED ADULT: Immaculate white eyebrows behind yellow lores; black head stripes. TAN-STRIPED ADULT: Soft beige eyebrows behind yellow lores; brown head stripes. **Similar Species:** White-crowned Sparrow (below) has orange bill; lacks yellow lores and white throat. **Voice:** Ringing *pink* note. Quavering, slowly whistled *sweet dream-free sleep sleep sleep*. **Status:** Uncommon in winter (Oct-May); casual (late Sep and early Jun). **Habitat:** Desert oases; valley, foothill, and lower mountain canyon underbrush. **Elevations:** Winter 100'-7,000'. **Behavior:** White-striped morph adults sing more than tan-striped morph adults. **Noteworthy:** First recorded in Arizona in 1939. Usually occurs as 1 or 2 birds in a flock of White-crowned Sparrows.

WHITE-CROWNED SPARROW, *Zonotrichia leucophrys*

Description: 6.5". Stocky, stripe-crowned sparrow with **orange bill;** Adults have white eyebrows and crown. GAMBEL'S ADULT: Gray lores. MOUNTAIN ADULT: Tar-black lores. IMMATURE: Buff crown stripe; brown head stripes. **Similar Species:** White-throated Sparrow (above) always has gray bill and yellow lores. **Voice:** Bleated *pinch* note. Reedy whistled song ending with trills and buzzes. **Status:** Uncommon and local in summer (May-mid Sep); common in winter (mid Sep-May, rarely Jun). **Habitat:** Summer: Stunted conifers at timberline. Winter: Desert, valley, foothill, and lower mountain canyon openings, grasslands, farms, pastures, brushy edges, and urban areas. **Elevations:** Summer 10,700'-11,800'; Winter 100'-7,100'. **Behavior:** Forms winter flocks. **Noteworthy:** "Gambel's," *Z. l. gambelii*, is the common wintering race. Except for small breeding enclaves on Arizona's two highest peaks, "Mountain" White-crown, *Z. l. oriantha*, with black lores is only regular in migration (Sep and May), uncommon in winter. White-crowned Sparrow is considered Arizona's most abundant wintering land bird.

Harris's Sparrow
Nonbreeding

Immature

Breeding

Golden-crowned Sparrow
Immature

Breeding

HARRIS'S SPARROW, *Zonotrichia querula*

Description: 7.25". Large, stocky, **black-crowned** sparrow with **flesh bill; black bib**; white belly; long tail. BREEDING: Gray cheeks. NONBREEDING: Tawny cheeks. IMMATURE: Tawny head with black-tinged crown; white throat; "necklace" of short, black streaks on breast. **Similar Species:** Male House Sparrow (p. 367) has gray crown and large whitish cheeks. **Voice:** Imperious *peak* note. Quavering, slowly-whistled *fee bee be*. **Status:** Rare in winter (Nov-Apr); Casual in Oct and until late May. **Habitat:** Desert oases; valley, foothill, and lower mountain canyon underbrush. **Elevations:** Winter 500'-7,100'. **Behavior:** Hop-and-scratch foraging style. Primarily terrestrial; uses low perches. **Noteworthy:** Usually found within flocks of White-crowned Sparrows (p. 401), often when it appears with them at a feeding station. Many records pertain to immatures.

GOLDEN-CROWNED SPARROW, *Zonotrichia atricapilla*

Description: 6.75". Large, stocky, **yellow-crowned** sparrow with **dark bill**; brownish flanks; long tail. BREEDING: Yellow forecrown bordered by broad black stripes. NONBREEDING: Muted crown pattern. IMMATURE: Yellow forehead; subtly bicolored bill blackish above and pinkish below. **Similar Species:** Immature White-crowned Sparrow (p. 401) has bill entirely orange and shows well-defined eyebrow. **Voice:** Breathy *chep* notes. Very clear, slowly-whistled *oh dear me*, deeper pitched than Harris's Sparrow. **Status:** Rare in winter (mid Oct-early May); casual earlier from mid Sep and later to mid-Jun. **Habitat:** Desert oases; valley, foothill, and lower mountain canyon underbrush. **Elevations:** Winter 100'-7,100'. **Behavior:** Hop-and-scratch foraging style. Primarily terrestrial; uses low perches. **Noteworthy:** Usually found within flocks of White-crowned Sparrows (p. 401), often when it appears with them at a feeding station. Most records pertain to immatures, but adults in breeding plumage have been recorded.

DARK-EYED JUNCO

"Slate-colored" Male

Female

"Oregon" Male

Female

"Gray-headed" Adult

"Pink-sided" Adult

"Gray-headed" Juvenile

"SLATE-COLORED" DARK-EYED JUNCO, *Junco hyemalis hyemalis*

Description: 5.75". Pink bill; **concolor nape and back**; white central belly; white outer tail feathers. MALE: Blackish upperparts. FEMALE: Uniform brownish-gray upperparts lack distinct hood. **Status:** Rare in winter (late Sep-mid May). **Habitat:** Desert oases to mountain tops. **Elevations:** Winter 100'-9,000'. **Behavior:** Usually a solitary bird joining a mixed flock of other juncos. **Voice:** All races have a snapping *pit* note.

"OREGON" DARK-EYED JUNCO, *Junco hyemalis montanus and others*

Description: 5.75". Pink bill; **dark hood**; reddish-brown back; rufous flanks; white central belly; white outer tail feathers. MALE: Black or slaty hood. FEMALE: Gray hood. **Status:** Common in winter (late Sep-May). **Habitat:** Desert oases and urban areas to mountain tops. **Elevations:** Winter 100'-10,800'. **Behavior:** Flocks with other junco races. **Noteworthy:** Most common race of desert and valley junco.

"PINK-SIDED" DARK-EYED JUNCO, *Junco hyemalis mearnsi*

Description: 6". Pink bill; dark lores; **blue-gray hood** with paler gray throat; brownish back; **pinkish-cinnamon flanks**; white central belly; white outer tail feathers. **Status:** Common in winter (late Sep-mid May). **Habitat:** Desert oases and urban areas to mountain tops. **Elevations:** Winter 100'-10,300'. **Behavior:** Flocks with other junco races.

"GRAY-HEADED" DARK-EYED JUNCO, *Junco hyemalis caniceps*

Description: 6". **Gray head** with pink bill; dark lores; reddish back; gray flanks; white outer tail feathers. JUVENILE: Heavily streaked. **Voice:** Sweet, fast *chew-cheh-cheh-cheh*. Call is a snappy *pit*. **Status:** Fairly common but local in summer (mid May-mid Sep); common in winter (mid Sep-mid May). **Habitat:** Summer: Coniferous forest north of Grand Canyon and in NE Arizona. Winter: Desert oases and urban areas to pine forests on mountain tops. **Elevations:** Summer 7,000'-9,800'; Winter 350'-9,800'. **Noteworthy:** Usually the common race in mountains.

"Red-backed" Dark-eyed Junco

Yellow-eyed Junco
Adult

Juvenile

"RED-BACKED" DARK-EYED JUNCO, *Junco hyemalis dorsalis*

Description: 6". **Bicolored bill** with blackish upper mandible and **silvery or grayish lower mandible**; dark lores; gray head with **pale gray throat**; red back, red occasionally extending onto the wings; white outer tail feathers. **Similar Species:** "Gray-headed" Dark-eyed Junco (p. 405) has a smaller, all-pink bill and lacks contrasting paler gray throat. **Voice:** Rich, variegated song is like Yellow-eyed Junco; colorless snapping *pit* note. **Status:** Common resident, some descend to nearby lower elevations in winter (mid Oct-early Apr). **Habitat:** Summer: Ponderosa pine and mixed conifer communities. Winter: A few visit SE Arizona desert oases and urban areas, as well as foothill and mountain canyons. **Elevations:** Summer 5,600'-11,300'; Winter 2,300'-9,000'. **Noteworthy:** Away from breeding grounds, most winter records come from feeding stations.

YELLOW-EYED JUNCO, *Junco phaeonotus*

Description: 6.25". **Bicolored bill** with black upper mandible and **yellow lower mandible**; dark lores; **yellow eyes**; gray head with pale gray throat; red back, red often extending onto the wings; white outer tail feathers. JUVENILE: Gray eyes and heavily streaked body. **Similar Species:** "Red-backed" Dark-eyed Junco (above) has a dark eye and silver lower mandible. **Voice:** Snapping *pit* note. Song begins with a series of rich introductory notes on one pitch, followed by variegated trills. **Status:** Common resident, some post-breeding dispersal to lower canyons (Aug-Sep); some withdraw from high elevations to perimeter canyons in winter (Oct-Apr). **Habitat:** Mountain coniferous forests; upper pine-oak woodland; shady canyon groves. **Elevations:** Summer 5,000'-10,000'; Winter 3,400'-9,100'. **Behavior:** Typically does not flock with other junco races and does not form flocks larger than family groups. **Noteworthy:** In the U.S., resident only in SE Arizona, primarily in mountains with summits above 8,000', and—rarely—adjacent New Mexico.

Green-tailed Towhee

Spotted Towhee
Male

Juvenile

Female

GREEN-TAILED TOWHEE, *Pipilo chlorurus*

Description: 7.25". Chestnut-capped towhee with **snow-white throat**; white whisker; **broad green edgings on wings and tail**. **Similar Species:** Smaller Five-striped Sparrow (p. 385) lacks chestnut cap, green edgings. **Voice:** Plaintive *meww* call or very high, thin *tsip*. Song is variable trill *tip seeo see tweeeee chchchch*. **Status:** Fairly common in summer (mid May-Aug); common migrant (Apr-mid May and Sep-Oct); irregular and typically uncommon in winter (Nov-Mar). **Habitat:** Summer: Montane thickets in upper canyon groves, stream edges, and successional new brush on meadow borders and regenerating burns. Winter: Brushy desert arroyos, oasis thickets, and urban plantings; valley, foothill, and lower canyon brush. **Elevations:** Summer 6,400'-11,300'; Winter 100'-7,000'. **Behavior:** Often under dense cover but is curious, and frequently pops up when it hears a pish. **Noteworthy:** Some years almost no Green-tailed Towhees winter in SW Arizona.

SPOTTED TOWHEE, *Pipilo maculatus*

Description: 8.25". **Hooded** towhee with red eyes; **white-spotted back and wings; rufous sides**. MALE: Black head. FEMALE: Slaty head. JUVENILE: Brown head; heavily streaked back and sides. **Similar Species:** Immature Aztec Thrush (p. 361) has much longer, thinner bill and heavily streaked head. Eastern Towhee, accidental in winter (Dec-Feb), lacks white spots on back or shoulders. **Voice:** Harsh *beerrrh* call; song ends with trill: *brh brh she-e-e-e-e-rh*. **Status:** Fairly common in summer (May-Sep); common in winter (Oct-Apr). **Habitat:** Summer: Thickets within mountain canyon groves, chaparral, dense pine-oak woodland, and scrub within Ponderosa pine forest. Winter: Thickets and dense cover in foothill and lower mountain canyon groves and chaparral; irregular and rare in valley oases in western lowlands. **Elevations:** Summer 3,500'-9,500'; Winter 100'-8,500'. **Behavior:** Usually hidden but noisy, calling and scratching leaf litter inside thickets. **Noteworthy:** Spotted Towhee is the resident mountain towhee in most of Arizona.

Canyon Towhee

Abert's Towhee

CANYON TOWHEE, *Melozone fuscus*

Description: 8.5". Brownish-gray towhee with a dull rufous cap; **buffy throat outlined by necklace of streaks**; usually a central breast spot. **Similar Species:** Larger Abert's Towhee (below) has pale silvery bill accentuated by blackish foreface. Overall, Albert's is a warmer brown. **Voice:** Hoarse *hic-cup* call; sudden squabbling bursts; typical song is abrupt introductory note followed by a five or six dull whistles, *chop wee-wee-wee-wee-weeds*. **Status:** Common resident. **Habitat:** Dense areas of desertscrub; valley grasslands with thickets; arid foothill canyons and thornscrub; dry lower mountain canyons, chaparral, and woodlands. **Elevations:** Resident 1,000'-7,300'. **Behavior:** Forages for seeds and insects on the ground. Usually found in pairs. **Noteworthy:** This is the most confiding towhee, often under cars, picnic tables, and farm machinery in rural areas.

ABERT'S TOWHEE, *Melozone aberti*

Description: 9". **Silver-billed** towhee with a **black foreface**; warm brown body; ochre crissum. **Similar Species:** Smaller, grayer Canyon Towhee (above) has a dull rufous cap and a buffy throat bordered by a necklace of streaks. **Voice:** Penetrating *pink* call; song is several accelerating calls followed by squealing chatter *pink-pink-pink-cheh-cheh-cheh-cheh-cheh*. **Status:** Fairly common resident. **Habitat:** Flatlands with dense cover and usually nearby permanent water, such as desert oases, pecan farms, and urban areas; valley and broader foothill canyon groves with cottonwood, willow, and mesquite overstories. **Elevations:** Resident 100'-5,300'. **Behavior:** Forages for seeds and insects on the ground. Usually found in pairs. **Noteworthy:** Abert's Towhee is essentially confined to the lower Colorado River drainage, largely within Arizona.

Dickcissel
Immature

Breeding Male

Bobolink
Breeding Male

Breeding Female

DICKCISSEL, *Spiza americana*

Description: 6.25". Triangular-billed grassland bird with long, **yellowish eyebrow** and broad lower eyering; **rufous shoulder patch; yellow wash on chest**. BREEDING MALE: Black triangle on throat. NONBREEDING ADULT: Lacks black throat. IMMATURE: Yellow on face and breast faint or absent; streaked sides. **Similar Species:** Larger nonbreeding Bobolink (below) has obvious crown stripes, lacks rufous on shoulder, and is entirely yellow below. **Voice:** Electric buzzer *bzzzt* call. Song is burry *dic-chee-chee or dic-chee-chee-cheh*, reminiscent of its name. **Status:** Uncommon fall migrant (mid Aug-mid Oct); casual in spring (Apr-May); otherwise accidental. **Habitat:** Desert oases and feeding stations; valley farms and fields; pond and lake shores. **Elevations:** Migration 200'-8,300'. **Behavior:** Forages on the ground but often perches in short trees. **Noteworthy:** Dickcissels in Arizona usually occur singly, infrequently in small flocks.

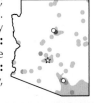

BOBOLINK, *Dolichonyx oryzivorus*

Description: 7". Triangular-billed grassland bird with **spiny-tipped tail**. BREEDING MALE: Black with buffy hindhead; white slashes in wings; white rump. NONBREEDING: Pink bill; blank buff face with brown stripes; yellowish below with pin-striped flanks. **Similar Species:** Nonbreeding Dickcissel (above) has yellow on face confined to above eye and on malar stripe, and shows a rufous shoulder patch. **Voice:** Rough *tech* calls and *quink* notes. Song is a cascading, jingling series of notes that accelerates at the end. **Status:** Casual migrant (May-early June and mid Aug-mid Oct); accidental in summer. **Habitat:** Desert oases; valley fields and reedbeds adjacent to ponds. **Elevations:** Migration 450'-6,700'. **Behavior:** Often forages in tall grasses or weeds; male sings in flight. **Noteworthy:** Most recent Bobolink records pertain to nonbreeding birds. Until the early 1980s, Bobolinks bred in mid-elevation moist meadows and hay fields in central Arizona.

413

"Lilian's"
Eastern Meadowlark

Nonbreeding

Western Meadowlark

Nonbreeding

"LILIAN'S" EASTERN MEADOWLARK, *Sturnella magna lilianae*

Description: 9". **Clear-cheeked** meadowlark with contrasting **dark head stripes**. BREEDING: Black chest chevron. FLIGHT: Stiff wings; four completely white outer tail feathers. **Similar Species:** Western Meadowlark (below) shows brown head stripes, darker cheeks that do not contrast with eye stripes, and less white in tail. **Voice:** Burry *drrrt* calls. High, piercing *for-fear, fear-oh-dear* song. Meadowlarks best separated by voice. **Status:** Common in summer (Mar-Sep); most withdraw from higher elevations in winter (Oct-Feb). **Habitat:** Valley grasslands, farm fields, and pastures. **Elevations:** Summer 2,500'-9,400'; Winter 750'-8,000'. **Behavior:** Males sing from obvious perches and usually have two mates. **Noteworthy:** Some authorities consider "Lilian's" Meadowlark, the only form in Arizona, a full species.

WESTERN MEADOWLARK, *Sturnella neglecta*

Description: 9". **Dirty-cheeked** meadowlark with low-contrast **brownish head stripes**. BREEDING: Yellow malar blends with throat. FLIGHT: Stiff wings; three white outer tail feathers with dark outer edges. **Similar Species:** "Lilian's" Eastern Meadowlark (above) shows darker head stripes, paler cheeks that contrast with eye stripes, white malar stripe, and whiter tail. **Voice:** Loud *cluck* calls. Rich, musical song of flute-like notes. **Status:** Common resident, most withdrawing from lower elevations in summer (Mar-Sep) and most withdrawing from higher elevations in winter (Sep-Mar). Primarily a migrant (Sep-Oct and Feb-Mar) in lower Colorado and Gila River Valleys. **Habitat:** Open desert and valley grasslands; farm fields and pastures; grassy plateaus and large montane meadowlands. **Elevations:** Summer 100'-9,200'; Winter 100'-7,100'. **Behavior:** Elaborate dome nests are often accessed through tunnels in dense grasses. In winter occurs from singles to 50 or more birds. **Noteworthy:** The breeding birds in S. Arizona are almost exclusively confined to lowland agricultural areas.

MALE

FEMALE

Red-winged Blackbird

Male

Yellow-headed Blackbird

Male

RED-WINGED BLACKBIRD, *Agelaius phoeniceus*

Description: 8″. Sharp-billed marsh blackbird. MALE: **Black body; red epaulets** with yellow rear border. FEMALE: **Obvious eyebrow; heavily streaked** above and below. **Similar Species:** European Starling in nonbreeding plumage (p. 367) has slender bill, white spots above and below, and short tail; blackish breeding Starlings have yellow bills. **Voice:** Dry *chek* call. Song often transcribed as *Uncle Lee-e-e-e.* **Status:** Common resident; northern migrants swell population in winter. **Habitat:** Marshes; rivers, ponds and lakes with emergent vegetation; irrigated fields and pastures; feedlots. **Elevations:** Resident 100′-9,400′. **Behavior:** Forages on seeds and insects in reeds, rank weed growth, farms, and on waste grain. Colonial nester. Males often have harems of five or more females. **Noteworthy:** Thousands of Red-winged Blackbirds may gather on a single winter roost.

YELLOW-HEADED BLACKBIRD, *Xanthocephalus xanthocephalus*

Description: 9.5″. Sharp-billed marsh blackbird with **yellow head**. MALE: Bright yellow head and chest. FEMALE: Dull yellow face; dusky brown body. MALE IN FLIGHT: **White crescents on upperwing**. **Similar Species:** Smaller female Brewer's Blackbird (p. 421) lacks yellow face and is very gray–not brownish. **Voice:** Loud *kuck* notes. Rasping *ye-ow ow-ow* song seems forced. **Status:** Uncommon in summer (mid Apr-Aug); common in winter (Sep-mid Apr). **Habitat:** Marshes; ponds and lakes; irrigated fields and pastures; feedlots. **Elevations:** Summer 100′-9,100′; Winter 100′-5,700′. **Behavior:** Forages in reeds, pastures, fields, and feed lots. Colonial nester. Males usually have harems of two to five females. **Noteworthy:** Males are the main component of winter roosts of Yellow-headed Blackbirds in Arizona. In 1973 a winter flock was estimated at over one-half million birds.

417

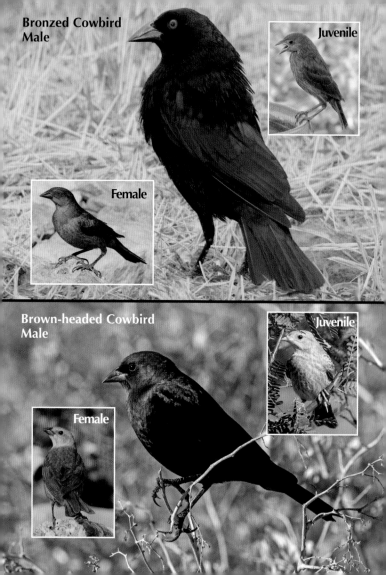

Bronzed Cowbird
Male

Juvenile

Female

Brown-headed Cowbird
Male

Juvenile

Female

BRONZED COWBIRD, *Molothrus aeneus*

Description: 8". Stocky cowbird with **long, thick bill; red eyes**. MALE: Glossy; expandable ruff. FEMALE: Sooty gray. JUVENILE: Brownish; dark eyes; streaked below. **Similar Species:** Smaller Brown-headed Cowbird (below) has shorter bill and brown eyes. Females are streaked below; juveniles are typically more yellowish than juvenile Bronzed. **Voice:** Dry rattles and strained *wheeer* sounds. Hypersonic whistles like escaping steam. **Status:** Fairly common in summer (Apr-Aug); uncommon and local in winter (Sep-Mar). **Habitat:** Desert oases, feedlots, and urban parks up to mountain canyon groves. **Elevations:** Summer 100'-5,400'; Winter 100'-3,700'. **Behavior:** Forages primarily in grassy areas. Male inflates neck feathers as it performs helicopter display flight several feet above one or two females. Lays eggs in the nests of other bird species. **Noteworthy:** Summer range of Bronzed Cowbird mirrors that of Hooded Oriole, its primary nest host.

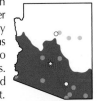

BROWN-HEADED COWBIRD, *Molothrus ater*

Description: 7". Slim cowbird with conical bill; **dark eyes**. MALE: Brown head and neck. FEMALE: Neutral brown with vague streaking below. JUVENILE: Paler than female, usually tinged yellowish; obvious streaking below. **Similar Species:** See Bronzed Cowbird (above). **Voice:** Dry rattles. Pleasant, liquid song is high *glu-glu-glu-gleee*, piercing at end. **Status:** Fairly common in summer (Apr-Jul); common but local in winter (Aug-Mar). **Habitat:** Summer: Desert oases and urban areas; farms, ranches, and feedlots; mountain canyon groves, pinyon-juniper, and forest edges. Winter: Lower elevation valleys, especially feedlots and farm fields. **Elevations:** Summer 100'-9,300'; Winter 100'-4,900'. **Behavior:** Lays eggs in the nests of other bird species. Forms large winter flocks, frequently with other blackbird species. **Noteworthy:** The primary hosts of Arizona Brown-headed Cowbirds are Black-tailed Gnatcatchers, Yellow Warblers, and Bell's Vireos.

MALE

FEMALE

Brewer's Blackbird

Rusty Blackbird
Nonbreeding

BREWER'S BLACKBIRD, *Euphagus cyanocephalus*

Description: 9". Slender, medium-sized blackbird. MALE: Glossy purple head with **pale yellow eyes**; greenish gloss on body. FEMALE: **Dark eyes**; sooty beige. **Similar Species:** Brownish nonbreeding Rusty Blackbird (below) has very slender bill, pale yellow eyes, pale eyebrows, rusty edges on wing feathers, and contrasting gray rump. **Voice:** Deep *chupt* call. Emits nasal notes and a noisemaker *squeezzit* song. **Status:** Common in summer (May-Sep) and in winter (Oct-Apr), when most withdraw from high elevations and population is augmented by northern migrants. **Habitat:** Summer: Wetlands wild and urban, including marshy meadows, wet pastures, stock ponds, lake shores, lawns, parks, and golf courses. Winter: Open desert and valley grasslands, farm fields, pastures, and feedlots. Also urban parks, golf courses, and cemeteries. **Elevations:** Summer 5,600'-9,500'; Winter 100'-7,000'. **Behavior:** Forages on the ground in open areas for seeds and insects. Forms flocks in winter. **Noteworthy:** Brewer's Blackbird frequently occurs in mixed flocks that include Red-winged and Yellow-headed Blackbirds, Brown-headed Cowbirds, and European Starlings.

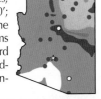

RUSTY BLACKBIRD, *Euphagus carolinus*

Description: 9". Slender, medium-sized blackbird with **very slender bill** and **pale yellow eyes**. BREEDING MALE: Glossy black. NONBREEDING ADULT: Warm brown head, back, and underparts; **pale eyebrows; rusty edges on wing feathers; contrasting sooty gray rump. Similar Species:** Female Brewer's Blackbird (above) has dark eyes and is sooty gray overall; males have shorter, thicker bills. Larger female grackles (p. 423) lack contrasting gray rumps. **Voice:** Soft *tchek* notes. **Status:** Rare in winter (Nov-Mar). **Habitat:** Open desert oases; irrigated pastures, stock and sewage ponds; river shallows. **Elevations:** Winter 1,000'-6,800'. **Behavior:** Often occurs with Brewer's Blackbirds. **Noteworthy:** Most observations in Arizona involve single Rusty Blackbirds in winter plumage.

421

Great-tailed Grackle Male

Female

Common Grackle Male

Female

GREAT-TAILED GRACKLE, *Quiscalus mexicanus*

Description: Male: 16"; female: 11.5". **Very large blackbird** with large bill and pale yellow eyes; **very long, keeled tail**. MALE: Glossy purple-black of head gradually blends with blue-black tone of body. FEMALE: **Dull brown** with paler eyebrow and throat. **Similar Species:** Much smaller Common Grackle (below) shows abrupt contrast between purple foreparts and bronzy-green body. **Voice:** Squeaky *wi-wi-wi-wi-wheep!* and other creaky calls—as if its voice box needs oiling. **Status:** Common resident in S. Arizona; fairly common but local in N. Arizona, some withdraw from highest elevations in winter (mid Sep-early Mar). **Habitat:** Desert oases; flatlands with some trees and water, especially urban areas, parks, golf courses, and farms; mountain lakeshores. **Elevations:** Resident 100'- 9,000'. **Behavior:** Forages opportunistically. Nests colonially. Males are polygamous. Forms flocks in winter. **Noteworthy:** Great-tailed Grackles apparently followed agricultural development from Mexico into Arizona in 1935, when they were first reported from Safford.

COMMON GRACKLE, *Quiscalus quiscula*

Description: 12.5". **Large blackbird** with stout bill and pale yellow eyes; **glossy purplish-blue head contrasts with bronzy-green body**; long, keeled tail. **Similar Species:** Much larger male Great-tailed Grackle (above) not as colorful and lacks abrupt contrast between purple-black foreparts and blue-black body. Smaller male Brewer's Blackbird (p. 421) has thin bill and lacks keeled tail. **Voice:** Emphatic *bzeeet!* and other creaky calls—like a child playing horn instrument first time. **Status:** Rare in winter (mid Oct-mid May). **Habitat:** River valleys and flatlands, especially urban area lawns, feeding stations, golf courses, and farms. **Elevations:** Winter 200'-7,700'. **Behavior:** Forages opportunistically. **Noteworthy:** Common Grackles apparently followed agricultural development from New Mexico into NE Arizona in 1980. Records usually involve single birds present for one day, infrequently longer.

MALE	FEMALE
Hooded Oriole	
Orchard Oriole	
Streak-backed Oriole	

HOODED ORIOLE, *Icterus cucullatus*

Description: 7.5". Slender oriole with **long, curved bill**; long tail. MALE: Golden with black back; back scaly in winter. YEARLING MALE: Reduced black foreface. FEMALE: Yellow below; olive back. **Similar Species:** Female/yearling male Orchard Oriole (below) has short, straight bill, contrasting wingbars, short tail, and is lemon-yellow below. **Voice:** *Check-check* scolds; *wink* calls; fast, rollicking song of scolds, calls, and whistles. **Status:** Fairly common in summer (Mar–mid Oct); rare in winter (mid Oct–Feb). **Habitat:** Summer: Desert oases and urban areas; valley, foothill, and lower mountain canyon groves. Winter: Urban areas, especially hummingbird feeding stations. **Elevations:** Summer 100'–7,400'; Winter 100'–4,600'. **Behavior:** Palms, cottonwoods, and sycamores are frequent nest substrates, but will even use porch eaves.

ORCHARD ORIOLE, *Icterus spurius*

Description: 6.75". Compact oriole with **short, straight bill**; white wingbars on blackish wing. BREEDING MALE: Black and chestnut. YEARLING MALE: Lemon-yellow below; black lores and throat. FEMALE: Lemon-yellow below; grayish-olive back. **Status:** Rare migrant and winter visitor (mid Aug–mid Jun). **Habitat:** Desert oases and urban areas; valley, foothill, and lower mountain canyon groves. **Elevations:** Winter 100'–5,700'.

STREAK-BACKED ORIOLE, *Icterus pustulatus*

Description: 8.25". Large oriole with **straight, thick-based bill**; black lores and narrow black throat; **streaked back**. MALE: Orange crown, cheeks, and breast. FEMALE: Tinged orange. **Similar Species:** Smaller Hooded Oriole (above) has thinner, more curved bill, and male's back is solid black or, in winter, scaly black–never streaked. **Voice:** Chattering scolds; whistled *wheap* call. Song is *tu-wheap-sweet-pea tu-wheap tu-wheap*. **Status:** Rare and irregular in winter (mid Oct–Apr); otherwise casual, but has nested. **Habitat:** Desert oases and urban areas; pecan orchards; valley cottonwood groves; foothill groves. **Elevations:** Year-round 100'–4,700'.

Bullock's Oriole Male

Female

Baltimore Oriole Male

Immature Male

Scott's Oriole Male

First Year Female

BULLOCK'S ORIOLE, *Icterus bullockii*

Description: 7.75". Stocky oriole with **straight bill** and distinct eyebrow; **bright orange cheeks**. MALE: Orange with white wing panel. YEARLING MALE: Black lores and throat. FEMALE: Whitish belly. **Similar Species:** Female/yearling male Baltimore Orioles (below) lack eyebrows and have drab cheeks; usually not as pale-bellied as Bullock's. **Voice:** Husky *chek* scolds, sometimes in series. Song is whistled variant of *witchy-gee-goo-goo*. **Status:** Fairly common in summer (early Mar-Sep); rare in winter (Oct-early Mar). **Habitat:** Desert oases; valley, foothill, and lower mountain canyon groves; highland deciduous trees. **Elevations:** Summer 100'-8,400'; Winter 100'-4,100'.

BALTIMORE ORIOLE, *Icterus galbula*

Description: 7.75". Stocky oriole with **straight bill; bright orange breast.** MALE: Black hood and orange underparts. IMMATURE MALE: Drab cheeks; older birds show black lores and throat. FEMALE: Drab brownish cheeks. IMMATURE FEMALE: Whitish belly. **Status:** Rare migrant (mid Apr-Jun and late Aug-mid Oct); otherwise casual. **Habitat:** Desert oases; valley, foothill, and lower mountain canyon groves. Found once in mountain coniferous forest. **Elevations:** Migration 250'-7,200'.

SCOTT'S ORIOLE, *Icterus parisorum*

Description: 8". **Yellow** oriole with **long, straight, and sharp bill.** MALE: Black hood. YEARLING MALE: Blackish face and bib. FEMALE: Dusky streaking on back; may have blackish face and breast. **Similar Species:** Black-vented Oriole, accidental mid April and July, has all black tail and lacks any white in wings. **Voice:** Harsh *chack* note; whistled *perp?* call. Song is musical whistle that includes word *Albuquerque*. **Status:** Fairly common in summer (early Mar-mid Oct); rare in winter (mid Oct-early Mar). **Habitat:** Desertscrub with ocotillo; mesquite and yucca grasslands; foothill oak savanna; mountain chaparral; pine-oak and pinyon-juniper woodlands. **Elevations:** Summer 700'-8,400'; Winter 2,700'-5,400'.

Olive Warbler
Male

Female

Orange-crowned Warbler
L.c. orestera

Orange-crowned Warbler
L.c. lutescens

OLIVE WARBLER, *Peucedramus taeniatus*

Description: 5.25″. Pine-loving warbler look-alike of the mountains. **Dark ear patches form "bandito" mask**; lacks any flank streaking. MALE: Orange head with ink-black ear patch. FEMALE: Head is yellow and ear is dull charcoal. **Similar Species:** Female Hermit Warbler (p. 445) lacks mask, usually shows faint to solid black triangle on throat. **Voice:** Calls are breathy, bluebird-like *feww* notes; song is repetitive *pita-pita-pita*. **Status:** Fairly common summer resident (Apr-Sep), primarily in SE Arizona; rare in winter (Oct-Mar). **Habitat:** Summer: Mountain coniferous forest, especially in Ponderosa pines. Winter: Foothill and lower mountain canyon groves. **Elevations:** Summer 6,000′-10,000′; Winter 3,000′-8,000′. **Behavior:** Gleans for insects in canopy pine needles; in winter also feeds in broadleaf trees. Small groups or individuals may join mixed species flocks in fall and winter. **Noteworthy:** Most common south of the Mogollon Rim, but since 1970 the range of Olive Warbler in Arizona has steadily expanded north.

ORANGE-CROWNED WARBLER, *Leiothlypis celata*

Description: 5″. Variably bright to dull **olive-yellow** warbler with indistinct eyebrows; dark eye-lines; faint **dusky-olive breast streaking**; yellow undertail coverts; long dusky tail. **Similar Species:** Tennessee Warbler (p. 449) has distinct eyebrows, lacks breast streaks, has whitish undertail coverts, and a short tail. Huskier female Yellow Warbler lacks eyebrows, has yellow wing edgings, and a shorter, mostly yellow tail. **Voice:** Call is sharp *tik*; song is weak trill. **Status:** Uncommon and local in summer (mid May-mid Aug); fairly common migrant (all elevations) and in winter (mid Aug-mid May). **Habitat:** Summer: Aspen groves and thickets in mountain coniferous forest. Winter: Lowland groves and thickets. **Elevations:** Summer 6,200′-10,100′; Winter 100′-5,100′. **Behavior:** Probes foliage for insects. **Noteworthy:** Breeding birds are grayish-headed *L. c. orestera,* and they are also widespread in winter; yellowish *L. c. lutescens* is a fairly common migrant, less common in winter.

Virginia's Warbler
Male

Female

Lucy's Warbler
Male

Female

VIRGINIA'S WARBLER, *Leiothlypis virginiae*

Description: 4.5". Small, gray warbler with **complete white eyerings; yellow breast**; gray belly; **yellow undertail coverts**; relatively short-tailed. MALE: Rufous crown patch. FEMALE: Lacks rufous crown and shows reduced yellow on breast. **Similar Species:** Closely-related Nashville Warbler (p. 457) has solid yellow throat and breast; upperparts olive. **Voice:** Sharp *spink* call. Song is leisurely series of *cheepa* notes ending with a slow trill. **Status:** Fairly common in summer (Apr-Aug), arrives later in N. Arizona; rare lowland migrant (mid Mar-early May and Sep-mid Oct). **Habitat:** Summer: Mountain chaparral, pine-oak woodland, and mixed coniferous forest with brushy understory. Migration: Valley and arid foothill scrub and thickets. **Elevations:** Summer 5,000'-9,800'; Migration 150'-5,000'. **Behavior:** Forages for insects and spiders in foliage of low shrubs and trees. Nests on the ground on steep hillsides. **Noteworthy:** Virginia's Warblers are adversely affected by prescribed burns to remove understory brush.

LUCY'S WARBLER, *Leiothlypis luciae*

Description: 4". Very small, pearl-gray warbler with a **pale face; chestnut rump**; creamy underparts; relatively short-tailed. MALE: Rufous crown patch. FEMALE: Lacks rufous crown. **Similar Species:** Larger Virginia's Warbler (above) has bold eyerings on darker gray face, and yellow on undertail coverts. **Voice:** Sharp *chink* call. Song is series of rapid, accelerating trills that end with a sputter. **Status:** Fairly common in summer (Mar-Sep). **Habitat:** Desert mesquite bosques and oases; valley, foothill, and lower mountain canyon groves; rare transient in mountain areas up to 7,300'. **Elevations:** Summer 100'-5,400'. **Behavior:** Gleans leaves for insects and spiders. **Noteworthy:** Arizona's earliest migrant warbler— even recorded casually in late February, Lucy's is the only western U. S. warbler that nests in cavities.

Northern Parula
Male

Female

Tropical
Parula
Male

Male

Crescent-chested Warbler
Male

Female

NORTHERN PARULA, *Setophaga americana*

Description: 4.25". Small, blue-headed warbler with **split white eyerings**; bicolored bill; green back; bold white wingbars; **white belly**. MALE: Diffuse black and chestnut breast bands. FEMALE: Diffuse chestnut breast band. **Similar Species:** Tropical Parula (below) lacks split white eyerings, has more yellow on sides of throat and on sides of belly. Males have a black mask and tawny-orange breast. **Voice:** Sharp *tzip* call. Song is a rising buzzy trill ending with *tchup* note. **Status:** Rare year-round, spiking Nov-Dec. **Habitat:** Desert oases and urban areas; valley, foothill, and lower mountain canyon groves. **Elevations:** Year-round 150'-7,700'. **Behavior:** Feeds actively in canopy of broadleaf trees.

TROPICAL PARULA, *Setophaga pitiayumi*

Description: 4.25". Small, blue-headed warbler with **broad yellow throat**; bicolored bill; green back; bold white wingbars; yellow upper belly. MALE: Black mask; tawny wash on breast. **Similar Species:** Crescent-chested Warbler (below) has flaring white eyebrows and lacks white wingbars. **Voice:** Sharp *tzip* call. Song is accelerating *chip-chip-chip* becoming a buzzy trill that ends with *ptut* note. **Status:** Casual in summer (early Jun-late Sep). **Habitat:** Mountain canyon groves. **Elevations:** Summer 4,700'-6,200'. **Noteworthy:** Arizona's first record was July, 1984 in the Santa Rita Mountains.

CRESCENT-CHESTED WARBLER, *Oreothlypis superciliosa*

Description: 4.2". Small, blue-headed warbler with **flaring white eyebrows**; bicolored bill; green back; yellow upper belly. MALE: Chestnut crescent-shaped bar on chest. **Voice:** Hard buzz, faster and deeper than either species of parula. **Status:** Casual year-round. **Habitat:** Summer (late Apr-mid Sep): Mountain canyon groves. Winter (mid Sep-late Apr): Foothill and mountain canyon groves. **Elevations:** Summer 5,300'-7,000'; Winter 3,700'-6,500'. **Behavior:** Forages on outer foliage. **Noteworthy:** Arizona's first record was September, 1983 in the Huachuca Mountains.

MALE

FEMALE

Yellow Warbler

Immature

Wilson's Warbler

YELLOW WARBLER, *Setophaga petechia*

Description: 5". Entirely yellow-headed warbler with **big, black eyes**; black wings edged bright yellow; short, **yellow undertail**. MALE: Sun yellow; **red streaks on the breast**. FEMALE: Pale yellow; thin or no red streaks on breast. JUVENILE: Yellowish gray overall. **Similar Species:** Juvenile female Wilson's Warbler (below) has bright yellow eyebrow and a dusky cap; long blackish tail. Orange-crowned Warbler (p. 429) has dark eyeline and dusky tail. **Voice:** Down-slurred *chilp*; cheery song usually rendered *sweet sweet sweet I'm so sweet*. **Status:** Common in summer (mid Mar-mid Oct); rare in winter (mid Oct-mid Mar), principally in lowland riparian west from Tucson and Phoenix. **Habitat:** Desert oases; valley, foothill, and lower mountain canyon groves, especially in cottonwoods and willows. **Elevations:** Summer 100'-8,400'; Winter 100'-2,300'. **Behavior:** Except in spring migration, found near permanent water. Gleans insects in canopy. **Noteworthy:** The breeding race in SE Arizona, "Sonoran Yellow Warbler," is the palest yellow and the largest subspecies in the U.S.

WILSON'S WARBLER, *Cardellina pusilla*

Description: 4.75". Dainty, **dark-capped** warbler with a yellow foreface, duskier behind eyes; olive above and bright yellow below; long dark tail. ADULT: Ink black cap. JUVENILE FEMALE: Dusky greenish cap. **Similar Species:** Yellow Warbler (above) has an entirely yellow face and crown; short tail is yellow below. **Voice:** Dry *chitt* call. **Status:** Common migrant (mid Mar-May and mid Aug-mid Oct); rare in winter (mid Oct-mid Mar) in lowlands. **Habitat:** Migration: Desert to mountain crest, but most common in riparian groves. Winter: Desert oases and valley river groves. **Elevations:** Migration 100'-9,100'; Winter 100'-3,800'. **Behavior:** Actively forages for insects in understory. **Noteworthy:** During peak migration, Wilson's is the most common species of lowland warbler.

YELLOW-RUMPED WARBLERS

"Audubon's" Male

Female

"Myrtle" Male

Female

"Audubon's" Yellow-rumped Warbler, *Setophaga coronata auduboni*

Description: 5.5". **Yellow-throated** warbler with **split white eyering,** yellow rump, **yellow sides,** and white tail spots. BREEDING MALE: Blue-gray with black chest, large white wing patch. FEMALE: Throat varies from cream to bright yellow; prominent streaking above and below. **Similar Species:** Yellow rump patch and flanks distinguishes even the dullest immatures from other regularly occurring warblers. Female "Myrtle Warbler" (below) has weak eyebrows, white throat wraps around ear patches, and is more brownish above than "Audubon's" female. **Voice:** Dry *chipt* call; song is deliberate but ringing series of *jee jee jee jee jee juu* notes. **Status:** Fairly common in summer (May-Sep); common in winter (Oct-Apr), primarily below 5,500'. Stragglers remain in lowlands until early June. **Habitat:** Summer: Mountain coniferous forest, especially Ponderosa pine. Winter: Desert oases and urban areas; valley, foothill, and lower mountain canyon groves; rare in high elevation pine forest and burns. **Elevations:** Summer 6,000'-11,000'; Winter 100'-9,100'. **Behavior:** Gleans insects from all levels. Can subsist on small fruits or berries in winter. **Noteworthy:** Yellow-rumps are the most abundant wintering warblers in Arizona.

"Myrtle" Yellow-rumped Warbler, *Setophaga coronata coronatai*

Description: 5.5". Warbler with **flaring white throat** extending under dark ears; **narrow white eyebrow, yellow rump,** yellow sides, and white tail spots. BREEDING MALE: Black face and chest; white wingbars. FEMALE: Brownish upperparts. **Similar Species:** "Audubon's" form lacks "Myrtle's" eyebrows and large, clean white throat. **Status:** Rare in winter (Oct-Feb); uncommon in spring (Mar-mid May). **Habitat:** Desert oases; valley, foothill, and mountain canyon groves. **Elevations:** Winter 100'-8,400'. **Noteworthy:** Rare intergrades between "Myrtle" and "Audubon's" Warblers with broken white eyebrows, dark auriculars, and yellow throats with white corners occur from 100-7,100' from mid Oct-mid May.

437

MALE   FEMALE

Magnolia Warbler

Black-throated
Green Warbler

Black-throated
Blue Warbler

MAGNOLIA WARBLER, *Setophaga magnolia*

Description: 5". Gray and yellow warbler with broken, black flank stripes, yellow rump, white belly, and **wide white tail band.** MALE: Blue-gray crown, white eyebrow, black mask, black chest necklace, large white wing patch. FEMALE: Gray face with pale eyering. IMMATURE: Vague gray breast band. **Similar Species:** "Audubon's" Yellow-rumped Warbler (p. 437) has split eyering; lacks yellow on center of breast and belly. **Voice:** Airy *chipt* calls. **Status:** Casual migrant (mid Sept-mid Nov and Apr-May); accidental in winter (mid Nov-Mar). **Habitat:** Desert oases and urban areas; valley, foothill, and mountain canyon groves. **Elevations:** 100'-7,000'. **Behavior:** Regularly fans black tail showing the wide white band as it forages for insects at all levels. **Noteworthy:** Magnolia is one of the dullest fall warblers and one of the most striking in spring.

BLACK-THROATED GREEN WARLER, *Setophaga virens*

Description: 4.75". Green-backed warbler with **ear patches outlined in dark olive**; yellow wash across vent. MALE: Black throat and breast. FEMALE: Yellowish throat. **Similar Species:** Townsend's Warbler (p. 445) shows solid dark ear patches and extensive yellow breast; it lacks yellow wash on vent area. **Voice:** Juicy *chilp* call. **Status:** Casual in winter (Sep-May). **Habitat:** Desert oases; valley, foothill, and mountain canyon groves. **Elevations:** 950'-8,400'. **Behavior:** Often forages high. **Noteworthy:** Usually disappears within 2 days, but may overwinter.

BLACK-THROATED BLUE WARBLER, *Setophaga caerulescens*

Description: 5". Stocky warbler with **white wing patches**. MALE: Blue with black face. FEMALE: Dusky olive; thin white eyebrows and under-eye crescents; darkish ears. **Voice**: Smacking *tchuk*. **Status:** Rare (mid Sep-mid Jun), especially in fall (Oct-Nov). **Habitat:** Desert oases; valley, foothill, and mountain canyon groves. **Elevations:** 450'-7,900'. **Behavior:** Usually forages low, from trunk outwards onto major limbs. **Noteworthy:** In Arizona most records pertain to males.

439

Black-throated Gray Warbler
Male

Female

Black-and-white Warbler
Male

Female

BLACK-THROATED GRAY WARBLER, *Setophaga nigrescens*

Description: 5". Warbler with black and white head; **yellow loral spots**; gray back. MALE: Black throat. FEMALE: Black bar on lower throat. IMMATURE: Lacks black on throat. **Similar Species:** Black-and-white Warbler (below) has striped crown and back. **Voice:** Abrupt call *tpp* like striking a match; scratchy song *buzz buzz buz zze-ze-zuu*. **Status:** Common in summer (Apr-mid Oct) and statewide in migration (mid Mar-mid May and mid Aug-mid Oct); uncommon in winter (mid Oct-mid Mar). **Habitat:** Summer: Foothill and mountain canyon groves, oak and pinyon-juniper woodlands, and pine-Gambel's oak.

Winter: Desert oases and urban areas; valley and foothill canyon groves. **Elevations:** Summer 4,800'-9,200'; Winter 100'-5,400'. **Behavior:** Actively gleans insects from shrubs and trees. **Noteworthy:** Black-throated Gray Warbler is the most common mid-elevation warbler breeding in the mountains of Arizona.

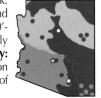

BLACK-AND-WHITE WARBLER, *Mniotilta varia*

Description: 5". **Black-and-white-striped** warbler with long, curved bill. MALE: Black ear patches; mostly black throat. FEMALE: Ear patches faintly streaked; white throat; unstreaked white central breast. **Similar Species:** Black-throated Gray Warbler (above) has solid crown and back and flits as it forages—does not feed by creeping on major limbs and trunks. **Voice:** Sharp, sputtering *ptt* notes; song is repetitious, lisping, very high *wee-see wee-see wee-see* phrases. **Status:** Rare in winter and migration (Sep-May); casual in summer (Jun-Aug).

Habitat: Desert oases and urban areas; river valley, foothill, and mountain canyon groves. **Elevations:** Year-round 100'-7,700'. **Behavior:** Typically crawls along major limbs and the trunks of trees investigating bark for insects. **Noteworthy:** Most Black-and-white Warblers in Arizona are first fall immatures or females.

Blackpoll Warbler
Male

Female

American Redstart
Female

Male

BLACKPOLL WARBLER, *Setophaga striata*

Description: 5.5". Large warbler with streaked back and flanks, white edged wings, white undertail coverts, and **yellow lower legs and feet.** BREEDING MALE: **Black cap crosses eye**; white cheek. BREEDING FEMALE: Greenish yellow upperparts with distinct streaking. NONBREEDING: Head, throat, and breast washed with yellow; streaked back olive-green. **Similar Species:** Pine Warbler (p. 451) female has unstreaked back and black legs and feet. Winter <u>Bay-breasted Warbler</u>, accidental in late May and casual in lowlands in late Sep-mid Dec, usually shows some remnant buff on flanks and undertail coverts, and its legs and feet are black. **Voice:** Call is a sharp *chip*. **Status:** Casual migrant (late Apr-late May and Sep-late Nov), primarily in fall. **Habitat:** Desert oases; isolated groves of deciduous trees in valleys, plateaus, and mountains. **Elevations:** 450'-8,000'. **Behavior:** Gently dips tail as it forages, usually on the interior and often fairly low in trees and shrubs. **Noteworthy:** Most Arizona Blackpolls are females or immatures.

AMERICAN REDSTART, *Setophaga ruticilla*

Description: 5". Black or gray warbler with **wing and tail flash marks**. MALE: Black with orange flash marks. FEMALE: Gray head, olive-gray back, yellow flash marks. IMMATURE MALE: Like female but with dark lores and some orange on sides. **Similar Species:** Painted Redstart (p. 459) has white—not yellow or orange--flash marks in wings and tail. **Voice:** Call is high *tsip*. **Status:** Rare year-round; most common in migration (May-Jun and Sep-mid Nov). **Habitat:** Desert oases; valley, foothill, and—least often—mountain canyon groves. **Elevations:** 100'-8,300'. **Behavior:** Active and acrobatic, while foraging it frequently flashes wing and tail patches. **Noteworthy:** The majority of American Redstart records in Arizona pertain to females or immatures. From 1936 until 1985 pairs nested near Springerville.

Townsend's Warbler
Male

Female

Hermit Warbler
Male

Female

TOWNSEND'S WARBLER, *Setophaga townsendi*

Description: 5". Warbler with **solid dark ear patches** bordered by yellow; **yellow breast; dark flank streaking**. MALE: Black throat and head pattern. FEMALE: Yellow throat; ear patches are dusky. **Similar Species:** Hermit Warbler (below) lacks dark ears, yellow on the breast, and obvious flank streaking. Black-throated Green Warbler (p. 439) has yellowish-centered, olive ear patches. **Voice:** Call is high, sharp *tip*. **Status:** Common migrant (mid Apr-May and Aug-Oct); rare in winter (Nov-Mar). **Habitat:** Migration: Mountain coniferous forest and canyon groves, infrequently to foothill canyon groves and desert oases. Winter: Desert oases; valley and foothill groves. **Elevations:** Migration 100'-10,000'; Winter 100'-7,000'. **Behavior:** Actively gleans insects in canopy. **Noteworthy:** DNA studies suggest that Townsend's are subsuming Hermit Warblers and will eventually eliminate their species.

TOWNSEND'S X HERMIT WARBLER HYBRIDS

Description: MALE: Yellow face of Hermit with yellow breast and streaked flanks, or head pattern of Townsend's without its yellow breast. Rare.

HERMIT WARBLER, *Setophaga occidentalis*

Description: 5". **Yellow-faced** warbler; **white breast** and belly; **unstreaked flanks.** MALE: Yellow forecrown and black throat. FEMALE: Dusky throat. JUVENILE FEMALE: Yellow eyerings; bottom edge of ear patches dusky. **Similar Species:** Juvenile Olive Warbler (p. 429) has dark upper--not lower--edges of ear patches. **Voice:** Call is high, thin *tip*, virtually identical to Townsend's Warbler. **Status:** Fairly common in spring (Apr-May) and common in fall (late Jul-Oct); casual in winter (Nov-Mar). **Habitat:** Mountain coniferous forest and canyon groves, infrequently to foothill canyon groves and desert oases. **Elevations:** Migration 100'-10,000'; Winter 950'-6,800'. **Behavior:** Actively gleans insects in canopy. **Noteworthy:** At high elevations, dozens or more Hermit and Townsend's Warblers may form large migratory flocks in the fall, usually mixed with other species of warblers in lesser numbers.

Grace's Warbler
Male

Blackburnian Warbler
Male

Yellow-throated Warbler
Male

GRACE'S WARBLER, *Setophaga graciae*

Description: 4.75". Gray warbler with **short, broad yellow eyebrow**; yellow throat and breast. **Similar Species:** Yellow-throated Warbler (below, casual) has long white eyebrow, triangular black cheek, and vertical white neck patch. **Voice:** Soft *pit* note; song is an accelerating trill, higher pitched at end. **Status:** Common in summer (Apr-mid Sep); accidental in winter. **Habitat:** Mountain coniferous forest, especially with Ponderosa pine, and canyon groves with tall pines. **Elevations:** Summer 5,000'-9,500'. **Behavior:** Actively gleans insects in pine canopy. **Noteworthy:** Over 90 percent of all Grace's Warblers located during the Breeding Bird Atlas project were associated with Ponderosa pine.

YELLOW-THROATED WARBLER, *Setophaga dominica*

Description: 5". Gray warbler with **long, white eyebrow; triangular black cheek**; yellow throat and breast. **Status:** Casual year-round, probably annual, especially during migration (Apr and Nov). **Habitat:** Desert oases; valley, foothill, and mountain canyon groves. **Elevations:** Year-round 100'-6,900'. **Behavior:** Usually feeds in canopy; may creep along trunks. **Noteworthy:** Often uses palm and sycamore trees.

BLACKBURNIAN WARBLER, *Setophaga fusca*

Description: 5". Dark ear patch entirely surrounded by orange or yellow; unmarked orange or yellow throat and breast; **pale yellowish braces on dark back.** BREEDING MALE: Fiery orange throat. NONBREEDING: Yellow face and throat. FLIGHT: Mostly white outer tail. **Similar Species:** Immature Townsend's Warbler (p. 445) has all black bill, the ear patches are connected to its nape, and its green back lacks pale yellow stripes. **Voice:** Resonant *chipt!* note. **Status:** Casual in fall and winter (Sep-Jan); otherwise accidental. **Habitat:** Desert oases; valley, foothill, and mountain canyon groves. **Elevations:** 1,200'-7,500'. **Behavior:** Gleans insects in canopy. Joins other warbler species in winter. **Noteworthy:** Most records are from late September to mid-October.

Tennessee Warbler
Breeding

Worm-eating Warbler
Adult

Chestnut-sided Warbler
Breeding Male

Nonbreeding

TENNESSEE WARBLER, *Leiothlypis peregrina*

Description: 4.75". **Moss-green** warbler with pale eyebrow and dark eyeline; **white undertail coverts**; short tail. BREEDING MALE (Apr-Dec): Gray cap; entirely white underparts. NONBREEDING: Olive cap; yellow breast. IMMATURE: Yellow breast and belly. **Similar Species:** Orange-crowned Warbler (p. 429) has diffusely streaked breast and olive-yellow undertail coverts. **Voice:** Loud, lip-smacking *sick!* calls. **Status:** Rare migrant (Mar-mid May and Aug-mid Nov); casual in winter. **Habitat:** Desert oases; valley, foothill, and—least often—mountain canyon groves. **Elevations:** 950'-7,500'. **Behavior:** Actively gleans at all levels.

WORM-EATING WARBLER, *Helmitheros vermivorum*

Description: 5.25". Bob-tailed warbler with **buff-orange, black-striped head**; long bill. **Similar Species:** Larger Ovenbird (p. 451) has a bold white eyering and black-streaked white underparts. **Voice:** Loud *cheap* calls. **Status:** Rare spring migrant (Mar-mid Jul); casual in other seasons. **Habitat:** Desert oases; valley, foothill, and mountain canyon groves. **Elevations:** 100'-7,700'. **Behavior:** Investigates lower strata dead leaf clusters and creeps up tree trunks.

CHESTNUT-SIDED WARBLER, *Setophaga pensylvanica*

Description: 5". Warbler with green back and yellow wingbars. NONBREEDING (Sep-Apr): White eyering on gray face; **lime green crown and back**. BREEDING (Mar-Aug): Yellow cap; chestnut sides. Most Arizona birds are immatures lacking chestnut flanks. **Similar Species:** <u>Golden-winged Warbler</u> (casual year-round) has gray back and shows a single, broad yellow wing bar. **Voice:** *chilp* call. **Status:** Rare in winter (Sep-Mar); casual in summer (May-Aug). **Habitat:** Broadleaf shrubs and trees in desert oases and valley groves; least often—primarily in May—mountain canyon groves. **Elevations:** 400'-8,300'. **Behavior:** Often forages low in deciduous trees and thickets. Tail is usually cocked.

449

Ovenbird

Palm Warbler

Pine Warbler

OVENBIRD, *Seiurus aurocapilla*

Description: 5.75". Plump, big-eyed warbler with white eyering; **orange crown** bordered by black stripes; black, thrush-like chest spotting. **Similar Species:** Waterthrushes (p. 455) have solid brown caps, eyestripes, and brown backs. **Voice:** Loud *tsuck* notes; *teacher-teacher-teacher* song. **Status:** Rare migrant (Apr-May and Oct-Nov); casual in summer and winter. **Habitat:** Desert oases; valley, foothill, and mountain canyon groves. **Elevations:** 250'-7,700'. **Behavior:** Forages on the ground, bobbing its head as it walks, usually with its tail cocked.

PALM WARBLER, *Setophaga palmarum*

Description: 5.5". **Ground-hugging, tail-pumping** warbler, usually with chestnut cap; **long, white eyebrow; blackish eyeline**; dull yellowish rump, **bright yellow undertail coverts**. **Similar Species:** Larger Waterthrushes (p. 455) lack any chestnut in cap, oleaginous rump, and bright yellow undertail coverts. Yellow-rumped Warblers (p. 437) have yellow flanks, brighter yellow rumps, and do not pump tail. **Voice:** Ripping, sharp *pritt*! notes; song is extended rapid trill *prrrrrrrrrt* lasting 1-2 seconds. **Status:** Rare in winter (late Sep-May), occasionally present for a month. **Habitat:** Desert oases; valley, foothill, and mountain canyon groves. **Elevations:** 100'-7,000'. **Behavior:** Wags tail continuously as it forages on the ground or in shrubbery, often near water.

PINE WARBLER, *Setophaga pinus*

Description: 5.5". Dull olive to dull yellow, nondescript warbler with **contrasting throat; blurry flank streaking**; long tail. **Similar Species:** Orange-crowned Warbler (p. 429) lacks wingbars and throat-cheek contrast. **Voice:** Thin *tsip* calls; song is a series of slow, pleasant trills. **Status:** Rare in winter (mid Oct-Mar). **Habitat:** Desert oases; valley, foothill, and mountain canyon groves. **Elevations:** 1,400'-5,900'. **Behavior:** Likes pines and other trees; may join mixed flocks on the ground.

Prothonotary Warbler

Kentucky Warbler
Male

Hooded Warbler
Male

Hooded Warbler
Female

PROTHONOTARY WARBLER, *Protonotaria citrea*

Description: 5.25". Golden warbler with **long bill; blue-gray wings**. MALE: Golden head. FEMALE: Golden face with subtly duller olive-yellow crown and eyeline. FLIGHT: Black-tipped white outer tail feathers. **Similar Species:** Short-billed Hooded Warbler (below) has green wings concolor with back. **Voice:** High, thin *cheat!* notes. **Status:** Rare migrant (May-Jun and mid Aug-mid Nov). **Habitat:** Desert oases; valley, foothill, and—least often—mountain canyon groves. **Elevations:** 450'-7,100'. **Behavior:** Usually forages low in trees and shrubbery near water.

KENTUCKY WARBLER, *Geothlypis formosa*

Description: 5.25". Warbler with **yellow spectacles, black, triangular ear patches; long legs; short tail**. MALE: Large black ear patches. FEMALE: Limited black ear patches. **Similar Species:** Hooded Warbler (below) has yellow face and forehead; white outer tail feathers. **Voice:** Emphatic *chrrt!* chips; song is rich, regular *weeeh weeeh weeeh* or *tuwee tuwee tuwee*. **Status:** Rare migrant (mid Apr-early Jul and early Aug-early Oct), records spike in June; casual (mid Dec-early Jan). **Habitat:** Desert oases; valley, foothill, and mountain canyon groves. **Elevations:** 400'-8,300'. **Behavior:** Usually forages on the ground or low in thickets.

HOODED WARBLER, *Setophaga citrina*

Description: 5.25". **Yellow-masked** warbler; dark lores; **white outer tail**. MALE: Black cowl. IMMATURE FEMALE: Yellow face outlined by greenish cowl. FLIGHT: White outer tail feathers. **Similar Species:** Smaller female Wilson's Warbler (p. 435) has small bill, yellow lores, smaller eye, and lacks any white in tail. **Voice:** Emphatic *spink!* notes; song is rich whistle: *wit wit wit whit-chew*. **Status:** Rare year-round, primarily in spring (Apr-Jun); occasionally present for more than a month. **Habitat:** Desert oases; valley, foothill, and mountain canyon groves. **Elevations:** 400'-7,700'. **Behavior:** Usually forages on the ground or low in dense growth, often near water, flashing white outer tail feathers.

Black-dotted throat

Northern Waterthrush

Louisiana Waterthrush

Clean white throat

NORTHERN WATERTHRUSH, *Parkesia noveboracensis*

Description: 5.75". Brown-backed warbler, typically with **tapering pale eyebrow, black-dotted throat,** and coral red legs. Waterthrushes are best separated by full suite of field characters. **Similar Species:** Louisiana Waterthrush (below) has flaring white eyebrow, clean white throat, often rich buff-washed flanks, and pink legs. **Voice:** Metallic, loud *pink* note. **Status:** Uncommon migrant (mid Apr-Jun and Aug-Sep); casual in winter (Oct-mid Apr). **Habitat:** Ponds and slow-moving streams at desert oases and in valley, foothill, and mountain canyon groves. **Elevations:** Migration 100'-9,200'. **Behavior:** Forages for insects on water's edge, bobbing tail as it walks or balances on stones. **Noteworthy:** Northern Waterthrush in Arizona is typically more common in fall than in spring.

LOUISIANA WATERTHRUSH, *Parkesia motacilla*

Description: 6". Brown-backed warbler, typically with **flaring white eyebrow, clean white throat,** often buffy flanks, and pink legs. Waterthrushes are best separated by full suite of field characters. **Similar Species:** Northern Waterthrush (above) usually has tapering white eyebrow, black-dotted throat; lacks contrasting buffy flanks, and has duller coral legs. **Voice:** Sharp, emphatic *chink* note. **Status:** Rare migrant and winter visitor (mid Jul-early Apr). **Habitat:** Primarily slow-moving rivers and streams in valley, foothill, and mountain canyon groves. **Elevations:** Winter 550'-7,500'. **Behavior:** Forages for insects on water's edge, bobbing tail as it walks or balances on stones. **Noteworthy:** The rare permanent streams in the SE corner seems to be the only reliable area in Arizona for over-wintering Louisiana Waterthrushes.

MacGillivray's Warbler
Male

Female

Nashville Warbler
Male

Female

MACGILLIVRAY'S WARBLER, *Geothlypis tolmiei*

Description: 5.25". Gray-hooded warbler with pink-based bill and **split eyering**. MALE: Blue-gray hood, black in front of eyes and across lower breast. FEMALE: Pale gray hood. **Similar Species:** Smaller Nashville Warbler (below) has complete eyering and yellow throat. **Voice:** Call is hard, sharp *chik*; song abruptly changes at end *swee-swee-swee-swee chow chow*. **Status:** Uncommon and local in summer (Jun-Jul); fairly common migrant (Apr-May and Aug-mid Oct). **Habitat:** Summer: Streamside willow and alder thickets, and deciduous undergrowth in shady mixed conifer forest. Migration: Thickets from desert oases to mountain crests. **Elevations:** Summer 5,800'-11,300'; Migration 100'-10,000'. **Behavior:** Skulks in thickets and deep cover; nests on ground. **Noteworthy:** The population in the Pinaleno Mountains near Safford are the southernmost breeding MacGillivray's Warblers in the U.S.

NASHVILLE WARBLER, *Leiothlypis ruficapilla*

Description: 4.5". Gray-headed warbler with **bold white eyering**; yellow throat; olive-green back. MALE: Inconspicuous chestnut cap. IMMATURE FEMALE: Indistinct hood merges with back; whitish belly. **Similar Species:** Larger MacGillivray's Warbler (above) has a gray hood and broken white eyerings. In larger <u>Mourning Warbler</u>, casual (mid May-mid June and late Aug-early Sep), male has no eyerings, female has gray throat, and immature has very thin eyerings and pink legs. Closely-related Virginia's Warbler (p. 431) has whitish throat and gray wings and back. **Voice:** Dry *pitt* call. **Status:** Uncommon spring (late Mar-mid May) and fairly common fall (early Aug-mid Oct) migrant; casual in winter. **Habitat:** Spring: Desert oases; valley, foothill, and lower mountain canyon groves. Fall: Desert oases up to high mountain thickets. **Elevations:** Migration 100'-9,300'; Winter 100'-2,200'. **Behavior:** Forages in understory weeds and thickets, less frequently higher in trees. **Noteworthy:** In SW lowlands Nashvilles are most common in spring; in mountains they are most common in fall.

Red-faced Warbler

Painted Redstart

RED-FACED WARBLER, *Cardellina rubrifrons*

Description: 5". Dapper gray warbler with **red face**, black head-band, and white rump. **Similar Species:** None. **Voice:** Hard, dry *chett* call; song is quick, piercing *zwee zwee zwee zweeta t'whew*. **Status:** Common in summer (mid Apr–mid Sep). **Habitat:** Upper canyon riparian coniferous forest mixed with groves of Gambel's oak and quaking aspen. **Elevations:** Summer 5,100'–9,700'. **Behavior:** Forages from low to high levels, often in deciduous trees; nests on steep hillsides, usually under overhanging grass or other cover. **Noteworthy:** As a breeding species in the U.S., Red-faced Warbler is confined to Arizona and adjacent New Mexico.

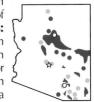

PAINTED REDSTART, *Myioborus pictus*

Description: 5.25". **Black warbler** with white crescents below eyes; **white panels in wings; red belly**; white outer tail feathers. JUVENILE: Sooty belly. **Similar Species:** Charcoal-gray–not black–Slate-throated Redstart (p. 461) lacks white under-eye crescents, lacks white wing panels, and shows less white in the outer tail. **Voice:** Conversational *cheeu* or *chee-wee* calls; cheerful, run-on *sweeta-sweeta-sweeta-sweeta* notes. **Status:** Common in summer (mid Mar–Oct); uncommon in winter (Nov–mid Mar). **Habitat:** Summer: Mountain canyon groves; heavy stands of pine-oak on slopes. Winter: Valley, foothill, and lower mountain canyon groves. **Elevations:** Summer 3,800'–9,100'; Winter 950'–5,800'. **Behavior:** Pivots and flashes white outer tail to startle prey. Forages from ground to tree tops; sometimes circles up tree trunks like a Brown Creeper. Nests on banks under hummocks of grass.
Noteworthy: In the major wet canyons of SE Arizona's larger mountains, Painted Redstarts are the most abundant summering warbler. Early arrivals and post-breeding wandering may take birds into desert oases or up to 9,500' in the mountains. After breeding, most N. Arizona birds disperse south of the Mogollon Rim.

Slate-throated Redstart

Fan-tailed Warbler

Rufous-capped Warbler

SLATE-THROATED REDSTART, *Myioborus miniatus*

Description: 5.25". **Charcoal-gray warbler** with maroon crown; orange-red chest and belly; **white tail corners**. **Similar Species:** Black–not slate gray–Painted Redstart (p. 459) has white under-eye crescents, large white wing panels, and shows more white in the outer tail. **Voice:** High, thin *tsip* calls; languid *twee-twee-tweea-tee* song thinner than Painted Redstart's. **Status:** Rare in summer (mid Mar-Jul); accidental in fall (Oct). **Habitat:** Mountain canyon groves with perennial streams within pine-oak woodland. **Elevations:** Summer 4,900'-7,200'. **Behavior:** Forages in thickets and the lower strata of trees, often fanning its tail.

FAN-TAILED WARBLER, *Basileuterus lachrymosus*

Description: 5.75". Large gray warbler with split white eyerings and **white accents on forehead**; narrow yellow crown; long, white-tipped tail. **Similar Species:** Larger Yellow-breasted Chat (p. 463) has complete white spectacles and lacks white-tipped tail. **Voice:** Very high *seet* calls; song is piercing *swee swee swee sweeta s'wee*. **Status:** Accidental in summer (mid Apr-early Sep). **Habitat:** Foothill and lower mountain canyon groves with dense understory adjoining steep hillsides or cliffs. **Elevations:** Summer 3,700'-6,000'. **Behavior:** Forages on ground or low in thickets, often fanning its tail.

RUFOUS-CAPPED WARBLER, *Basileuterus rufifrons*

Description: 5". **Rufous-capped** warbler with bold white eyebrows, **rufous ears**; rich yellow throat and breast; long tail. **Voice:** Snappy *cht* and *chit* chips; song consists of rapid, repeated chips ending with trills. **Status:** Rare and local resident. **Habitat:** Foothill and mountain canyon groves with dense thickets adjoining steep hillsides or cliffs. **Elevations:** Resident 3,300'-7,200'. **Behavior:** Forages low, cocks its very long tail and waves it like a Bewick's Wren. **Noteworthy:** First detected in the Chiricahua Mountains in 1977, they have bred in Arizona since 2001.

461

Common Yellowthroat
Male

Female

Yellow-breasted Chat

COMMON YELLOWTHROAT, *Geothlypis trichas*

Description: 5". Marsh warbler with yellow underparts brightest on throat; **cocked tail**. MALE: **Black mask** bordered by white. FEMALE: Gray face; pale yellow throat; grayish belly; yellow undertail coverts. **Similar Species:** Female MacGillivray's Warbler (p. 457) lacks yellow throat and cocked tail. **Voice:** Dry *tickk* notes; long staccato chatter calls; loud song is *wich-i-ty wich-i-ty wich-i-ty*. **Status:** Common in summer (Apr-Sep); fairly common in winter (Oct-Mar). **Habitat:** Marshes, streams, rivers, ponds, and lakes with emergent vegetation. Migrants occasionally also use dense savanna and dry brush. **Elevations:** Summer 100'-9,100'; Winter 100'-5,100'. **Behavior:** Gleans insects from low marsh or water edge vegetation. **Noteworthy:** Male Common Yellowthroats in Arizona with entirely yellow underparts are *G. t. chryseola*, the largest and brightest race in the U.S. Migrant race males show olive flanks.

YELLOW-BREASTED CHAT, *Icteria virens*

Description: 7". **Large, thick-billed** warbler-like bird with **white spectacles; rich yellow throat and breast**; olive upperparts; white belly; long tail. **Similar Species:** Smaller, accidental Fan-tailed Warbler (p. 461) has white accent marks on forehead, entirely yellow underparts, and white-tipped tail. Otherwise no other similar bird. **Voice:** Loud, coughing *chuh-chuh-chuh*. Song is series of deliberate and quite different phrases, often repeated rapidly, with long pauses between each element. **Status:** Common in summer (mid Apr-mid Oct); casual in fall (mid Oct-mid Nov). **Habitat:** Desert oases; valley, foothill, and lower mountain canyon thickets, usually near permanent water. **Elevations:** Summer 100'-7,600'. **Behavior:** Forages in thickets. Male's display flight is low with deep wing beats. **Noteworthy:** DNA analysis suggests chats are only distantly related to New World Wood-Warblers. The longevity record for Yellow-breasted Chat is from Arizona, a recapture 15 years after it was first banded.

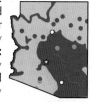

MALE

FEMALE

Hepatic Tanager

Juvenile

Summer Tanager
"Fruit-stained bill"

Immature Male

HEPATIC TANAGER, *Piranga flava*

Description: 7.75". Tanager with **blackish bill** and **grayish ear patch**; grayish back; gray flanks; colors brightest on forehead and throat. MALE: Flame red. FEMALE: Mustard yellow. JUVENILE: Yellow with pin-striped breast. **Similar Species:** Summer Tanager (below) has paler bill, unless stained, and lacks dark ear paches. **Voice:** Smacking *chup* call; clear, lilting song of robin-like phrases without burry notes. **Status:** Fairly common in summer (Apr-mid Oct); uncommon in winter (Nov-Mar), primarily west of San Pedro Valley. Casual year-round at elevations below 2,100'. **Habitat:** Summer: Mountain canyon groves, pine-oak woodland, and Ponderosa pine forest. Winter: Valley, foothill, and lower mountain canyon groves. **Elevations:** Summer 3,800'-9,600'; Winter 2,100'-6,200'. **Behavior:** Methodically searches canopy for insects. **Noteworthy:** Recent genetic studies have repositioned U.S. tanagers with grosbeaks and buntings, taxonomically far removed from the polychrome tanagers of the New World tropics.

SUMMER TANAGER, *Piranga rubra*

Description: 7.25". Tanager with large **pale bill**. MALE: Red. FEMALE: Clear yellow. IMMATURE MALE: Splotchy red and green. JUVENILE: Lightly streaked chest. **Similar Species:** Hepatic Tanager (above) has blackish bill and dark ear patches. **Voice:** Staccato *kid-dy-tuck-tuk* call; clear, lilting song of three-part phrases without burry notes. **Status:** Common in summer (mid Apr-Sep); rare in winter (Oct-mid Apr) west of the San Pedro River Valley. Casual transient in Ponderosa pine associations. **Habitat:** Desert oases; valley, foothill, and lower mountain canyon groves. **Elevations:** Summer 100'-5,600'; Winter 100'-3,800'. **Behavior:** Methodically searches canopy for insects and fruits. **Noteworthy:** In a Bureau of Land Management study, an average density of over 50 Summer Tanagers per 100 acres were noted in San Pedro River National Conservation Area.

Scarlet Tanager
Male

Female

Western X
Flame-colored
Tanager Hybrid
Male

Male

SCARLET TANAGER, *Piranga olivacea*

Description: 7". Tanager with **small, apple-green bill, toothed on upper mandible.** BREEDING MALE: Incandescent scarlet and black. NONBREEDING MALE Like female with solid black wings. FEMALE: Yellow-green body; dark wings and tail have thin, green edgings. May show very thin wingbars. **Similar Species:** Larger Summer Tanager (p. 465) has wings concolor with back. Female Western Tanager (p. 469) has orangish bill, contrasting gray or dusky back, and two distinct wingbars. **Voice:** Snapping *tick* call, sometimes followed by burry note. **Status:** Rare spring (Apr-May) and fall (Oct-Nov) migrant. Accidental in other months. **Habitat:** Desert oases; valley river groves, and foothill canyon groves. Accidental in mountain canyon groves. **Elevations:** Migrant 1,200'-6,300'. **Behavior:** Forages in the canopy of deciduous trees for insects and fruits. **Noteworthy:** The majority of Arizona sightings occure in fall.

WESTERN X FLAME-COLORED TANAGER HYBRID

Description: 7". MALE: Forward wingbar yellow; lower back solid black; rump distinctly yellow. FEMALE: Usually indistinguishable as a hybrid. **Similar Species:** Western Tanager (p. 469) has smaller, paler bill, unmarked face, and lacks any streaking on back. Flame-colored Tanager (p. 467) has a larger bill, white forward wingbar, never has a solid black lower back, and rump is dull olive. **Status:** Rare in summer (early Apr-mid Aug). **Habitat:** Border range canyon groves within pine-oak woodland. **Elevations:** Summer 5,000'-6,800'. **Behavior:** Methodically searches canopy for insects. **Noteworthy:** In 1985 Arizona's first Flame-colored Tanager in the Chiricahua Mtns. paired with a Western Tanager and nested twice. Hybrid crosses between these two species have been recorded almost as often as apparently pure Flame-colored Tanagers.

MALE

FEMALE

Western Tanager

Flame-colored Tanager

WESTERN TANAGER, *Piranga ludoviciana*

Description: 7". Tanager with small, **olive-tinged or orange bill** and **two wingbars**. BREEDING MALE: Orange-red face; black back; yellow forward wingbar. FEMALE: Yellow head; grayish back; belly variable from yellow to pale gray. **Similar Species:** Larger Flame-colored Tanager (below) has blackish bill, dark-bordered ear-patch, white forward wingbar, and obvious back streaks. **Voice:** Quick, almost trilled, *pret-ty-pink* call; usually seven high, slurred, sing-song phrases *I-think, you-think, we-think, you-drink*, etc. **Status:** Fairly common in summer (mid Jun-mid Jul); common in migration (mid Apr-mid Jun and mid Jul-Oct); casual in lowlands in winter (Nov-mid Apr). **Habitat:** Summer: Upper mountain canyon groves and mixed coniferous forest. Migration: All habitats from desert to mountain crest. **Elevations:** Summer 5,300'-11,000'; Migration 100'-11,000'. **Behavior:** Methodically searches canopy for insects. **Noteworthy:** Arizona represents the southern limits of Western Tanager's breeding range. Transients away from breeding habitats occur statewide throughout the summer.

FLAME-COLORED TANAGER, *Piranga bidentata*

Description: 7.5". Tanager with large dark bill; **dark-bordered ear-patch; striped back**. MALE: Extent of reddish-orange foreparts variable. FEMALE: Yellow. FIRST SPRING MALE: Bright yellow with orange tinge on forehead. **Similar Species:** Western Tanager (above) has smaller bill, unmarked face, and lacks streaked back. **Voice:** Burry *cor-rupt!* call; deliberate, burry three- or four-part *sherree, shurroo, sherroo* song. **Status:** Rare in summer (early Apr-Aug). **Habitat:** Border range canyon groves within pine-oak woodland. **Elevations:** Summer 5,000'-6,800'. **Behavior:** Methodically searches canopy for insects. **Noteworthy:** In Arizona, known only from the Santa Rita, Huachuca, and Chiricahua Mountains. First record in Arizona was in April, 1985.

MALE

FEMALE

Northern Cardinal

Pyrrhuloxia

NORTHERN CARDINAL, *Cardinalis cardinalis*

Description: 8.5". **Bushy-crested cardinal** with **black foreface** and **triangular, orange-red bill**. MALE: Entirely red. FEMALE: Warm cinnamon overall with reddish crest, wings, and tail. JUVENILE: Black bill. **Similar Species:** Female Pyrrhuloxia (below) has slimmer crest; stubby, rounded, yellowish or horn-colored bill; red eyering. **Voice:** High *pink* note, as if from a smaller bird. Loud *whoit whoit whoit, cheer-ry cheer-ry, too too too* song in changing sequences. **Status:** Common resident. Casual in western lowlands. **Habitat:** Desert thickets, oases, and urban areas; valley, foothill, and lower mountain canyon groves. **Elevations:** Resident 100'-5,700'. **Behavior:** Forages for seeds, fruits, and insects. Male feeds female during courtship. **Noteworthy:** Northern Cardinals apparently colonized southern Arizona from Sonora, Mexico via the Santa Cruz River Valley in the mid-1800s.

PYRRHULOXIA, *Cardinalis sinuatus*

Description: 8". **Taper-crested cardinal** with **red around eye** and **rounded, straw-yellow bill**; red crest, wings, and tail. MALE: Red lipstick smear down breast. FEMALE: Red eyering; neutral fawn or gray underparts. NONBREEDING ADULT: Gray or horn-colored bill. JUVENILE: Dusky bill. **Similar Species:** Female Northern Cardinal (above) has bigger, bushier crest; larger, triangular, orange-red bill; black smudge between eyes and bill. **Voice:** Thin *tchik* note, more fulsome than Cardinal's, sometimes chattered. Thin *tuwheet tuwhee tuwheet tuwheet, chew-y chew-y chew-y, chew-chow!-chow!-chow!* reedier than Northern Cardinal song. **Status:** Common resident. **Habitat:** Desertscrub and urban areas; valley thickets; open foothill canyon groves with underbrush. **Elevations:** Summer 1,400'-5,000'; Winter 500'-5,500'. **Behavior:** Forages for seeds, fruits, and insects. **Noteworthy:** In winter Pyrrhuloxias may join small flocks, and some move up into lower mountain canyons above breeding habitat.

Female

Rose-breasted Grosbeak
Male

Black-headed Grosbeak
Male

Female

Description: 7.35". Grosbeak with **pink bill**. MALE: Black head and back; **rose breast**. FEMALE: Brown head with white stripes; pin-striped breast and flanks. FLIGHT: **Male shows red underwing linings. Similar Species:** Female Black-headed Grosbeak (below) has dark upper mandible, unstreaked center of breast, and center of belly washed yellow. **Voice:** Call is squeaking *peak*; song is rollicking series of rich, whistled notes. **Status:** Rare in summer (mid Apr-mid Nov); casual in winter (mid Nov-mid Apr). **Habitat:** Desert oases and urban areas; valley, foothill, and mountain canyon groves; mountain pine-oak woodland. **Elevations:** Summer 150'-7,900'; Winter 1,100'-7,000'. **Behavior:** Searches for fruits and insects in canopy; also eats seeds. **Noteworthy:** Numbers spike in May. Seldom remains at an Arizona location for over two weeks.

Description: 7.5". Grosbeak with **bicolored bill, upper mandible blackish**. MALE: Mostly black head; **orange breast.** FEMALE: Brown head with white stripes; unstreaked center of breast; center of belly washed yellow. FLIGHT: **Both sexes show yellow underwing linings. Similar Species:** Female Rose-breasted Grosbeak (above) has pin-striped center of breast and whitish center of belly. **Voice:** Call is smacking *whick*; song is rollicking series of rich, whistled notes. Juvenile begging call is *whee-ah*. **Status:** Common in summer (Jun-Jul) and in migration (late Mar-May and Aug-mid Oct). Casual in winter (mid Oct-late Mar). **Habitat:** Summer: Mountain canyon groves, pine-oak woodland, coniferous forest. Migration: Desert washes to mountain tops. **Elevations:** Summer 3,600'-9,500'; Migration 100'-9,100'. **Behavior:** Both sexes sing from nest. **Noteworthy:** Although also widespread in lowlands during migration, they remain most common in the mountains.

Yellow Grosbeak
Male

Blue Grosbeak
Male

Female

YELLOW GROSBEAK, *Pheucticus chrysopeplus*

Description: 9". Grosbeak with **massive, lead-gray bill; entirely yellow underparts**. MALE: Yellow head and back. FEMALE: Finely-striped crown; dusky ear-patch. **Similar Species:** Female Flame-colored Tanager (p. 469) lacks massive bill. Evening Grosbeaks (p. 373) have green bills and gray heads. **Voice:** Squeaking *peep* call; song is hurried series of three or four rich, whistled phrases, followed by a pause before resuming. **Status:** Casual in stummer (May-mid Aug). **Habitat:** Desert oases; valley, foothill, and lower mountain canyon groves. **Elevations:** Summer 2,800'-5,200'. **Behavior:** Searches for fruits and insects in canopy; also eats seeds and may visit feeding stations. **Noteworthy:** Almost all Yellow Grosbeak records are in June and July.

BLUE GROSBEAK, *Passerina caerulea*

Description: 6.75". Grosbeak with **silver-blue bill; broad, chestnut wingbars**. MALE: Deep blue body. FEMALE: Warm cinnamon-brown. IMMATURE MALE: Blue head; patchy blue body. **Similar Species:** Smaller Indigo Bunting (p. 475) lacks large, thick bill and broad, chestnut wingbars. **Voice:** Explosive, hammer on an anvil *spink!* call; song is reedy warbling whistles. **Status:** Common in summer (late Apr-mid Oct); rare in winter (mid Oct-late Apr). **Habitat:** Summer: Desert oases; shrubby valley grasslands, foothill and lower mountain canyon groves, usually associated with mesquite. Most common south of Mogollon Rim. Winter: Weedy fields, mesquite bosque, and valley groves. **Elevations:** Summer 100'-7,700'; Winter 600'-5,200'. **Behavior:** Usually forages on ground or in thickets for seeds, fruits, and insects. Male singing reaches its peak in August. **Noteworthy:** Blue Grosbeaks arrive comparatively late and seem to time breeding to the summer monsoon.

MALE

FEMALE

Lazuli Bunting

Indigo Bunting

LAZULI BUNTING, *Passerina amoena*

Description: 5.25". Bunting with **obvious wingbars; sky-blue rump**. MALE: Turquoise head; thick white forward wingbar; cinnamon chest. FEMALE: Brownish above with grayish throat; cinnamon wash across breast contrasts with whitish belly. NONBREEDING MALE: Brownish back.
Similar Species: Female Indigo Bunting (below) has whitish throat, faint streaking on breast, lacks blue rump, and lacks abrupt contrast between fawn breast and white belly. **Voice:** Dry *ptt* call and high frequency *ink* notes. Song is reedy whistled notes and trills, usually twice repeated. **Status:** Uncommon in summer (late May-mid Jul); fairly common migrant (mid Mar-late May and mid Jul-late Oct); rare in winter (late Oct-mid Mar). **Habitat:** Tall grasses and weeds in desert oases and feeding stations; pond reeds; rank growth in valleys, foothills, and mountain canyons. **Elevations:** Summer 100'-8,500'; Winter 950'-4,900'. **Behavior:** Males seldom breed until their second summer. Forms small to large flocks in migration. **Noteworthy:** Arizona harbors the southernmost known breeding populations of Lazuli Buntings in North America.

INDIGO BUNTING, *Passerina cyanea*

Description: 5.25". Bunting with blue tail edgings. MALE: Entirely **deep blue**. FEMALE: Brownish above with **whitish throat; fine streaking on breast; narrow brownish wingbars**. IMMATURE MALE: Patchy blue with white belly. **Similar Species:** See female Lazuli Bunting (above). **Voice:** Song similar to but slower than Lazuli Bunting's. **Status:** Uncommon in summer (late Apr-mid Oct); casual in winter (mid Oct-late Apr). **Habitat:** Tall grasses and weeds in valleys, foothills, and mountain canyons; desert oases with trees and rank growth; urban parks and feeding stations. **Elevations:** Summer 100'-7,700'; Winter 1,100'-4,700'. **Behavior:** Often forages near mesquite woods, and edges of cottonwood and sycamore groves. **Noteworthy:** The first known Arizona record of Indigo Bunting was 1917.

MALE

FEMALE

Varied Bunting

Painted Bunting

VARIED BUNTING, *Passerina versicolor*

Description: 5.25″. Bunting lacking wingbars with **curved upper mandible.** MALE: **Blue, red, and purple above**; mostly rich burgundy below. FEMALE: **Uniform warm brown above**; entirely pale brown below. **Similar Species:** Female Indigo Bunting (p. 477) lacks curved upper mandible; has whitish throat, faint streaking on breast, and thin brown wingbars. **Voice:** Dry *ptt* call. Song is reedy warbled phrases without pauses, phrases not repeated, deeper than other buntings. **Status:** Fairly common in summer (May-mid Oct); casual (Apr and after mid Oct).

Habitat: Prefers foothill thornscrub and mesquite thickets. Also uses thickets in desert oases, valley, foothill, and lower mountain canyons. **Elevations:** Summer 1,900′-5,700′. **Behavior:** Often forages in dense brush. Times breeding to coincide with the summer monsoons in July and August. **Noteworthy:** Arizona harbors the northernmost known breeding populations of Varied Bunting in North America.

PAINTED BUNTING, *Passerina ciris*

Description: 5.25″. Bunting with **narrow eyering; green back**. MALE: Blue head with red eyering, red rump, and red underparts. FEMALE: Green head with pale eyering; grass-green above; yellowish-green underparts. JUVENILE: Like drab female. **Similar Species:** Male color combination distinctive; larger female Scarlet Tanager (p. 467) and larger female Orchard Oriole (p. 425), both vagrants in Arizona, have very different bills than female Painted Bunting. **Voice:** Dry *ptt* call. Song is sweet, high-pitched reedy phrases without pauses, notes not repeated. **Status:** Uncommon in summer (May-early Oct); casual in winter (early Oct-Apr). **Habitat:** Overgrown fields and rank growth in valley, foothill, and lower mountain canyon groves. **Elevations:** Summer 450′-5,600′. **Behavior:** Often forages in weeds on pond edges and floodplains. Usually secretive. **Noteworthy:** Numbers crescendo during monsoon season from mid July through early October. Females and immatures are the majority of Painted Bunting observations.

479

Acknowledgments

This book owes much to many. The collective experience and knowledge of Arizona's energetic community of birders made writing Birds of Arizona possible. Many photographers also rose to the dual challenge of producing beautiful images that nonetheless convey crucial field marks. They have all materially improved the utility and appearance of this book. Meriting special mention are Tony Battiste, Jim Burns, Fred Forssell, John Hoffman, Alan Schmierer, Robert Shantz, and Charlie Trapani. Fully one-half of all the images in this book are examples of their dedication and their craft. The stunning cover shot of a pair of Gilded Flickers at a saguaro is the work of photographer Charlie Trapani.

I was fortunate to have four exceptional reviewers, Chris McCreedy, Dennis Paulson, Andrew Stepniewski, and Susan Wethington. They weeded out mistakes, imprecision, and even corrected potentially misleading statements. The book benefits from each one's long field experience in Arizona, as well as their pragmatic dedication to accuracy. I am deeply indebted for their help.

Finally, I want to thank the three member "team" that wed the disparate elements of words, graphics, and photos into a cohesive field guide. My son, Eric G. Taylor, took my sketch ideas and executed the computer graphics that resulted in the hummingbird chart, state map, and the color range maps for the birds. Book designer Christina Merwin created the page layouts, and patiently implemented the innumerable tweaks I made to the text. Overseeing the entire book project was Publisher and Editor Christina Morse who developed the page and book design that make this state bird guide truly unique.

The birds described in this book also deserve recognition. They have opened the doors to my understanding of the world we share.

- Richard Cachor Taylor

Photographer Credits

The letters following the page numbers refer to the position of the photograph on that page; T = top, M = middle, MT = middle top, MB = middle bottom, B = bottom, L = left, R = right, N = inset.

Peg Abbott/Naturalist Journeys: 230B, BN. **Walt Anderson**: 22T. **Marion Ball**: 90BR, 100BL, 108BN, 160TL, 186BN, 220T, 238MR, 298BN, 310TL, 362BL, 366TN, 394B, BN. **Lee Barnes**: 32B, 154BN, 156BL. **Tony Battiste**: 20B, TN, 24B, 26, 30MB, 34T, B, 36T, 40BL, 44TL, TR, BR, 46B, BN, 48TR, 52TR, 54T, TN, 66TN, 74BL, 78B, 80TN, BN, 82T, 92BL, TL, 102B, 108B, 114B, 118TL, TR, 122B, 124B, 130BL, 134ML, 144T, 146TR, ML, 160TR, 170B, 176T, 178T, 180T, 184T, 198BR, 206TRT, 208BL, 212TNL, 218T, TN, 224BR, 232BL, 238TR, 240TN, 242BL, 246BL, BR, 248T, 250TL, TR, 260TR, 266T, 270B, 276TN, 292T, B, 294T, 298B, 300T, 306T, 320B, 322BN, 324T, 326T, BN, 328ML, 332B, 334B, 342B, 344T, 350BR, 356M, BR, 366B, 368B, 374B, 376T, 378BL, 380B, 388TR, 390T, B, 392T, BL, 396B, 402B, 408T, 410T, 414BN, 416TL, TR, 418TL, TR, BR, 422T, 424TR, 426TL, TR, BL, BR, 430TN, B, BN, 432TL, 438ML, 446N, 456T, TN, 462TN. **Keith Brady**: 24T. **Jim Burns**: 32T, 36M, TN, 38MT, B, 40TR, 42T, 44ML, BL, 48B, 50T, MT, MB, 52BR, 64T, M, 66T, 84T, B, 114TR, 116TN, 142ML, MR, BL, 144B, BNR, 146BL, 150TL, 166TN, T, 168T, TRN, B, 172TN, BN, 174B, 196BN, B, 198TL, TR, 206BL, TL, BN, 212BL, BR, 214B, 216TL, 220BN, 222R, 226T, 228BR, 232TR, 248TN, BL, 252BR, 276BL, BR, 288B, 290B, 296T, 302B, 310BN, 312T, 314TR, 320T, 336T, 348B, T, 356T, 360TN, BN, 368M, MN, 370BL, 372BL, BR, 384BN, 386T, 398B, 402T, BN, 404BRB, 406BN, 410BR, 414T, 420TL, TR, 422BL, 424BL, MR, 426ML, 428TR, 430T, 440B, 448B, BN, TR, 468BL, 474BR, 476BL. **Andrew Core**: 330BR. **Paul Cozza**: 248BR. **Pierre Deviche**: 210TN. **Dick Dionne**: 102T, 466B, BN. **A.R. Donaldson**: Back Cover, 216TR. **Axel Elfner**: 108TN, 374BN. **Fred Forssell**: 52TL, 58B, 94B, 98TL, BL, 100TL, TN, 118BL, 138T, 194TN, 208BRB, 228T, 234TL, 240BL, 244BL, 246TL, TR, 262T, 276T, 322TN, 326B, 350TL, 352B, 360T, 362T, 384B, 428TL, 434TL, 440T, 454TN, 458T, B, 470TL, 476TL.

Richard Fray: 86BN, 393BR. **Joe Fuhrman**: 164B. **Cory Gregory**: 312BN. **Peter Grube**: 128TN, 478BL. **Jean Halford**: 166B. **Lauren Halsey**: 244BN, 360B. **Ed Harper**: 354TL, 432BR. **John Hoffman**: 20T, 72T, 76R, 88N, 90TR, TL, 180B, 186TN, 190BL, 194T, 196TN, 232BR, 242BR, 274T, 280B, 284T, 306B, 308T, 330T, 334T, 352T, TN, 368T, 414B, 436B, 468TL, 472BN, 474BL. **Jillian Johnstone**: 256BR. **Eric Kallen**: 256TN. **Gordon Karre**: 38MB, 40ML, 126TL, 182TL, 238BL, 286T, 332T, 444T. **Dave Krueper**: 256BL. **Dave Kutilek**: 376BN. **Greg Lavaty**: 304BN. **Jerry Liguori**: 158T. **Lois Manowitz**: 42TN, 86TL, 88B, 92BR, 94BLN, 96BR, 110T, 270T, 272T, 294B, 338B, 344B, 362BN, 402TNT, 428BR, 464BL, BR, 470BL. **Martin Molina**: 212T. **Narca Moore**: 88T, 422TN. **C. Allan Morgan**: 34BN, 54B, BN, 64TL, 108T, 128T, 178TN, 260BR, 344M, 388TL, 436T, 470BR. **Alan Murphy**: 46T, 238ML. **James Ownby**: 432BL. **Leslie A. Pardo**: 72M. **Dennis Paulson**: 68BR, 128BN, 134MR. **Tyler Pockette**: 364T. **Jim Pruske**: 70B. **Lee Rentz**: 302BN. **Bob Rodrigues**: 202BRT, 412T, 416BL, 424BR, 470TR. **Bob Royse**: 112B, 146TL, 158TN, 244TR, 260TL, 328TL, 350BL, 378TL, ML, BR, 382T, 384T, 388BL, 394TL, 396M, 400T, 478TL, TR. **Tom Ryan**: 196T, 274BN, 308B, 398TR. **Larry Sansone**: 206TRB, 310TN, 410B. **Nick Saunders**: 200 T. **Alan Schmierer**: 20BN, 36MN, 56BL, BR, TR, 58TR, BN, 60T, B, 62B, 72B, 74ML, 86TR, BL, BR, 92TR, 94TR, BRN, 98BR, 110TN, 114TL, BN, 116B, 120TL, M, BR, TR, 122TN, 126ML, 130TR, 134TL, TR, BL, BR, 136T, 138BL, BR, 140BL, BR, 142TL, TR, BR, 144TN, BNL, 146TN, MR, 148B, BN, 150BL, 152T, 154, TN, 158BN, B, 160M, 162T, MT, 164T, TN, 170T, TN, BN, 172B, 184B, 186T, 190TR, N, 192BL, 194BN, 202BRB, 204BN, BR, 206BR, 210TR, 220B, 222L, 234TR, 236L, 244TN, 246BN, 252TR, 262BL, BR, 268BR, TN, 270N, 272N, 274TN, 278BR, 300B, 302T, 304B, 306TLN, TRN, 310BR, 316T, 320BN, 328BL, BR, MR, 330BL, 334M, 338T, 340T, B, 342T, 354TR, B, 364B, 378MR, 382TN, BN, 384TN, 394TR, 408BL, BRT, BRB, 434BL, 438MR, 440TN, 442T, TN, B, 444B, 446B, 452BN, 454BN, 456B. **Robert Shantz**: 24TN, 30B, 40TL, 40BR, 40MR, 48TL, 52BL, 58TL, 64B, 66BN, 66B, 68TL, 68TR, 68MR, 68BL, 74T, 76L, 80T, 90BL, 112T, 116T, 132B, 132T, 132M, 140TL, 146MN, 156BRB, 156BRT, 176TN, 178ML, 178BR, 184M, 192TN, 194B, 196MN, 202TRT, 202BL, 204TR, 208TNR, 210BR, 210BN, 218BN, 220TN, 224BL, 254T, BL, 258B,

268BL, 308BNT, BNB, 340BN, 370BR, 386B, 404TL, 406T, 414TN, 416TN, BN, 460B, 468BR. **Brian Small**: 28T, 34TN, 44MR, 50BL, 60BN, 78T, 98TR, 104T, 112TN, BN, 128B, 130TN, TL, MR, 148TN, TN, 150TRT, BRT, 156TL, BL, 162MB, 192BRT, 256TL, 278T, 306BN, 320TN, 350TN, 370TR, 376B, 402TNB, 422BR, 454B, 476TR. **Arnold Small**: 152TN. **Bryan J. Smith**: 24BN, 38T, 136TN, 162B, 310BL, 346B, 400B, 412T, 418BL, 420BL, 438TL, 440BN, 462T, 468TR, 474T. **Noel Snyder**: 88TN, 188N, 208T, 208TNL. **Bob Steele**: 32BN, 286BN. **Bruce D. Taubert**: 68ML, Back Cover. **Rick Taylor**: 22B, 28B, 30T, 36B, 42B, BN, 46TN, 62T, N, 64TR, 70T, TN, 74BR, MR, 82M, 86TN, 96TL, TR, BL, 104B, 106TL, TR, ML, MR, BL, BR, 110B, 118BR, 120BL, 122T, 124T, 126BL, BR, MR, TR, 136B, BN, 140TR, 146BR, 150TRB, BRB, 152B, BN, 160B, 166BN, 168TLN, BN, 172T, 174T, 178BL, 180MN, TN, M, BN, 182B, BN, TR, 186B, 190TL, 198BL, 200B, 202TL, TRB, 204TL, TN, BL, 218B, 222LN, 226BN, 232M, 234BL, BN, BR, 236RT, RB, 240TL, TR, 244TL, BR, 250BR, 254BR, 258T, 260BL, 264T, B, 266B, 268TL, 272B, 274B, 278BL, 280T, 282T, B, 298T, 302TN, 304T, 312TN, 314TL, BL, 318T, 322T, 324B, 328TR, 330T, 346T, BN, 350TR, 356BL, 358TL, TR, BR, 366BN, 374T, TN, 376TN, 380T, 382B, 388BR, 390BN, 396T, 398M, TL, 400TN, BNR, BNL, 404BRT, ML, MR, TR, BL, 406B, 414BR, 418TN, BN, 426MR, 428BL, 432ML, MR, 434TN, 436TN, BN, 438TR, BL, BR, 444TN, BN, 448TL, 450M, B, 456BN, 460T, 462B, 464TL, TR, TN, BN, 470TN, 472TR. **Glen Tepke**: 314BR. **Gregg Thompson**: 214T. **Terry Thormin**: 286TN. **Charles Trapani**: Front Cover, 56TL, 82B, 94TL, 130BR, 188, 190BR, 208BRT, 212TNR, 216B, 224T, 226B, 232TL, 238TL, BR, 240BR, 242TL, TR, 284B, 286B, 288T, 290T, 296TL, 308TN, 310TR, 316B, 318B, 322B, 336B, 358BL, 366T, 368TN, 370TL, 378TR, 412BL, TN, 420BR, 424ML, 432TR, 434TR, BR, 442BN, 446T, 450T, 452T, M, 452B, 454T, 460M, 466T, TN, 472TL, B, 476BR, 478BR. **Hank Tseng**: 30MT, 80B. **Stephen Vaughan**: 226TN, 192BRB. **George Vlahakis**: 312B. **Brian Wheeler**: 210TL, 210BL. **Jason Wilder**: 372TL, 372TR. **Steve Wolfe**: 110BN, 178MR, 192T, 228BL, 230TL, TR, 250BL, 252TL, 252BL. **Lee Zeiger**: 296BN. **Jim Zipp**: 230TL, TR, 250BL, 252TL, BL, 356TL.

Index/Checklist of Birds of Arizona

Bold numbers are for the main Species Account page.
Underlined species are minor accounts with no photos.

Other Species Seen

_____

_____

_____

_____

_____

_____

_____

_____

_____

About the Author

Lynne Taylor

RICHARD CACHOR TAYLOR

A lifelong resident of Arizona, he conducted an eight year study of the Elegant Trogon that led to the publication of *Trogons of the Arizona Borderlands* in 1994. During the course of his research he reported the first Eared Quetzal seen in the U.S. In 1980 he founded Borderland Tours, a birding travel company dedicated to responsible ecotourism as a means of providing an economic platform for the preservation of the world's wildlife communities. His love of guiding resulted in lifelong friendships with people on six continents, as well as the opportunity to see and study all of the trogons and quetzals in the new world. In 1995 the American Birding Association published his *A Birder's Guide to Southeastern Arizona*, which he revised in 2005. *Birds of Southeastern Arizona*, also published by the R.W. Morse Company, preceded this book in 2010.

Short Index to Species

Use this index to find the main account for every species illustrated in the guide. A complete index is on pages 484 – 492.